M000223048

EX LIBRIS:

CHAIM
POTOK

Edited by **Daniel Walden**

CHAIM

CONFRONTING MODERNITY THROUGH THE LENS OF TRADITION

POTOK

THE PENNSYLVANIA STATE UNIVERSITY PRESS
UNIVERSITY PARK, PENNSYLVANIA

Library of Congress Cataloging-in-Publication Data

Chaim Potok : confronting modernity through the lens of
tradition / edited by Daniel Walden.
p. cm.
Summary: "A collection of essays exploring the work of
Jewish American novelist Chaim Potok, with emphasis on
his efforts to reconcile the appeal of modernity and the pull
of traditional Judaism"—Provided by publisher.
Includes bibliographical references and index.
ISBN 978-0-271-05981-5 (cloth : alk. paper)
1. Potok, Chaim—Criticism and interpretation.
2. Judaism and literature—United States—
History—20th century.
3. Jewish fiction—History and criticism.
4. Jews in literature.
5. Modernism (Literature).
I. Walden, Daniel, 1922– .

PS3566.O69Z63   2013
813'.54—dc23
2013002342

Copyright © 2013 The Pennsylvania State University
All rights reserved
Printed in the United States of America
Published by The Pennsylvania State University Press,
University Park, PA 16802-1003

The Pennsylvania State University Press is a member of the
Association of American University Presses.

It is the policy of The Pennsylvania State University Press
to use acid-free paper. Publications on uncoated stock
satisfy the minimum requirements of American National
Standard for Information Sciences—Permanence of Paper
for Printed Library Material,
ANSI Z39.48–1992.

This book is printed on paper containing
30% post-consumer waste.

For my wife,

lover, friend, and rock for

fifty-six years, Bea Walden (1927–2011).

And for my children, grandchildren, and

great-grandchildren.

CONTENTS

ACKNOWLEDGMENTS

I would like to thank all those who worked with me for more than thirty-six years to make *Studies in American Jewish Literature* the great journal it became, and to acknowledge that that work helped prepare me for this volume on Chaim Potok. I wish to thank the contributors to this book, who stayed with me through the years. I also thank all those at the Pennsylvania State University Press who helped bring this publication to fruition, including director Patrick Alexander, editor-in-chief Kendra Boileau, and manuscript editor Julie Schoelles. I am grateful to Hannah Berliner Fischthal, whose typing ability and emotional support were invaluable. Finally, I'd like to express my thanks and admiration for the help Adena Potok has extended and to Chaim Potok for being Chaim Potok.

INTRODUCTION

Daniel Walden

Chaim Potok was a world-class writer and scholar, a Conservative Jew who wrote from and about his tradition and the conflicts between observance and acculturation. With a plain, straightforward style, his novels were set against the moral, spiritual, and intellectual currents of the twentieth century. His characters thought about modernity and wrestled with the core-to-core cultural confrontations they experienced when modernity clashed with faith. Potok was able to communicate with millions of people of many religious beliefs all over the world, because, unlike his major predecessors, he wrote from the inside, inclusively.

Beginning with *The Chosen* and continuing through *The Promise, My Name Is Asher Lev, The Gift of Asher Lev, The Book of Lights,* and *Davita's Harp,* Potok wrote very American novels. They were understandable and attractive to one and all. As Sheldon Grebstein put it, referring to *The Chosen*, a runaway best seller, the dream of success played out in an improbable but possible "only in America" way, demonstrating that "people can still make good through hard work, . . . integrity, and dedication," if also at the cost of occasional alienation.[1] Refusing to ignore modern thought, Potok was led to a crisis of faith, which he resolved by embracing both modernity and observant Judaism. In his view, Judaism was a tradition integrating into the American culture, not opposed to it. He kept his focus on working out his characters' identity as American.

Through his novels, Potok was a major voice in American literature because he was the first Jewish American novelist to open up the Jewish experience to a mass audience, to make that world familiar and accessible as the outside world increasingly became willing to acknowledge that Jews are a multiethnic, multiracial, and multireligious people. Potok touched chords felt by many and diverse peoples with his probing and wonderfully written evocations of the world that he knew.

Herman Harold (Chaim Tzvi in Hebrew) Potok was born in 1929 in the Bronx, New York, to Benjamin and Molly Potok. His father was a Belzer Hasid, his mother a descendant of the Hasidic Ryzner dynasty. Growing up in an Orthodox family, he had little quarrel with his Jewish world. He had a very Jewish education: he went to cheder and then a yeshiva and earned his B.A. in English literature from Yeshiva University in 1950, graduating summa cum laude. But when he was nine or ten he began to draw and paint, and when he was sixteen he accidentally came across Evelyn Waugh's *Brideshead Revisited* in the local library. Reading outside the prescribed curriculum, Potok entered a new tradition, modern literature, and came to recognize that "fundamental to that tradition was a certain way of thinking the world" that he had not encountered or used before. It entailed a "binocular view of the iconoclast, the individual who grows up inside the inherited systems of value and, while growing, begins to recoil from the games, masks, and hypocrisies he sees all around him."[2]

By the time Potok was eighteen or nineteen, as he transitioned from the Hebrew high school to the university, he began to experience a significant change. He came to realize that he and his people were at the core of a subculture in America and that the new and exciting interpretations and ideas he was discovering and experiencing were from the core of the majoritarian culture that he came to call "Western secular humanism." Having been formed by his very Jewish world of the Bronx, his encounter with this umbrella culture resulted in his becoming a "Zwischenmensch"—that is, a "between person."

One of the triggers that gave rise to his life as a writer was his discovery of the world of Evelyn Waugh when he was sixteen. Having been raised in a fundamentalist tradition, Potok found that *Brideshead Revisited* had a galvanic effect on him. "I will never forget the effect this book had upon me," he once told me. "I found myself in a world of a barest existence of which I knew nothing about before." *Brideshead Revisited* was about upper-class British Catholics. But, Potok explained, "I lived more deeply inside the world of that book than I lived inside my own world for the length of time it took me to read that book." What had Evelyn Waugh done to him? How did a writer, Potok mused, "utilizing the faculty of [the] imagination, so fuse words and imagination onto empty sheets of paper that out of that fusion comes a world more real to the reader than the world in which the reader is actually living, his or her day-to-day life? What power there is in that creativity!"[3] That was the beginning of Potok's strange hunger to write, to create his own world out of words on paper. It is the when, the where, the what of his beginnings as a writer. Soon afterward, he read James Joyce's *A Portrait of the Artist as a Young Man*, as well as works by Thomas Mann, Flannery O'Connor, Faulkner, and Hemingway.

Potok had made contact with modern literature. It is a literature whose practitioners are, by and large, in rebellion against the world that raised them, nurtured them, and taught them their primary system of values. Within that context, Potok attempted to track one element of this confrontation: ideas from the heart of one culture crashing up against ideas from the heart of another culture. He called it a core-to-core confrontation of cultures.

Potok recalled that another trigger occurred while he was serving as an American chaplain in Korea. After visiting the memorial to the dropping of the atom bomb in Hiroshima, Japan, he began to explore the world of Asia through the medium of storytelling. In the strict Jewish tradition, writing stories is regarded as a frivolity. Once, a Talmud teacher who had heard that Potok was writing stories told him, "I hear you want to be a writer. . . . What is it that you want to write?" Potok recalled, "I said, 'Stories.' And he was horrified."[4] The teacher sensed rightly, coming from an Eastern European tradition, that Potok had made contact with an element from the umbrella civilization that was inimical to his tradition—something adversary to the essence of the Jewish tradition he cherished. He was right.

Inherent in the modern literary tradition is a particular way of looking at the world and sensing rightly or wrongly the games that people play, the hypocrisies that enable us to make our way in the world, and the mechanisms that we use to live every day. Potok decided that there were three avenues he might take: break with the tradition that gave him life, give into it, or "live in constant tension with it," as he put it in 1982. So he read Joyce, Waugh, O'Connor, Mann, Flaubert, Jane Austen, Upton Sinclair, and Mark Twain, even as he studied the Talmud. He was committed to the possibilities of communicating his own narrow world through fiction as objectively as he could, while presenting and exposing Orthodoxy, especially ultra-Orthodoxy, in as critical a way as Waugh had presented Roman Catholicism.

In replying to a "semi-sympathetic critic" in 1976, he wrote, "The sonnets of Milton taught me my regard for simplicity and careful naming; the flattening effect I learned from Stephen Crane."[5] He also admired Hemingway's style and Joyce's treatment of religious themes. For example, illustrating the care he exercised in writing, he stated that stylistically his short stories are quite different from his novels, being "more compressed, laconic and elliptical, closer to the third person narrative style in *The Book of Lights* than the first person novels like *The Chosen*, where a careful balance had to be effected between the narrator's unsophisticated literary voice and the requirements of literary style."[6] He rewrote each novel at least four or five times, some more than a dozen times. He worked hard to achieve his simplicity of style. For instance, in *The Chosen* and *The Promise*, he needed his characters to speak like Orthodox Jews in Brooklyn, not like they came from elite American backgrounds or from Eton.

When Potok published *The Chosen*, one critic said, "He's not like the other Jewish-American novelists being read by the general American public. He's an entirely new breed."[7] To be a new breed, Potok had to break from his fundamentalist past. He lost more than a decade's worth of friends and teachers who had been close to him but would never talk to him again. He reflected, "A whole world that had been very warm and tribal vanished from my life."[8]

The Chosen was that rare thing, a novel about Hasidic Jews and Orthodox Jews set in Brooklyn toward the end of World War II. Written in a contemporary vernacular, it is about two kinds of Orthodoxy, about two subcultures confronting each other. It is also a kind of love story between Danny Saunders, son of and heir to Reb Saunders, the rebbe of the ultra-Orthodox Hasidic sect, and Reuven Malter, son of the liberal journalist and teacher David Malter. Danny, a genius with a photographic memory who was raised in silence by his father in order to develop his heart and soul, struggles against the constricted world he knows and seeks secular learning, an expansion of his mind, to understand his own people. Interacting with Reuven, and with Mr. Malter, from whom he unknowingly seeks advice in selecting books at the neighborhood library, Danny's initial hostility toward Reuven is transformed into friendship and love. In the opening scene, a baseball game between the Orthodox team and the Hasidic team, Danny wants to kill Reuven; he purposely hits a ball at Reuven's face, breaking his glasses and damaging his eye. In Potok's view, this "war" demonstrated the divisiveness and anger between variants of Orthodoxy, as well as the fanaticism of the ultra-Orthodox. Potok may have exaggerated the case, for as Judah Stampfer put it, "The book is too freighted with anti-Hasidic prejudice to be of value. . . . But Potok's depictions of Yeshiva life have the ring of truth," especially with regard to the confrontation between piety and fanaticism.[9]

Why was *The Chosen* a *New York Times* best seller for thirty-eight weeks in 1967? Sheldon Grebstein pointed to it as a highly American novel, for all its religious character, and wrote that it was reminiscent of the American cultural myth or fable at the heart of the Horatio Alger stories and *The Great Gatsby*. According to Potok, *The Chosen* is no more like Alger or Fitzgerald than *Mansfield Park* is like Cinderella. Yet while Grebstein was mistaken in this regard, his description of *The Chosen* as a "really Jewish best-seller" is a gem.[10] The point is that, in spite of certain roughnesses, as Hugh Nissenson described it, the book "remains in the mind and delights. It is like those myths that . . . do not essentially exist in words at all." The structural pattern of the novel is complete, he added. "We rejoice, and even weep a little," Nissenson wrote, "as at those haunting Hasidic melodies which transfigure their words."[11] In 1967, *The Chosen*—riding on the burgeoning impact of Bellow, Malamud, and Roth, the early successes of the new state of Israel as it faced a hostile Arab world, and the warmth of the American public as it gradually learned of the horrors of the Holocaust—resonated with Jews and non-Jews, Americans and people all over the world, by virtue of its exposure for the first time of the Jewish experience from the inside.

The Chosen, like Potok's second book, *The Promise*, is subtle and complex. Danny, who chooses to be a clinical psychologist rather than succeed his father as the next rebbe, remains a righteous man. Reuven, son of a Zionist scholar-journalist, decides to be a rabbi. The central metaphor of *The Chosen* is "combat of various kinds"—on the baseball field and in Europe. As Potok explained to Elaine Kauvar in 1986, the book explores "what happens when the combat in Europe is actually brought home to Brooklyn because of the Holocaust and the subsequent hunger to create the State of Israel." Additionally, he continued, "*The Chosen* is about two components in the core of Judaism or the core of any tradition, one component looking inward and one component looking outward to solve its problems. Both of those elements are in confrontation with an element from the core of Western civilization." The core-to-core cultural confrontation likewise informs *My Name Is Asher Lev*, which depicts a confrontation with Western art. "Asher Lev typifies what might happen to a religious Jew who wants to enter the mainstream of Western art," Potok remarked. "Remaining observant is a crucial element in all of my books."[12]

The central metaphor of *The Promise*, Potok told Kauvar, is "people gambling and winning or losing." *Davita's Harp* is about the power of the human imagination to restructure unbearable reality and thereby come to terms with it—as demonstrated in the excellent example of Picasso's *Guernica*. Finally, the central metaphor of *The Book of Lights* is "the mystery and the awe that some of us sense in the grittiness of reality."[13] As Potok told Lynn Hinds in 1986, "*The Book of Lights* is about the tension between my particular tradition and the only pagan, or idolatrous, civilization left on this planet, which is the world of Asia."[14] According to him, when the world we know begins to break apart and when normative responses—religious and secular—become inadequate, you can become cynical, you can become a hedonist, you can enter a monastery, or you can leap into the mystical. In the end, we are left with a question: How can we make commitments in an utterly ambiguous world?

Potok, as he put it in *Wanderings*, had a "sense of renewal, a foresharpening of self-identity, a feeling of approaching some distant fertile plain." What he meant was that the Jewish tradition has the inherent ability "to confront new civilizations and to renew itself as a result," but also "to pull back when it realizes that it's about to give up too much." He shared with Kauvar his view that "there is a real possibility for the creation of something quite extraordinary, a third Jewish civilization. Indeed, the Jewish tradition may be one of the ways that Western civilization will save itself because I think Western civilization is in very serious danger of utilizing the dark side of its seminal thrusts for self-destruction." At present, he concluded in *Wanderings*, just as many of his characters are preoccupied with their in-between existence, so the Jewish situation is "between worlds."[15]

As Potok told Michael Cusick in 1997, someone once asked James Joyce why he only wrote about Dublin. He answered, "For myself I always write about Dublin, because if I can get to the heart of Dublin I can get to the heart of all the cities in the world. In the particular is contained the universal." Potok spelled out his particularities, primarily in certain areas of New York City. He explained to Cusick, "If the language is okay, and the story is interesting, what you end up doing inside yourself is taking those particularities and linking them to your own. And those two generate a universal. You as the reader can then function inside that universal."[16]

Chaim Potok died of brain cancer in July 2002. Thus ended his lifelong quest to confront modernity through the lens of tradition—or, as Jane Eisner phrased it, "to reconcile deep faith and fidelity to ancestral ritual with the pulsing challenges of modern life." Potok asked questions that others would not, for he believed that through honest inquiry we would all arrive in a better place. He also expressed a commitment to learning about and embracing diverse ideas and cultures. "I am open to all people and to all means of expression," he told Eisner.[17]

Potok is a part of American literature. His novels are bildungsromans (novels of character development) and künstlerromans (novels about artists' development), Edward Abramson concluded.[18] The protagonists develop and grow in understanding and thus do not remain eternal innocents. Yet, even in the end, they cannnot be described as having totally lost their innocence, and their quest for a "romantic absolute" remains. Alienation, dread, and loneliness are basic elements in American literature. According to Potok, so are the affirmation of human potentialities, the worth of the individual, and the return to society. He agreed with literary critic Lionel Trilling's notion that serious literature should assume an adversarial position with regard to the prevailing culture.

Though Potok was an observant Jew, a rabbi, and a Ph.D. in philosophy, he was able to depict the rigidities and intolerance of Orthodox Judaism. He demonstrated the desirability and possibility of Orthodox Jews becoming more aware of interpretation, modern text criticism, and modern scholarship. In the end, he was trying to understand and give some insight into the aimlessness and anxiety of the modern world. For him, the universe was ultimately meaningful, and the search for meaning was all-important. In Abramson's words, "He has shown the ability to create characters who remain with the reader long after the novel is closed, to tackle difficult issues and complex situations, and to illuminate previously untreated areas of Jewish life. . . . These are no mean achievements."[19]

The structure of this book is twofold. The first part presents a significant body of criticism of Potok's novels, which will help stimulate scholarly and critical discussion. The second half consists of more personal contributions. The aim of the collection is to further widen the lens through which we read Potok and thereby help establish him as an authentic American writer who created unforgettable American characters who successfully forge their own American identities while retaining their Jewish identities. This work seeks to illuminate the struggles in Potok's novels that result from a profound desire to reconcile two equally strong yet opposed impulses: the appeal of modernity and the pull of traditional Judaism.

In chapter 1, Kathryn McClymond answers the question of why *The Chosen* was a runaway best seller despite the fact that it was not received positively by many critics. She insightfully attributes this critical response to Potok's failure to fit the prevailing expectations for an American author writing from within the Jewish religion. In chapter 2, Jessica Lang emphasizes the dialectical forces at work in both *The Chosen* and *The Promise*, focusing on the triangulated relationship among an ultra-Orthodox Hasidic sect, modern Orthodoxy, and traditional Conservative Judaism. Her essay explores the philosophical underpinnings of conflict in Potok's writing. In chapter 3, Victoria Aarons claims that *The Promise* simultaneously depicts an adolescent boy's descent into psychosis and an ideological battle within Judaism. Additionally, she contends, it examines the consequences of the covenant between

God and the Jews and calls the nature of that "first promise" into question. *The Promise* thus provides a more realistic portrayal of the ethical and cultural challenges facing American Jews in the wake of the Holocaust.

In chapter 4, S. Lillian Kremer explores the simultaneous pull of modern art and Hasidism on Asher Lev in *My Name Is Asher Lev* and *The Gift of Asher Lev*. Acknowledging the influence of James Joyce's *A Portrait of the Artist as a Young Man* on these two novels, Kremer draws insightful comparisons between Asher Lev and Joyce's protagonist Stephen Dedalus. In chapter 5, Susanne Klingenstein explains that *Davita's Harp* is about the use of the imagination to cope with unbearable reality, as exemplified in Picasso's *Guernica*. This painting and the terrible event that inspired it play a central role in the novel, and Klingenstein thus uses *Davita's Harp* to explore Potok's notion of the "redemptive power of the artist." In chapter 6, Sanford Marovitz focuses on the affect of two lights—the mystical light of Kabbalah and the physical light of the atom bomb—on Gershon Loran in *The Book of Lights*. Gershon finds himself changed as a result of the core-to-core confrontations he experiences as a chaplain in Korea, which, Marovitz notes, echo the experiences of Potok himself. Finally, in chapter 7, Nathan Devir writes about the development of *I Am the Clay*, which was begun in 1956 while Potok was in Korea and was finished in 1992. Devir notes that Potok's time in Korea constituted a defining moment in his adult sense of self and explores how his experiences and observations there informed the structure of his "first and last" novel.

The second part of the book relates and reflects upon personal memories of Potok's life and work. Chapters 8 to 10 consist of three eulogies delivered by Hugh Nissenson, Daniel Walden, and Jonathan Rosen at a memorial service for Potok at the University of Pennsylvania in 2002. These are followed in chapters 11 and 12 by a brief literary biography of Potok written by his widow, Adena Potok, and an article by Jane Eisner, a close friend and editor of the *Forward*. Chapter 13 presents an interview with Adena Potok conducted by Nathan Devir, focusing on the novel *I Am the Clay*. Chapter 14 closes the volume with a speech, entitled "My Life as a Writer," that Potok gave at The Pennsylvania State University in 1982.

This collection attempts to bring to light new and subtle nuances in the robust work of an exceedingly talented Jewish American writer. For the first time, an outstanding group of Potok scholars is brought together to offer elegant readings and crisp interpretations of Potok's novels. It is hoped that these essays and remembrances will help readers explore and appreciate aspects of Potok's work in greater depth than before and help establish Potok's real significance and standing in mainstream American literature, as well as in Jewish American literature.

NOTES

1. Sheldon Grebstein, "The Phenomenon of the Really Jewish Best-Seller: Potok's *The Chosen*," *Studies in American Jewish Literature* 1, no. 1 (1975): 25.

2. Chaim Potok, "Culture Confrontation in Urban America: A Writer's Beginnings," in *Literature and the Urban Experience: Essays on the City and Literature*, ed. Michael C. Jaye and Ann Chalmers Watts (New Brunswick: Rutgers University Press, 1981), 164.

3. Quoted from Potok's speech in chapter 14.

4. Ibid.

5. Chaim Potok, "Reply to a Semi-Sympathetic Critic," *Studies in American Jewish Literature* 2, no. 1 (1976), 20.

6. Edward Abramson, *Chaim Potok* (New York: Twayne, 1986), 6.

7. Quoted in Leslie Field, "Chaim Potok and the Critics: Sampler from a Consistent Spectrum," *Studies in American Jewish Literature* 4 (1985): 3.

8. Edwin Newman, "Conversation with Chaim Potok," transcript of *The Eternal Light*, NBC-TV, November 6, 1997, 1–20.

9. Judah Stampfer, "The Tension of Piety," review of *The Chosen*, *Judaism* 16 (Fall 1967): 495.

10. Grebstein, "Phenomenon of the Really Jewish Best-Seller," 25–30.

11. Hugh Nissenson, "The Spark and the Shell," *New York Times Book Review*, May 7, 1967, 4–5.

12. Elaine M. Kauvar, "An Interview with Chaim Potok," in *Conversations with Chaim Potok*, ed. Daniel Walden (Jackson: University Press of Mississippi, 2001), 67, 69, 75.

13. Ibid., 67–68.

14. Lynn Hinds, "An Interview with Chaim Potok," in Walden, *Conversations with Chaim Potok*, 88.

15. Kauvar, "Interview with Chaim Potok," 86–87.

16. Michael Cusick, "Giving Shape to Turmoil: A Conversation with Chaim Potok," in Walden, *Conversations with Chaim Potok*, 127.

17. Jane Eisner, "Chaim Potok Is No Longer with Us, but His Lessons Remain," *The Forward*, February 26, 2010. Reprinted in chapter 12.

18. Abramson, *Chaim Potok*, 138.

19. Ibid., 142.

THE NOVELS

The essays in this part of the book approach Chaim Potok's novels from a scholarly and critical perspective, situating them within the context of Jewish American literature and analyzing the historical and cultural influences on Potok's writing. The authors consider the struggles and conflicts in the novels that arise from the confrontation of modernity and traditional Judaism, and they recognize the ways in which Potok's personal experience of such confrontation richly informed his work.

THE CHOSEN

Defining American Judaism

Kathryn McClymond

He's not like the other Jewish-American novelists being read by the general American public. He's an entirely new breed. The critics won't know what to do with him.

—ANONYMOUS CRITIC QUOTED IN LESLIE FIELD, "CHAIM POTOK AND THE CRITICS"

Like many Americans, I first read Chaim Potok's *The Chosen* as an adolescent. High school and college programs across the country assign this novel because it describes two young men "coming of age" during a dramatic and pivotal moment in Jewish and global history. These are important elements of the story, but I've come to appreciate other dimensions of this novel—dimensions that speak more directly to the relationship between literature and the study of religion—and it is these dimensions that I want to highlight in the following pages.

The Chosen is Potok's first book. Published in early 1967, it has also been adapted for the screen (1980) and the stage (1999). Potok wrote the novel while working on his doctoral dissertation in Jerusalem. He explained, "I wrote *The Chosen* in the morning and my doctorate in the afternoon" (a humbling piece of information for all of us who struggled with the dissertation

A version of this essay was previously published as Kathryn McClymond, "*The Chosen*: Defining American Judaism," *Shofar* 25, no. 2 (2007): 4–23. Used with permission.

alone).[1] *The Chosen* is highly autobiographical, drawing from Potok's child-hood in New York. Yet despite the personal quality of the book, it demonstrated broad appeal among Jews and non-Jews. *The Chosen* quickly became a best seller, remaining on the *New York Times* best seller list for ten months, and it continues to be popular forty-odd years later. While Potok went on to write many more novels, as well as plays, short stories, children's books, and nonfiction, *The Chosen* is his most well-known work. It tells the story of Danny Saunders and Reuven Malter, two Orthodox Jewish young men growing up in Brooklyn in the 1940s. As the book opens, Danny, the brilliant son of a Hasidic rebbe, despises Reuven, the son of an academic who has developed a reputation for using secular textual-critical methods in his study of Talmud. During an intense baseball game, Danny almost blinds Reuven by intentionally hitting a ball directly into Reuven's face. The boys are thrown together as a result of this event, and they quickly become close friends despite the initial antagonism and their cultural differences. Several personal crises occur throughout the story, and the novel is cast against the backdrop of the end of World War II, unfolding revelations about the Holocaust, and deeply divisive attitudes toward Zionism. But the sustained focus of the story is on Danny's relationship with his father, the rebbe. Reb Saunders, the highly revered leader of a local Hasidic community, is raising Danny in silence. That is, he does not speak to his son except when they argue Talmud on Shabbat. At the climax of the story, Reb Saunders explains why he chose to parent in this seemingly heartless way. As the book closes, the reader, through Reuven's eyes, literally watches Danny turn a corner. Danny moves into a new life, more understanding of his father's methods and committed to upholding traditional observance, but unsure of how he will incorporate the experiences of his childhood into his adult life.

While *The Chosen* has consistently held wide popular appeal, critical reviews have been more mixed. In fact, many of its initial critical reviews were rather negative, and Chaim Potok has never risen to the ranks of other modern Jewish novelists included in collections about Jewish American literature—writers such as Philip Roth, Bernard Malamud, and Saul Bellow.[2] Most standard lists and anthologies of classic Jewish American writers omit Potok's name entirely, or he is characterized as a "popular" writer, as in Arnold J. Band's recent book *Studies in Modern Jewish Literature*: "One finds a group of books of less critical acclaim but of clearer Jewish resolution, books that have enjoyed enormous popularity and have had significant impact on American Jewish life . . . [including] *The Chosen*."[3] There are several understandable reasons for this. Potok's characterization of Jewish life in New York in the 1940s is sentimental. Baruch Hochman of the magazine *Commentary* characterized the novel as a "wish-fulfillment fairy tale which concludes with the familiar, sugary projection of desiderated relationships."[4] In addition, Potok's characters are problematic—Potok romanticizes them. No one is really bad or evil; individuals are just misguided or misunderstood. David Stern of *Commentary* charged, "Characters display no real understanding of the dilemmas which they have been chosen to exemplify," and he complained that Potok's characterization is "heavy handed and even careless."[5] To complicate matters further, Potok's interesting characters are almost all men; women barely figure into the story line of *The Chosen* at all. Reuven's mother has died before the novel opens, but we never learn how or why, and Reuven never seems to think of her. The only significant woman in the Malter household is the housekeeper, and Danny Saunders's mother functions as little more than a housekeeper in her home; she is entirely absent from parenting. Danny has a sister, but she appears primarily to prompt discussions of arranged marriages within the Hasidic community.[6] Finally, in sharp contrast to Bellow's and Roth's writings, neither of *The Chosen*'s protagonists expresses any sexual desire or frustration throughout the novel, despite the fact that we meet them relatively early in their adolescence and follow them through their college years. The dramatic tension in *The Chosen* is almost entirely intellectual. The central conflict develops as Danny gradually considers rejecting the inherited position of tzaddik within his small community, choosing instead the dangerous world of Freud and psychoanalysis.

The points I have just listed have raised problems for many of Potok's critics, and as a result he is often recognized as a well-known popular writer but not necessarily a writer deserving critical acclaim. But I want to argue that there may be another, more deep-rooted reason why Potok's work is often not received well by scholars of Jewish American literature. Potok's lack of overwhelming critical acclaim—and his striking success with popular audiences—is, in part, due to how he positions Judaism in relationship to mainstream American culture. I will lay out this argument in the following pages. First, I will indicate some key content and structural elements of the story that relate to this point. Second, I'll situate the book in the broader context of contemporary Jewish American literature. Finally, I'll argue that *The Chosen*, as Jewish American literature, raises several interesting issues from a religious studies perspective. Potok's characterization of Judaism in *The Chosen* differs markedly from characterizations by other authors of that period. In addition, critical interpretations of and responses to the novel reveal a theological stance taken by literary critics in the mid-twentieth century—a theological stance driven by a particular (and monolithic) understanding of traditional Judaism's place in relationship to mainstream America. Potok's presentation of Judaism differs markedly from what critics expected and perhaps wanted. He characterizes Judaism *not* as a tradition in opposition to mainstream American culture, but rather as an arena that had to be integrated into mainstream American life. By contrast, the trend in Jewish American literature at this time was to present Judaism in opposition to mainstream culture; one could not be traditionally Jewish and American. Becoming the latter seemed to require rejecting the former. This, I suggest, is a theological stance. Since Potok did not position traditional Judaism in relationship to mainstream American culture in the same way that writers such as Roth and Bellow did, critics who had specific notions of what Jewish American literature was *supposed* to be dismissed Potok's work as simplistic, naive, and sentimental. But popular readers accepted the multiplicity of Jewish identity suggested in Potok's novel, and they often saw themselves in Potok's protagonists. As a result, popular readers—Jews and non-Jews—embraced *The Chosen* as a novel that told their own American story.

The Chosen

Potok sets *The Chosen* in the Williamsburg neighborhood of Brooklyn in the 1940s. He tells his story in the first person, through the eyes of Reuven Malter, the teenage son of David Malter, a professor at a local yeshiva. From the very beginning, Potok uses Reuven's perspective to position communities in relationship to one another. In the opening pages, Reuven situates himself for the reader: "I attended the yeshiva in which my father taught. This latter yeshiva was somewhat looked down upon by the students of other Jewish parochial schools of Brooklyn: it offered more English subjects than the required minimum, and it taught its Jewish subjects in Hebrew rather than Yiddish. Most of the students were children of immigrant Jews who preferred to regard themselves as having been emancipated from the fenced-off ghetto mentality typical of the other Jewish parochial schools in Brooklyn."[7] Within the first two pages of the book Potok sets up an unexpected opposition. It is not the Hasidic Jews who are "alien" to mainstream America. Rather, the more liberal Orthodox community is "alien" to the Hasidic community. The reader is drawn into the complexity of Jewish American life. In this particular corner of American Judaism Reuven is marginalized, not for being too Jewish in the eyes of non-Jewish Americans but for not being Jewish enough. Potok reorients the reader so that he sees the world from the perspective of Reuven, who is committed to Orthodox Judaism but also to some level of participation in American life. This brings him into conflicts with other Jews, most significantly the Hasidic world of Danny and Reb Saunders. Here Potok differs markedly from the more critically acclaimed Jewish American writers, who focused on the angst of rejecting one's Jewish identity as a necessary prelude to living a full American life. In *The Chosen*, the problem is how to work out one's Jewish identity in light of being an American—but never to leave one's Judaism behind.

At the same time that Potok explores the conflicts between two Jewish communities—Danny's Russian Hasidic community and Reuven's more liberal Orthodox world—he situates these conflicts in the broader context of American life. Many scholars have noted that Potok begins his story in wartime, in the spring of 1944, and opens the novel on the quintessential American field of conflict: the ball field. "I use the openings to make the statement concerning the central metaphor of the novels," Potok explained. "The central metaphor of *The Chosen* is combat of various kinds, combat on the baseball field, combat in Europe, and then what happens when the combat in Europe is actually brought home to Brooklyn because of the Holocaust and the subsequent hunger to create the State of Israel."[8] Potok's opening scene suggests that all of these arenas of conflict are interconnected. In the first few pages, Reuven explains that the Second World War prompted some teachers in Jewish parochial schools "to show the gentile world that yeshiva students were as physically fit as any other American student, despite their long hours of study. They went about proving this by organizing the Jewish parochial schools in and around our area into competitive leagues" (11). But Potok doesn't use the baseball game primarily to distinguish Jews from gentile America. Rather, he uses the game to contrast Reuven's Jewish community with Danny's. Reuven's league is coached by a gentile public school gym teacher who uses military language to inspire and motivate his players. Danny's league is led by a rabbi who sits on the sidelines throughout the game with his nose buried in a book. Reuven's team members "had no particular uniform, and each of us wore whatever he wished" (14). Danny's Hasidic team members, by contrast, "were dressed alike in white shirts, dark pants, white sweaters, and small black skullcaps. In the fashion of the very Orthodox, their hair was closely cropped. . . . They all wore the traditional undergarment beneath their shirts, and the tzitzit, the long fringes appended to the four corners of the garment, came out above their belts and swung against their pants as they walked" (14). This baseball game does not represent a competition between Judaism and America, but rather a conflict between two different kinds of Judaism. As Potok explained in a later interview, "In that baseball game you have two aspects of Jewish Orthodoxy in contention. You have the Eastern European aspect, which prefers to turn inward and not confront the outside world. You have the Western European more objective scientific aspect within the core, within Orthodoxy, that is not afraid to look at the outside world that produces scientists. These are in interaction with one another inside the core. That's the baseball game."[9]

Potok's writing style is broadly inclusive. Throughout the story, Potok takes pains to make sure that non-Jewish readers can follow the events described. Daniel Walden, a well-known scholar of Potok's work, comments that Potok "makes that very particular world [Hasidism] seem eerily familiar to non-Jews."[10] Potok defines Hebrew and Yiddish terms as he uses them, and he offers a basic primer on several elements of Orthodox Jewish life, such as the history of the Hasidim, the basics of *gematria*, and Talmud study. At the same time, his style is simple and direct. Through Reuven Malter the reader is included in the most private moments, receiving occasional explanations as necessary. We are brought into the very inner sanctum of Hasidic family life and a rebbe's Shabbat afternoon Talmud study. As Sanford Pinsker observes, "Potok's hasidic boys playing baseball, their earlocks and *tsitsis* flapping as they round third base, strike a wide audience of Jews and non-Jews alike as an entertaining way to learn about the ultra-Orthodox."[11] As a result, Hasidic Judaism increasingly becomes less foreign to the reader as the story progresses.

However, at the same time that Potok invites non-Jewish readers to feel comfortable in his 1940s Jewish world, he also includes elements that would probably be meaningful only to Jews. For example, the book is organized into eighteen chapters, eighteen being the numerical value of the Hebrew word for life, *chai*. He introduces each major section of the book with excerpts from religious texts—the Proverbs, the *Zohar* (a mystical text), and the Talmud— without providing explanations of the textual sources, let alone the excerpts themselves.

Most interestingly, in the juxtaposition of one father's household with the other, Potok sets up a kind of rabbinic encounter for the reader. Careful readers will note that the two fathers never talk with each other. In fact, they are never even in the same room or geographic space. They are, geographically and culturally, worlds apart. Yet the two sons move in and out of these two worlds, jockeying back and forth between the opposing positions these two scholars promote. It is as if the young men—and, by extension, the reader—are being exposed to and asked to evaluate two schools of thought, two *beit midrash*. Reuven learns from Danny's father in his "house of study," the three-story brownstone that functions as the Saunders home and the synagogue for the local Hasidic community. Alternatively, Danny learns from David Malter in his modern version of a "house of study": the public library. Here Danny is first introduced to Freud and psychoanalysis under Professor Malter's watchful eye. The two young boys move back and forth between the rebbe's study and the public library, traveling geographically and symbolically between two worldviews. The conflicting views of the two fathers culminate in their disagreement about Zionism. At one point Professor Malter shares his pro-Zionist views with his son, Reuven. When Reuven later shares these views with Reb Saunders, the rebbe explodes. This creates an interesting reading experience. Literally, with the first edition of the book open, we read Professor Malter's arguments for Zionism on the lefthand page (186) and then Reb Saunders's critique of Zionism on the facing page (187). The reader is witness to a variation on a great rabbinic debate, played out in the layout of the pages as well as the plot of the novel.

These conflicts, whether easily identifiable by non-Jewish readers or addressed with more nuance to Jewish readers, always come back to the core problem: Danny's increasing alienation from the life expected of him as Reb Saunders's son. The manner in which this problem is worked out sets *The Chosen* (and, in fact, most of Potok's writing) apart from what was being critically acclaimed as important Jewish American literature in the mid-twentieth century. I turn now to a brief discussion of that phenomenon.

Jewish American Literature

In general, Jewish American literature is traced back to the late 1800s. This first wave of writing was steeped in the experiences of immigrants, particularly European immigrants and their struggles building new lives in America. The next wave, roughly the period between 1930 and 1945, happily left immigrant culture behind and looked to America for hope in the face of crises such as the Depression and the Holocaust. Lewis Fried remarks, "Assimilation was a welcome fact of their American existence."[12]

Most scholars, however, agree that the heyday of modern Jewish American literature began in the 1950s, and references to great Jewish American literature most often take us back to this period. Saul Bellow, Bernard Malamud, and Philip Roth came onto the scene and dominated Jewish American fiction for decades to come. No list of Jewish American writers was complete without their names. More important, the themes these writers addressed and their orientations toward Judaism were embraced as the definitive expression of midcentury Jewish American experience and, therefore, midcentury Jewish American writing. For example, one critic commenting on Roth's work remarked that he is "one of the first American Jewish writers who finds that it [Judaism] yields him no sustenance, no norms or values, from which to launch his attacks on middle-class complaisance."[13] Over time, the most critically acclaimed Jewish American writers, almost without exception, depicted liberal Judaism as opposed to mainstream American culture and values, promoting either a rejection or a secularization of Judaism. Gerhard Falk notes that these writers "opposed their Jewish heritage and treated it with contempt, disdain and calumny. . . . Roth, and so many other Jewish-American writers, contributed mightily, not only to the secularization of Judaism and America in general, but also to the de-mystification of the Jewish tradition."[14] Another critic generalizes, "Our best writers are 'mad crusaders,' hoping for a transcendent ideal—art, potency?—to replace the tarnished ones they embraced in their youth."[15] Irving Malin offers a broad definition of Jewish American writers: "I would try to isolate 'Jewish' stories as those that witness, even in disorted [*sic*] or inverted ways, traditional religious and literary moments. . . . They demonstrate that their creators seek to escape from exile, to break old covenants, and to embrace transcendent ideals."[16]

Generally speaking, critics identified the great Jewish American writers as those who were in conflict with traditional Judaism. This is in sharp contrast to the Yiddish fiction tradition (as exemplified by Chaim Grade), which looked back to the old world, not necessarily as a utopian society but as a foundational community. Grade is best known for his novels *The Agunah* and *My Mother's Sabbath Days* and for the short story "My Quarrel with Hersh Rasseyner" (later adapted for stage and film). Grade is an apt figure for comparison with Potok because he, too, left Orthodox Judaism, but his writing moved in a different direction. Like many other classic Yiddish writers, he witnessed the decimation of Eastern European Jewry, and because his work is steeped in both the Eastern European experience and its destruction, it is difficult for many non-Jewish American readers to identify with.

Chaim Potok's work is much more accessible to American Jews and non-Jews alike. As a result, some argued that Potok, while a popular writer, was not a particularly good writer. Certain evidence, however, contradicts this view. First, *The Chosen* was nominated for a National Book Award when it was first published. Leslie Field notes that Potok's novel was reviewed in prestigious magazines such as the *New York Times Book Review*, *Times Literary Supplement*, *Saturday Review*, *Christian Science Monitor*, *Commentary*, and *Harper's*, an impressive feat for a first novel.[17] In addition, the book received positive reviews from respected critics such as Hugh Nissenson, Granville Hicks, and Karl Shapiro. Mark Van Doren went so far as to declare, "Chaim Potok is in my opinion the most powerful story teller living, in this or any other country."[18] Clearly, certain critics—as well as general readers—found value in Potok's work.

Another possible response is to recognize Potok as a strong American writer but not a particularly Jewish writer. This response raises even more serious problems. First, Potok has been widely recognized as an author dealing with and writing out of deeply personal Jewish experiences. Consequently, *The Chosen* received the Edward Lewis Wallant Award in 1967, an annual award that acknowledges contributions in Jewish fiction. In 1985 SUNY published a volume on Potok as part of its Studies in American Jewish Literature series (edited by Daniel Walden), and other collections dedicated to his work have followed. Potok was a committed Jewish writer, addressing explicitly Jewish content and speaking powerfully to certain Jewish audiences.

I would argue that the problem was, first of all, the *kind* of American Judaism Potok wrote about. Simply put, Potok's Jews are different from Roth's and Bellow's Jews. For example, Potok's characters' most intense personal crises play out in the intellect, not the body. Danny Saunders's adolescent rebellion expresses itself in surreptitious reading at the local library—hardly the scintillating and titillating world Roth describes. In addition, Potok's adolescent rebellions do not inevitably lead to permanent alienation between family members. We do not have here the adult men of "My Quarrel with Hersh Rasseyner," who run into one another after years of separation and spend the afternoon seriously debating God's character, even his existence, in light of the devastation of the Holocaust. While Danny and Reuven make choices that disappoint, pain, and even anger each other and their families, the conflicts center on different interpretations of religious identity, not their fundamental allegiances, and no irreparable breaks occur.

Second, Potok writes with the understanding that there are multiple Judaisms in midcentury America, and he highlights this diversity by focusing on Orthodox communities. In doing so he destroys the myth of a monolithic midcentury American Judaism, and he "decenters" the stream of Judaism that Roth, Malamud, Bellow, and many others made familiar. Barbara Meyerhoff has offered language that may be helpful in understanding the significance of this. She distinguishes between the "Great Tradition" and the "Little Tradition." The former is described as "the formal Jewish law, study, and shared history that make Jews one people, *klal Israel*." Of the latter, Meyerhoff writes, "For Eastern-European Jews and their descendants, which includes most American-Jewish writers, this folk culture or domestic religion is *Yidishkayt*."[19] Bonnie Lyons, building on Meyerhoff's terminology, argues, "What is central to the issues of the Jewishness of American-Jewish literature is the inheritance of *Yidishkayt*."[20] In other words, although there are multiple Judaisms, one stream of Judaism dominates Jewish American literature: the domestic Yiddish culture of Eastern Europe. Potok, by contrast, is drawing from the "Great Tradition" or rabbinic stream of Judaism, focused on Torah study, Jewish law, and Jewish global history, woven into an American experience. Potok himself makes this point in slightly different language:

> My experience is so entirely different from that of Roth's. While we write about Jews, even the Jews that we write about are different, conceptually different. . . . Bellow really knows Yiddish literature. But it would stop there; he wouldn't be able to go beyond the Yiddish into the rabbinic, the heavy content of rabbinic tradition. . . . Interestingly enough, I feel closer to someone like Joyce, who really did, in terms of models, precisely what I'm trying to do. Joyce was right at the heart of the Catholic world and at the same time at the heart of western secular humanism.[21]

For Potok, the kind of Jew he writes about resonates more strongly with the kind of Catholic Joyce was writing about than with a different type of Jew.

Finally, because Potok draws on a different stream of American Judaism, he describes a different kind of relationship between Orthodox Judaism and mainstream America. Potok does not assume that Jewish and American identities are mutually exclusive. As S. Lillian Kremer notes, "Whereas the assimilated American Jews of the fictions of Saul Bellow and Philip Roth retain only peripheral connection to Jewish institutions, Potok's characters, like those of Joyce, are at the core of their cultural and religious heritage. They preserve the languages, traditions, and beliefs of Orthodox Judaism, even when they enter the secular professional world. Unlike most of the characters in the writings of Bellow, Malamud, and Roth, who leave the religious life for the secular, those of Potok's novels bring the secular life into the religious."[22] Potok's characters integrate their core Jewish and American identities rather than choosing one over the other.

I would argue that many of Potok's critics have missed this. They judged Potok's writings in light of dynamics that more accurately reflect liberal forms of Judaism and mainstream America. That is, they assumed a fundamental conflict between a monolithic modern Judaism and mainstream American culture. For example, Sanford Marovitz describes Potok's protagonists as being caught between "the threats and temptations of secular America in contrast to the security offered by their nuclear communities"—but he misrepresents Potok here.[23] The threats and temptations Danny and Reuven face do not come from secular America but from crises *within* their "core communities": the influx of textual-critical methods into yeshivas, the worldwide devastation and theological challenges of the Holocaust, and the deeply passionate stances for and against Zionism. Marovitz—and many others— assumed that Potok's Hasidic Judaism related to mainstream America in the way that Roth's and Bellow's liberal Judaism related to mainstream America. Fictional representations of Orthodoxy were asked to display the same themes and conflicts as fictional representations of "peripheral" Jewish experience—or to conflate Orthodox Judaism with Eastern European Judaism. As Potok's Orthodox world was rejected as a valid expression of American Judaism, so too was Potok's writing marginalized and dismissed as romantic and sentimental. At least in part because of this, he is not included in most critics' lists of influential Jewish American writers.

It is striking that the popular reading public, including non-Jews, read Potok differently than these critics, and perhaps more in line with the way Potok understood his own work. Notably, despite the fact that both Jews and non-Jews shared an experience of alienation in the 1960s, critics of Jewish American literature appropriated alienation as a distinctively Jewish American quality. Potok's characters do experience alienation, but he does not suggest that their experience is unique. On the contrary, even when cast in a traditional Jewish setting, the alienation Potok describes is something most Americans at that time could identify with; thus, readers of all backgrounds could see themselves in Potok's world. Potok managed to convince mainstream American readers that the personal religious crises that Orthodox, even Hasidic, Jews struggled with were not unlike their own. It was not the *content* of the conflicts that resonated with them, as the content was specifically Jewish: modern methods of biblical criticism, the Holocaust, and Zionism. Rather, it was the *scope* and *tenor* of the conflict. Potok received letters to this effect from his readers: "What non-Jews are doing—if I can get it from the letters they are sending me—is that they are simply translating themselves into the particular context of the boys and fathers and the mothers and the situation that I'm writing about. So instead of being a Jew, you are a Baptist; instead of being an Orthodox Jew, you are a Catholic; and the dynamic is the same."[24] Gershon Shaked comments, "In his [Potok's] fiction, it is the struggle for meaning and self-knowledge in the multiple entanglements of twentieth-century cultural confrontations that is central, though the actors who share in that struggle are all Jewish."[25]

More important, Potok painted a complex picture of the diversity within American Judaism and, as a result, a nuanced conception of the choices presented with regard to competing identities. Literary critics who focused on the Bellow-Malamud-Roth depiction of American Judaism focused solely on abandoning traditional Jewish identity. The choice these critics perceived was between being a traditional Jew and being a secularized American, implying that one could not be both. Potok understood that American life required choices—as suggested by his novel's multivalent title—but he presents more complex options. First, Danny and Reuven face differences *within* Judaism. The central conflicts within *The Chosen* are conflicts between Jews with different understandings of what it means to be Jewish. Potok suggests a spectrum of Jewish belief and practice, dramatized most strikingly in the imposed separation of the two boys by Danny's father. This resonated with American Christians, who were struggling with their own divisive issues in the sixties and seventies. Potok makes clear that even within the small world of Brooklyn Orthodox Judaism, there are strong conflicts of opinion among members— how much more, then, can one expect to find conflicts of opinion within the broad spectrum of Christian Americans?

In addition, Danny and Reuven never consider abandoning their Jewish identity; rather, their choices center on how to integrate their religious identities with secular modernism, in what Potok himself termed "core-to-core" confrontations. These choices play out in very concrete ways in *The Chosen*. Most obviously, at the end of the book, Danny shaves his beard and earlocks, choosing to look one way while the rest of his community looks another. He also breaks off a long-standing engagement in an arranged marriage. Reuven develops an interpretive response to a problematic Talmud passage using textual-critical methodologies, a strategy rejected by traditional Orthodoxy. In all of these examples, Potok speaks to general readers wrestling with how to integrate their religious identity into secular modernism.

Problems always arise when one tries to characterize an entire category of literature—one tends to homogenize. For example, Bonnie Lyons opens her essay "American-Jewish Fiction Since 1945" with a partial list of luminaries in the Jewish American canon. She then closes the essay with the following comment: "Contemporary American-Jewish fiction is then a coherent body of work; that is, there is something gained by grouping the individual writers and works in this way. . . . There are shared ideas about both life and art. Some of these ideas run counter to those of most American fiction; in particular, the American-Jewish vision of the individual as embedded in history and the family directly opposes the typical American conception of the American Adam, the solitary individual beginning a new day."[26] Lyons follows these generalizations with the obligatory caveat, but her point has been made: Jewish American fiction can be characterized in one way, but non-Jewish American fiction should be characterized in another. The two are necessarily distinct from each other.

Potok challenges this neat bifurcation. *The Chosen*, blatantly autobiographical, unveils a world of conflict, not between Judaism and America but within Judaism. It describes localized conflicts within families and between particular communities, challenging broad-brush characterizations of mid-century Jewish experience. To categorize Potok as a "romantic" or a "sentimentalist" makes it easy to dismiss his portrayal of Jewish experience as false. Such a move suggests broad assumptions about what makes some experiences "Jewish American" and others not. This, I would argue, is an issue of concern to the study of religion, because it indirectly defines who and what is acknowledged as belonging to specific religious communities. What is (and is not) Jewish American? Such questions bring us to the heart of the work of religion and literature.

Religion and Literature

What do these comments about *The Chosen* have to contribute to the study of Judaism or to the study of religion more broadly? In this concluding section I'd like to outline some potential contributions at several levels.

It is common to think first of literature as a medium that includes religious themes or metaphors or as a context in which representations of specific religious communities are presented. As many scholars have noted, *The Chosen* offers a rare glimpse into a traditionally private community, Russian Hasidic Jews in New York. Through the novel Jews and non-Jews alike were introduced to a branch of Eastern European Judaism that exists on the margins of mainstream American life. This exposed readers to an unfamiliar world— Hasidic history, traditions of study, and domestic observance. At the same time, it demystified this world to some extent and spoke universally to concerns shared by Potok's readers. The novel demonstrated that while the particularities of Hasidic experience may be foreign to most Americans, the underlying concerns and conflicts were identical to other Americans' conflicts. It suggested that people across various religious communities wrestled with questions of how to live as modern Americans within traditional religious frameworks.

At another level, Potok intentionally sought not just to inform his readers but also to transform them. Potok specifically rejected the idea of writing for entertainment, asserting instead that he saw himself "as a novelist with a mission." He said repeatedly that the act of reading could be a transformative experience, describing how reading Evelyn Waugh's *Brideshead Revisited* had transformed him: "It absolutely changed my life. . . . I lived inside that book with more intensity than I lived inside my own world. . . . When I closed the book, I was *overwhelmed* by my relationship to that book. I remember asking myself, 'What did he do to me? How do you do this kind of thing with words?'"[27] Potok has also referenced James Joyce's *A Portrait of the Artist as a Young Man*: "*Portrait*, which was almost as much a part of my growing up as were the Bible and Talmud, is resident in the deepest springs of my being."[28] Potok, like many other authors, believed that literature had the power to transform individuals, to change their orientation to the world, and to instill moral virtues in their character. As Sanford E. Marovitz notes, "He intentionally conveys a sense of moral truth in his fiction and wishes it to serve as a means of guiding his readers, especially American Jews, toward developing some form of meaningful commitment in their lives."[29]

At still another level, Potok's work indirectly raises questions about representations of religious experience in America. As we have seen, the tendency among critics of Jewish American fiction was to highlight a certain kind of Jewish American experience, one chronicled in the writings of authors such as Roth, Bellow, and Malamud. By highlighting this stream of fiction, *without noting divergent streams of writing*, critics were not simply evaluating fiction. They were also glossing over the diversity of Jewish experience in America. Orthodox, particularly Hasidic Orthodox, communities were treated as throwbacks to the past, remains of the initial waves of Jewish immi-gration, but certainly not as representative of modern Jewish life. Such treat-ment conveys not only a certain perspective on traditional Judaism but also assumptions about the trajectory of modern Judaism, implying that the future of Judaism is assimilation.

It should be mentioned that, at the time, such assumptions were well founded. Jonathan Sarna, in his recent landmark book *American Judaism*, reminds us that in the 1940s and 1950s "Orthodox Judaism was actually losing ground." Sarna cites a 1952 study documenting that the existing Orthodox population was aging and "only twenty-three percent of the children of the Orthodox intend to remain Orthodox; a full half plan to turn Conservative."[30] Given these statistics, it may not be surprising that Jewish American literary criticism focused on more liberal, even "peripheral," Judaism as it identified its literary heavyweights. But such predictions about Orthodoxy now seem to have been premature. Alan Dershowitz, in his controversial book *The Vanish-ing American Jew*, notes that Hasidic and Orthodox "enclaves" persist in America, and he claims that "differential birth and assimilation rates suggest that what remains of the Jewish community by the middle of the twenty-first century will consist primarily of ultra-Orthodox Jews."[31] These staggering rates of assimilation and birthrate projections demonstrate that Orthodox communities are growing much more quickly than any other branch of Juda-ism.[32] Despite the dire mid-twentieth-century projections, Dershowitz's data indicates that Orthodoxy is alive and well. This may require us to rethink monolithic canons that marginalize traditional expressions of Judaism.

Current religious studies work on American religious life is grappling with similar issues. Increasingly, scholars are recognizing the diverse reli-gious streams that were present at the birth of this nation, and they are revis-ing histories to express the complexity of this religious diversity. No longer do we generalize about America as heir to the Puritans; instead, scholars such as Catherine Albanese draw attention to the multiple communities that contrib-uted to the religious makeup of early America.[33] More recently, scholars have been documenting the global religious diversity present in America today. For example, Diana Eck's Pluralism Project at Harvard University draws attention to the wealth of immigrant religious communities within American metropolitan communities.[34]

Potok's literary treatment of Orthodox Jews resonates with these more complex approaches to American religious history. Conversely, by omitting Potok's work from the great canon of mid-twentieth-century Jewish Ameri-can fiction, the myth of monolithic religious history is perpetuated. Smaller traditional Jewish communities get dismissed as out of date, irrelevant, and perhaps even backward, and thus are indirectly labeled as insignificant to the understanding of developing Jewish life in that time. Such a characterization not only oversimplifies Jewish American fiction; it belies the diversity of Jewish American religious experience and the complexity of Jewish American identity.

I do not want to oversimplify here. As mentioned early in this essay, there are numerous good literary reasons why Potok may not be included with Roth, Bellow, and Malamud among the great literary figures of mid-twentieth-century Jewish American fiction. But we need to be aware of what is at stake in such a list, and we need to be aware of the potential cultural forces at work when such canons are created. Critical and public responses to Potok's novels, beginning with *The Chosen*, may also reflect differing preferences—perhaps unconscious at some levels—for how American Judaism should be defined. In this context, the establishment of literary canons is an intensely theological pursuit.

We have recently celebrated 350 years of Jewish life in America. It seems appropriate at this time to reflect not just on the historical presence of Jews in this country but also on how we characterize that presence. As Americans become increasingly aware of the many religious communities being nurtured in the American landscape, it is important to highlight the complexity *within* each religious tradition as well. In this task, Jewish American literature has much to contribute. Jews continue to have widely divergent experiences of integrating their Jewish and American identities, experiences that Potok could not even dream of. A heterogeneous critical approach to Jewish American literature will represent and speak to the complexity of Jewish American life in a way that offers meaning to Jews and non-Jews alike.

NOTES

1. Mike Field, "Potok Has Chosen to Create Worlds from Words," *Gazette*, November 14, 1994, http://www.jhu.edu/~gazette/1994/nov1494/potok.html.

2. Potok's name and work do not appear in many volumes about Jewish American literature. See, for example, Sanford Pinsker, *Jewish-American Fiction, 1917–1987* (New York: Twayne, 1992).

3. Arnold J. Band, *Studies in Modern Jewish Literature* (Philadelphia: Jewish Publication Society, 2003), 409. Note that the reference to Potok appears in the chapter "Popular Fiction and the Shaping of Jewish Identity." Potok is omitted entirely from the list at the beginning of Bonnie K. Lyons's "American-Jewish Fiction Since 1945," in *Handbook of American-Jewish Literature: An Analytical Guide to Topics, Themes, and Sources*, ed. Lewis Fried (New York: Greenwood Press, 1988), 61.

4. Quoted in Field, "Potok Has Chosen," 5–6.

5. Quoted in ibid., 8.

6. For a slightly different take on Potok's treatment of women, see Joan Del Fattore, "Women as Scholars in Chaim Potok's Novels," *Studies in American Jewish Literature* 4 (1985): 52–61.

7. Chaim Potok, *The Chosen* (Greenwich, Conn.: Fawcett, 1967), 10. Subsequent citations to this edition will be given in the text.

8. Elaine M. Kauvar, "An Interview with Chaim Potok," in *Conversations with Chaim Potok*, ed. Daniel Walden (Jackson: University Press of Mississippi, 2001), 67.

9. Harold Ribalow, "A Conversation with Chaim Potok," in Walden, *Conversations with Chaim Potok*, 13.

10. Daniel Walden, introduction to *Conversations with Chaim Potok*, ix.

11. Sanford Pinsker, "The Crucifixion of Chaim Potok," *Studies in American Jewish Literature* 4 (1985): 40.

12. Lewis Fried, "American-Jewish Fiction, 1930–1945," in Fried, *Handbook of American-Jewish Literature*, 35.

13. Irving Howe, "Philip Roth Reconsidered," *Commentary*, December 1972, 22.

14. Gerhard Falk, "Jewish-American Literature," http://www.jbuff.com/c021501.htm.

15. Quoted in Irving Malin, *Jews and Americans* (Carbondale: Southern Illinois University Press, 1965), 4.

16. Ibid.

17. Field, "Potok Has Chosen," 5.

18. Quoted in ibid., 8.

19. Quoted in Lyons, "American-Jewish Fiction," 62.

20. Ibid.

21. Quoted in S. Lillian Kremer, "An Interview with Chaim Potok, July 21, 1981," *Studies in American Jewish Literature* 4 (1985): 96.

22. S. Lillian Kremer, "Dedalus in Brooklyn: Influences of *A Portrait of the Artist as a Young Man* on *My Name Is Asher Lev*," *Studies in American Jewish Literature* 4 (1985): 27.

23. Sanford Marovitz, "Freedom, Faith, and Fanaticism: Cultural Conflict in the Novels of Chaim Potok," *Studies in American Jewish Literature* 5 (1986): 138.

24. Chaim Potok, quoted in Ribalow, "Conversation with Chaim Potok," 5–6.

25. Gershon Shaked, "German-Jewish and American-Jewish Literature," in Fried, *Handbook of American-Jewish Literature*, 403. Shaked, however, argues that this is closer "to the Hebrew and Yiddish literature of the turn of the last century than to German or American-Jewish literature of this century," thus implying certain criteria for inclusion within the category of American Jewish literature (ibid.).

26. Lyons, "American-Jewish Fiction," 85.

27. Quoted in Walden, introduction to *Conversations with Chaim Potok*, viii. In personal conversation, Rabbi Gerald Wolpe noted that Potok, like many others of his generation, was also deeply influenced by Milton Steinberg's *As a Driven Leaf*.

28. Chaim Potok, "The First Eighteen Years," *Studies in American Jewish Literature* 4 (1985): 101.

29. Marovitz, "Freedom, Faith, and Fanaticism," 342.

30. Jonathan D. Sarna, *American Judaism: A History* (New Haven: Yale University Press, 2004), 278.

31. Alan M. Dershowitz, *The Vanishing American Jew: In Search of Jewish Identity for the Next Century* (New York: Touchstone, 1997), 23.

32. Ibid., 24–27.

33. See, for example, Catherine Albanese, *America: Religions and Religion*, 3rd ed. (Belmont, Calif.: Wadsworth, 1999), and Albanese, *Nature Religion in America: From the Algonkian Indians to the New Age* (Chicago: University of Chicago Press, 1991).

34. For more on Diana Eck's work with the Pluralism Project, see http://www.pluralism.org.

THE THREE-PRONGED DIALECTIC

Understanding Conflict in Potok's Early Fiction

Jessica Lang

While the liveliest and most sharply depicted conflicts in Chaim Potok's earliest novels, *The Chosen* (1967) and its sequel, *The Promise* (1969), depend largely on dialectical forces playing themselves out, the more significant struggle introduced in the first novel and brought to a fraught climax in the second is far less dramatically positioned and, consequently, more elusive and difficult to understand. This struggle involves a triangulated relationship among an ultra-Orthodox Hasidic sect, modern Orthodoxy, and traditional Conservative Judaism. Before turning to a discussion of Potok's various characterizations of Judaism and the figures who stand for the ideologies named above, I wish to consider the role of conflict as a more general narrative strategy in Potok's novels, in particular its philosophical and psychological underpinnings. This dimension of both novels resonates clearly with the author's own intellectual interests and serves to illuminate the complicated relationship among three branches of Jewish belief, practice, and ideology. In short, Potok's life and, as many critics have noted, his fiction dwell on moments of fracture that illuminate an emotional pull of irreconcilable forces, often dichotomous, with the protagonist forced to negotiate his way between them.

Potok himself has commented on the autobiographical quality of much of his fiction insofar as he often describes a protagonist abandoning one community after finding meaning in another. In *The Chosen* and *The Promise*, Danny Saunders, the son and presumptive heir of the leader of an ultra-

Orthodox sect, chooses to pursue a Ph.D. in psychology rather than stay exclusively within his community. Reuven Malter, the modern Orthodox protagonist, commits himself to an intellectual methodology, scientific method, as a means of understanding Talmud—a controversial form of analytical thinking within the Orthodox community and one that serves to alienate its practitioners. As evidenced in these and other narratives, Potok describes a distancing effect from one community even if this is not accompanied by a parallel drawing near to another community. Indeed, his own personal choices in narrative, both in what to read and in what to write, bear within them a separation from his status quo. Recalling his near-religious identification with secular literature, Potok recounts in one essay that

> somehow Evelyn Waugh reached across the chasm that separated my tight New York Jewish world from that of the upper-class British Catholics in his book. . . . From that time on, I not only read works of literature for enjoyment but also studied them with Talmudic intensity in order to teach myself how to create worlds out of words on paper. . . . In time I discovered that I had entered a tradition—modern literature. Fundamental to that tradition was a certain way of thinking the world; and basic to that was the binocular vision of the iconoclast.[1]

Certainly the mode of crisis that drives the plots of Potok's novels forward creates a sense of rhythm that resonates with his own personal history. I would propose, however, that not only do different modes of conflict exist in Potok's fiction but they are grounded in an intellectual, as well as autobiographical, understanding of reason and argument, one that struggles to reconcile ultra-Orthodox traditions with postmodern religious sensibilities. The focus of this essay is to consider the philosophical underpinnings that are the basis of conflict in Potok's work. I work here to present a distinction between historical conflict, on the one hand, and Potok's presentation of Jewish intellectual and religious conflict, on the other. Potok's depiction in *The Chosen* of an Orthodox and an ultra-Orthodox community and his depiction in *The Promise* of Conservative, Orthodox, and ultra-Orthodox ideologies are *not* oppositional. Furthermore, while historical conflict and war are depicted with a clear sense of advocacy and moral decisiveness, the religious conflict found in the two novels emphasizes ambiguity, with each community's uniqueness, strengths, and weaknesses acknowledged, but with no single route being celebrated exclusively as the chosen—or promised—one.

In keeping with Potok's devotion and regular practice of painting and drawing, the opening scenes in both *The Chosen* and *The Promise* are dramatic not only because of their divisional nature but also because of the colorful tableau they present to the reader. *The Chosen* opens with a baseball game between the boys attending an ultra-Orthodox yeshiva and those attending a modern Orthodox yeshiva. Not only is the game itself an exercise in opposition, but Reuven is warned by one of his teammates that the ultra-Orthodox boys are "wild. . . . They're murderers."[2] Furthermore, the sports competition is overshadowed by the larger world conflict taking place in Europe at the same time. The coach of the modern Orthodox team reminds his boys that "there's a war on, remember?" (8) and that he "want[s] live soldiers, not dead heroes" (17). The dichotomy between players and murderers, between sport and war, between the living and the dead, suits the tableau at hand, with its infielders and outfielders, throwing and catching, winning and losing. With the image of a hotly contested baseball game, Potok introduces the idea of opposition, which is central to the novel series.

The Promise opens with the modern Orthodox hero of *The Chosen*, Reuven Malter, his girlfriend Rachel Gordon, and her emotionally troubled fourteen-year-old cousin Michael Gordon attending a county fair and getting fleeced in a gambling game. The conning of the trio takes on dark tones as Michael accuses the paternalistic Yiddish-speaking carnival-booth owner that he is "just like all the others. . . . You hate us!"[3] The scene vacillates between emotional coherence—Michael boasts of his "very famous" father with a "proud smile" (24)—and psychic coldness, with the pitchman lapsing into periodic silence and Michael standing "frozen, staring at the old man" (26). As in the opening tableau of *The Chosen*, action is juxtaposed with inaction, morality faces off with immorality, youthful naïveté pushes against jaded experience.

In both books, the opening scene centers around a game that presents a conflict of rather epic proportions—murderers against ballplayers, amusement seekers against con men—that the novel then magnifies and explores. The push and pull of both the baseball and carnival scenes is shattered by a moment of aggression. In *The Chosen*, Danny deliberately hits one of Reuven's pitches in such a way that the ball smashes into Reuven's face and almost costs him his eye. In *The Promise*, the Yiddish-speaking pitchman cheats Reuven, Rachel, and Michael of their prize and, in response to their accusations, grabs his cane, "lift[s] it high over his head, and [brings] it down with a crash upon the counter. . . . 'Out!' the old man shouted, waving the cane. 'Out! Play or get out!'" (28). In both novels, then, the introductory scene works to literalize a conflict that pulls in two directions, bears two sides, two sets of witnesses, and two different stories.

I would like to present another example of conflict, one that carries through and connects the two novels, before moving to discuss the underlying implications produced by this sustained yet varying dialectic. In *The Chosen*, when Reuven joins Danny and his father for a session of textual study, Reuven "realized soon enough that the *Pirkei Avot* text was merely being used as a sort of jumping-off point for them, because they were soon ranging through most of the major tractates of the Talmud again. And it wasn't a quiz or a quiet contest. . . . It was a pitched battle. . . . Danny and his father fought through their points with loud voices and wild gestures of their hands almost to where I thought they might come to blows" (163). This highly articulate exchange stands in marked contrast to the more daily interactions between Reb Saunders and Danny. Reb Saunders, in keeping with a long-standing European tradition, raises his son in silence, only speaking to him when they study Talmud.

Reuven and his father also often study text together. Both sets of fathers and sons iterate the habitual nature of their time spent engaged in religious textual analysis—it happens "*every* Saturday afternoon," Reuven comments to Danny (*The Chosen*, 212). The main difference, revealed in *The Promise*, is that Reuven's intellectual interactions with his father are of a collaborative nature, whereas Danny's are combative. Reuven not only studies Talmud with his father but also serves as an unofficial research assistant, a partner, even, at times, a colleague: "After dinner I took a copy of my father's book into the living room and sat by the light we kept burning all through Shabbat, and read. I read until late that night and all of Shabbat afternoon. I read very carefully, on a nervous hunt for errors that might have slipped by us but at the same time reading in order to study again what my father had written. I found no errors and more than half a dozen places where my father's words took on meanings I had not seen in them before" (*The Promise*, 160). Danny and Reb Saunders, on the one hand, and Reuven and David Malter, on the other, echo the tug-of-war established in the opening scenes of each novel, with one generational set engaged in a loud, muscular show of textual control and memory and the other committed to a quieter, more reverential form of learning. But what complicates the sense of opposition here is that Danny and Reb Saunders live in silence except when they study a religious text, and Reuven and David Malter, for all of their affection and respect for each other, end up spending much of their time in hospitals (Reuven is hospitalized after being hit in the eye by the baseball, and his father is hospitalized at various points for heart attacks) or pursuing their individual intellectual goals. In spite of Shabbat afternoons spent tussling over a text, the two fathers and two sons lead largely disconnected lives.

To comfort his son, who is dismayed at the emotional and physical invest-ment of the Saunders, father-and-son learning session, David Malter says, "It is not terrible, Reuven. Not for Danny, not for his father, and not for the people who listened. It is an old tradition, this kind of Talmudic discussion. I have seen it many times, between great rabbis. But it does not only take place between rabbis. When Kant became a professor, he had to follow an old tradi-tion and argue in public on a philosophical subject. One day when you are a professor in a university and read a paper before your colleagues, you will also have to answer questions" (*The Chosen*, 146). It is here that the philo-sophical nature of Potok's dialectical model most explicitly asserts itself. David Malter is gesturing toward Kant's decade of silence between 1770, when he was finally promoted to full professor at the University of Königsberg and published the *Inaugural Dissertation* in honor of this appointment, and 1781, when his next publication, the *Critique of Pure Reason*, came out. While at times this decade of latent productivity was derided as a "dogmatic slumber," it has more often been characterized as "the most important period of Kant's intellectual development," in large part because during that period "Kant's thought underwent a dialectical development" in which he began to question "some of his basic assumptions" and "arrived at a new (critical) position by answering these questions."[4] Potok harnesses two aspects of Kant's intellec-tual activity. First, the novelist's illumination of the tension between intellec-tual productivity and silence in both the Saunders and Malter homes resonates with Kant's determined removal from the academic community in his attempt to better understand and resolve weaknesses in his earlier work. Second, Kant's dialectical model of thesis, antithesis, and synthesis, which recognizes within it the history of argument and ideas, is a form of conflict that Potok latches onto to help envision the series of crises that move the plots of *The Chosen* and *The Promise* forward.

In many other narratives and, importantly, in the novels Potok lists as being of particular importance in influencing both his decision to become an author and the nature of his writing, a single major source of tension is devel-oped into the climax. *The Chosen* and *The Promise* stand in contrast to this model. While each novel has an overarching conflict that needs to be resolved—in *The Chosen* the relationship between Danny and Reuven; in *The*

Promise the personal crises of Michael Gordon, Danny, and Reuven—each novel is carried forward by additional mini-crises. These include physical conflicts such as the ball game; Danny's commitment to psychology and Reuven's to mathematics; their relationships with their respective fathers; their unorthodox methods of helping Michael, and so forth. Each crisis reflects the formula pictorially represented at the beginning of *The Chosen* and *The Promise*: two sides struggling for control and authority, a violent climax, and a resolution that is quiet and, for the most part, unsettled. However, this pattern is disrupted in Potok's presentation of ultra-Orthodox, modern Orthodox, and traditional Conservative Jewish communities and traditions.[5] Here the form of crisis, which elsewhere in the novel unfolds as a bilateral dialectic, is not sustained; Potok triangulates the system of beliefs he is evaluating, thus setting up quite a different model to explore the crisis of faith that strikes Reuven Malter, one that mirrors the author's own.

I would like to suggest that in categorizing two distinct models of opposition in *The Chosen* and *The Promise* Potok is reflecting two key aspects of his own intellectual identity; one is a product of his secular education, from Waugh to German philosophy, and the other is central to his identity as a Jew and a yeshiva graduate. For while he relies on Kantian methodology to manage, understand, and resolve a whole host of questions and issues in his novels in a dialectical mode, Potok's presentation of Jewish text, tradition, belief, and argument reflects a Talmudic sensibility, with its long tradition of disagreement, interpretation, reinterpretation, and discussion. David Malter, the esteemed Talmud scholar, and his son take care to articulate the multitudinous directions and variations of rabbinic interpretation. "Rabbinic literature can be studied in two different ways, in two directions, one might say," Reuven explains. "It can be studied quantitatively or qualitatively—or, as my father once put it, horizontally or vertically" (*The Chosen*, 162).

The climax of both *The Chosen* and *The Promise* entails Reuven's triumph in asserting his intellectual powers over a portion of the Talmud and establishing the validity of his methodology as opposed to that presented by his teachers. In *The Chosen*, he prepares for class in two ways, one method adhering to the traditions of his school, the Samson Raphael Hirsch Seminary and College, and the other taught to him by his father. Reuven characterizes the former method—the *pilpul* method—of reviewing passages from the Babylonian Talmud assigned to him in class as "traditional," "relatively simple," "brute memorization" of the text and the commentaries. The second method, involving textual emendation, is, in contrast, "tortuous," requiring endless research "through all the cross-references and all the parallel passages in the Palestin-ian Talmud" (*The Chosen*, 245). Toward the end of *The Promise*, Reuven explains the tension between the two methods as he prepares for his final exams before being ordained as an Orthodox rabbi:

> Many Orthodox Jewish scholars believe that the printed version of the Babylonian Talmud is the fixed and final depository of the oral tradi-tion and that its teachings are identical in date, origin, and sanctity to the teachings which are derived from the interpretation of Scripture itself. . . . This was a position which my father and I found impossible to maintain. There were too many variant readings, too many obvious scribal errors, too many emendations and substitutions of texts even within the Talmud itself for us to believe that text was frozen. We saw the Talmud as containing almost a thousand years of ideas and tradi-tions that had been in flux; we saw the text of the Talmud as fluid, alive, like a body of rushing water with many tributaries leading into it and from it. (330)

Most scholars view the two methodological approaches, *pilpul* and scien-tific method, as, at the very least, operating independently of each other. *Pilpul* is criticized most often as "Talmudic quibbling," because, at its most extreme, it involves long digressions over minute points in the Talmud.[6] It was a domi-nant method of studying Talmud beginning in the thirteenth century, because it strenuously protected the Oral and Written Torah from outside influence.[7] Scientific method attempts to reconcile apparent contradictions in various editions of the Talmud and to study the text not only as bearing religious and theological meaning but also as reflecting a history of authorship. Many schol-ars of Talmudic history attribute the first step in textual criticism, another name for scientific method, to the traditional Talmud scholar Raphael Nathan Rabbinovicz, who between 1867 and 1886 published the fifteen-volume *Dik-dukei Soferim*, which contained "variant Talmudic readings from medieval authorities and early printings and . . . manuscripts."[8] One of the figures con-tinuing Rabbinovicz's work was Henry Malter, who was hired by the Jewish Publication Society to edit the first critical edition of a Talmudic tractate, Ta'anit. "In preparing this tractate," writes one colleague of Malter's at Dropsie College in Philadelphia, "Malter utilized all the extant manuscripts, and all the printed readings, rare as well as standard. . . . In many passages, Malter has completely revised and re-arranged the accepted text. Many Talmudists will at first glance be reluctant to adopt his readings, but in nearly every case it will be seen upon examination of his notes that the new readings are entirely sound."[9] Clearly the intellectual inheritance of Henry Malter, along with his surname, is passed down through David Malter to Reuven Malter, the main proponent of scientific method in Potok's first two novels.

The tension between the ultra-Orthodox world of Danny Saunders and the modern Orthodox world of Reuven Malter that is so vividly portrayed in the baseball game at the opening of *The Chosen* never comes to a head around the topic of analyzing the Talmud using scientific method or textual emendation. When Reuven reveals to Danny that he is studying the Talmud critically, Danny's response is one of grinning surprise: "You're planning to try scientific method on Rav Schwartz? . . . Well, good luck with your scientific method" (*The Chosen*, 212). Later, when David Malter publishes his book, a study of the Talmud invoking scientific method, Reb Saunders resists joining the critics. He tells Reuven, "I have been asked to write about your father's book. . . . There will be trouble with that book. When a scholar as great as your father writes such a book it cannot be ignored. . . . But I will not write about it. I will say nothing" (*The Promise*, 200). Reb Saunders has fought with David Malter over politics, and David Malter, through his son, voices distaste for the rabbinical hierarchy around which Hasidic Judaism is structured. But regarding each other's intellectual pursuits and projects, the two never butt heads.

This absence of opposition only serves to set in relief the tension between those who do oppose scientific method—namely, many of David Malter's colleagues—and those who endorse it—namely, Reuven Malter's teachers. Furthermore, the Malters' support of this form of analysis is complicated by the presence, in *The Promise*, of Abraham Gordon, Michael's father, a widely published professor of Jewish philosophy who teaches at the Zechariah Frankel Seminary and a figure "whose books were scorned and despised by the rabbis in my very Orthodox school." The Frankel Seminary, named after one of the intellectual forefathers of Conservative Judaism, is so deeply distrusted by those affiliated with the Hirsch Seminary and College, itself named after a leading figure in modern Orthodoxy, that when Reuven admits in the middle of his oral rabbinic ordination exam to using the Frankel library, he becomes likewise viewed with suspicion:

"Where did you see this edition of the Mishnah?" the Dean asked abruptly. . . .

"In the Frankel Seminary Library," I said.

He gaped at me. I heard a thin sigh escape from between his lips. . . . [Rav Gershenson] was no longer smiling. He did not mind emendations that were supported by internal evidence in the Talmud itself. But to appeal to a reading that was not found anywhere inside the Talmud—that was dangerous. That sort of method threatened the authority of the Talmud, for it meant that the Talmud did not have all the sources at its disposal upon which laws could be based. (*The Promise*, 334–35)

Inserting a text not found inside the Talmud is dangerous, but inserting a text located at the Frankel Seminary Library is downright treacherous. Reuven, disregarding his teachers' responses, forges ahead with a plethora of sources that support his intertextual reading and, in so doing, his multifaceted approach and argument. He refers to commentaries written by "Luria and Perlow and Pineles and Epstein." He references two Amoras in the tractate Pesachim. He cites "two Talmudic discussions in the Gemara of the tractate Ketubot." Finally, he concludes with the reference that initiated the shocked response of his teachers, claiming that the manuscript needed to understand this passage of Talmud is available only in the Napoli edition of the Mishnah, a fifteenth-century document that is not widely read (*The Promise*, 335–36).

Reuven Malter's elaborate re-creation of his research, which incorporates a wide web of views, authors, and references and spans a vast period of time, presents an alternative mode of understanding and resolving argument to the one posited by Kant and his followers. Instead of maintaining a dialectic, with its demand for polarization and mediation, Potok and his fictional representative, Reuven Malter, revel in reading and responding to a great wave of Talmudic scholarship. They position themselves as both readers, incorporating and learning from those who have devoted themselves to the Talmud in previous generations, and writers, creating a new stream of thought and so contributing to an ever-deepening pool.

By the conclusion of *The Promise*, the backlash produced by David Malter's book forces him out of his current position on the faculty of an increasingly right-wing school, and he accepts an offer to join the faculty of the Frankel Seminary, where his book is celebrated and recognized for its scholarly impact. He is ambivalent about the offer, stating that while it is a "great privilege" to teach at Frankel, it would have been a greater one to work in a setting such as Hirsch. Instead, Reuven is offered a position as a Talmudist at the Hirsch Graduate School, a new component of the rabbinical school from which he has just graduated. "It will be very good to have your father at the [Frankel] seminary," Abraham Gordon says. "You at the [Hirsch] yeshiva and your father at the [Frankel] seminary. Strange . . . usually it's the other way around" (*The Promise*, 344). Usually, Gordon seems to say, the resolution between two oppositional forces, such as tradition and modernity, entails younger generations attempting to meaningfully synthesize the two sides. In the case of Potok's early fiction, however, the younger generation, the newly minted rabbi and seminarian Reuven Malter, will continue "fighting . . . from within" (*The Promise*, 342). The fight, Potok and his narrator agree, will continue without resolution, within the text, within the institution, and within the tradition.

NOTES

1. Chaim Potok, "Culture Confrontation in Urban America: A Writer's Beginnings," in *Literature and the Urban Experience: Essays on the City and Literature*, ed. Michael C. Jaye and Ann Chalmers Watts (New Brunswick: Rutgers University Press, 1981), 163–64.

2. Chaim Potok, *The Chosen* (New York: Ballantine Books, 1967), 7. Subsequent citations to this edition will be given in the text.

3. Chaim Potok, *The Promise* (New York: Ballantine Books, 1969), 29. Subsequent citations to this edition will be given in the text.

4. Michael C. Washburn, "Dogmatism, Scepticism, Criticism: The Dialectic of Kant's 'Silent Decade,'" *Journal of the History of Philosophy* 13 (April 1975): 167.

5. Indeed, the author of an article entitled "Baseball's Jewish Accent" describes Potok's "celebrated opening scene in 'The Chosen[,]' . . . a baseball game between assimilated Jews and black-hatted Hasidim[,] as a way to introduce the chasm between the two communities." *The Economist*, January 8, 1994, 86. Here the writer, in keeping with the many other binaries that Potok presents, misreads Reuven Malter's presence as indicative of "assimilation." It isn't. Reb Saunders makes a point of telling Reuven that "your father is an observer of the Commandments, and you have his head" (*The Chosen*, 135). Reuven is an observant non-Hasidic Jew.

6. Harry A. Wolfson, *Crescas' Critique of Aristotle* (Cambridge: Harvard University Press, 1929), 24–27.

7. *Encyclopedia Judaica*, vol. 13 (Jerusalem: Keter, 1996), s.v. "pilpul."

8. Marc B. Shapiro, "Talmud Study in the Modern Era: From Wissenschaft and Brisk to Daf Yomi," in *Printing the Talmud: From Bomberg to Schottenstein*, ed. Adam Mintz, Sharon Lieberman, and Gabriel M. Goldstein (New York: Yeshiva University Museum, 2005), 104.

9. Solomon Zeitlin, "A Critical Edition of the Talmud: An Appreciation of Malter's Text of Tractate Ta'anit," *Jewish Quarterly Review* 21 (July–October 1930): 68.

GUARDIANS OF THE TORAH

Ambiguity and Antagonism in *The Promise*

Victoria Aarons

. . . for the sake of Torah.

—*THE PROMISE*

Chaim Potok's multilayered novel *The Promise* is at once the story of an adolescent boy's descent into psychosis and the stage for an ideological battle within Judaism, a "theological loyalty test" that shakes the very foundation of belief and reaches well beyond the walls of the academy to threaten the lives of those most vulnerable.[1] *The Promise*, published in 1969 and recipient of the Athenaeum Award, is set in New York in the early 1950s, a difficult time for American Jewry. This period witnessed an influx of refugees from the Holocaust, forcing America, and particularly American Jewry, to assess its own responsibility for the devastation of millions of Jews. In an interview with scholar S. Lillian Kremer, Potok reflected on the onus of unspoken, but no less felt, culpability on the part of Americans, but particularly for American Jews. As Potok put it, these American Jews, who "never did enough," felt the burden of guilt "in a special way."[2] *The Promise* is staged against the landscape of the Holocaust, made increasingly proximate by the arrival of its refugees. Neighborhoods in Brooklyn are "dark with their presence," as they serve as haunting reminders of the utter and catastrophic failure of the civilized world. The growing presence of those who fled "from the sulfurous chaos of the concentration camps" in an attempt to rebuild some version of their lost lives creates the conditions in *The Promise* for an uneasy realignment within Jewish communities that find themselves in flux (*The Promise*, 1). They are reeling from the aftermath of the war and reassessing their place and identity in the material shape of a secular country that simultaneously poses sanctuary and a perceived threat to the sanctity of the lives so brutally lost and thus to the very fabric of *Yiddishkeit*.

Considered to be the sequel to Potok's lauded novel *The Chosen*, *The Promise* in many ways continues the story of Reuven Malter and Danny Saunders, whose coming-of-age in *The Chosen* depends on the intricacies of their developing friendship and shared destiny. *The Chosen* is an account of parallel lives, two sons and two fathers, who ultimately show themselves to be foils as well as doubles. The lives of Reuven Malter, the narrator and central character in *The Chosen*, and his father, rabbi and scholar David Malter, both contrast and mirror the lives of the ultra-Orthodox Danny Saunders and his father, Reb Isaac Saunders, the head of a yeshiva of Hasidic Jews who fled the ravages of Europe to resettle in America. *The Chosen* is a novel of pairings, of contrasts and realignments: two fathers and two sons; two rabbis/scholars whose dedication to Judaism determines the structure of their lives; two groups of Jews attempting to negotiate the balance between the secular world and the divine; and two Jewish boys coming of age in America in the wake of the Holocaust. These two boys, although initially at odds, will become friends; they will, in fact, change places, the one becoming a rabbi in the other boy's stead. Their fathers, too, will at least temporarily change places, as one man aligns with the other man's son in an exchange that puts into motion the conditions by which both boys may choose their destinies, if not entirely without regret, at least freely, in a way that Danny's father, Reb Saunders, never could.

It is Danny Saunders, no less central to the novel than his counterpart, whose struggle to reconcile his inherited legacy with his autonomous future brings the novel's tensions into sharp focus. Central to *The Chosen*, as it is to all of Potok's work, is the empathetic recognition and embrace of suffering, a fundamental feature of Jewish ethics. Reuven Malter's compassionate intelligence is ultimately no contest for the ultra-Orthodox Danny Saunders, whose brilliance is as much a deficit as it is a blessing, a prodigious intellect for which he pays dearly in silence. His is an intellect that will require a breathtakingly defining choice. Both boys must *choose*—choose their futures, choose their mutual friendship, choose the kind of lives they will live as Jews—as much as they have been *chosen*. And the very nature of what it means to be chosen is the dilemma of the novel. For what so strikingly underlies the very texture of *The Chosen* is the problem of choice—how much, at what cost—and, indeed, its potentially subverting other: to have been chosen, to feel the weight of the legacy of the promise of the covenant across time.

The biblical resonance of "the chosen" haunts the novel, and its biblical referent—the Jews as chosen people—hovers at its core. What are an individual's responsibilities as one of the chosen? Does being chosen necessarily subvert the freedom to choose? To whom or to what is one beholden? Just as the title *The Chosen* asks us to consider the myriad linguistic subtleties that spring from its root, "to choose," so does *The Promise* raise similar linguistic complexities inherent in the form and syntactical arrangement of the word. Here, the "promise" is nominative—a pledge that carries the expectation of fulfillment—but, at the same time, couched within it is a motivating action—a contractual agreement into which one willingly enters. If *The Promise* is Potok's sequel to *The Chosen*, then it is so less because of its thematic continuation of the lives of the two central characters, Reuven Malter and Danny Saunders, and more because it revisits the issues that may have been too easily resolved in the first novel. That is, if *The Chosen* sets up the precarious construction of the covenant between God and the Jews, then *The Promise* asks us to consider the consequences of this covenant. Indeed, with stunning clarity, *The Promise* calls into question the nature of that "first promise"—the promise made by God to Abraham, the one so unpredictably made, so rashly accepted, and so circuitously executed, a promise whose ambiguities and disputes are at the very heart of this novel. As such, *The Promise* is a much darker and more realistic depiction of the ethical and cultural challenges for post-Holocaust American Jewry.

The Promise, like *The Chosen*, is narrated by Reuven Malter, now a rabbinical candidate at Hirsch University. He is living in Brooklyn with his father and studying for his *smicha* (Orthodox rabbinic ordination) with Rav Jacob Kalman, a religious fanatic and ideologue and a renowned Talmudist who joined the faculty at Hirsch University after surviving the horrors of the concentration camps. The religious zeal of Rav Kalman, self-anointed guardian of the faith, secures his antagonism toward Reuven's father and others who, to his way of thinking, threaten the sanctity of sacred religious text. As the novel opens, Reuven is in the midst of preparing for his ordination and studying for his master's degree in philosophy. His father, Talmudic teacher and scholar David Malter, whose modern methods of textual criticism challenge the basic tenets of Rav Kalman's unyielding faith, is at work on a new book. Reuven's longtime friend Danny Saunders is now a doctoral student in clinical psychology at Columbia, conducting predoctoral fieldwork at a residential treatment center for children with psychiatric problems. When we first become reacquainted with Reuven, he is dating Rachel Gordon, the niece of Abraham Gordon, a liberal rabbinical scholar. Abraham's questioning of the literal interpretation of the Torah has resulted in his excommunication by Rav Kalman and other ultra-Orthodox rabbis and scholars, "strong and inflexible" men who cling to a strict adherence to the Word, to the sanctity and authority of Hebrew scripture, and to the absolute belief that the sacred texts were revealed on Mount Sinai by God and are thus not to be challenged (*The Promise*, 240). These characters are brought together through the forlorn figure of Michael Gordon, the fourteen-year-old son of Abraham Gordon, a boy who "reads clouds" and whose fierce loyalty to his father and rage against his father's enemies result in his nearly complete psychic disintegration (140). It is around this isolated figure that the lives of the other characters intersect in ferocious and catalyzing ways. For *The Promise*, like *The Chosen*, is a novel of doublings, of pairings and parallel lives; it is, as Reuven suggests, "as if the separate lines of our lives were being manipulated somehow, purposefully and carefully brought together by some master weaver" (102).

But the tone that heralds the onset of this mysterious design from the very beginning of the novel portends the deep anxieties and fears that will be exposed as the lives of Potok's characters collide. *The Promise* paints a portrait of Brooklyn, New York, five years after the end of World War II, as filtered through Reuven Malter's unsettled perspective. The story opens in Williamsburg, home to large numbers of Hasidim who have recreated a world from the past, an enclave in the midst of the modernity and urbanity of cosmopolitan New York. Since the war, the Hasidim have come to inhabit Williamsburg in rapidly increasing numbers. They are transplants not just from the ruins of twentieth-century Eastern Europe but from another era altogether, vestiges of a far older, antimodern world willed into contemporary being by fragments of memory. For Reuven, the ultra-Orthodox are a menacing presence: "dark, somber figures in long black coats and black hats and long beards, earlocks hanging alongside gaunt faces, eyes brooding, like balls of black flame turned inward upon private visions of the demonic" (*The Promise*, 1). The novel's prologue begins in winter, when the neglect wrought upon the neighborhood by the new arrivals is made all the more apparent, a result of their single-minded defiance of the material world. They reside in a "dimension of reality that made trees and grass and flowers irrelevant to their needs. . . . The grassy back yards went slowly bald, the hydrangeas were left to fade and die, and the brown-stones became old and worn" (2). Even as winter gives way to spring and then summer, the cycles fail to rejuvenate the land, and the neighborhoods remain "empty and deserted, a stagnant pool of shimmering asphalt" in the suffocating heat (4). The somber attire of the Hasidim and the worn, tired conditions of Williamsburg create a kind of stasis, as if time itself has been arrested by these refugees who graft upon the cityscape the vestiges of a world and a people exhausted by history. The "caftan-garbed Hasidim" are very much like the synagogue that houses Reb Saunders's congregation, "transplanted from another age, [with] its individual stands, its old chairs and tables, its podium and Ark, the cushioned chair alongside the Ark where Reb Saunders sat, the separate screened-off section for women, the exposed light bulbs hanging from the ceiling, the walls that needed paint . . . as if it were a movie set or something . . . in an historical novel" (189–90). The Hasidim not only represent a world out of real time but also change the very pulse of life for Reuven and the other American Orthodox and more liberal Conservative Jews whose environs inevitably overlap.

Although Reuven studies and lives among the Hasidim, their teeming presence discomfits him and makes him anxious, not in the least because they are posed as antagonists, especially in the person of Rav Kalman, upon whom Reuven's *smicha* depends. Rav Kalman is openly hostile to the work of Reuven's father, modern textual criticism, which he considers "a dangerous method . . . insidious . . . destroying not only Yiddishkeit but also the very essence of religion" (235). For Reuven, Rav Kalman is aligned with *them*, the ultra-Orthodox of Williamsburg, the streets of which are "filled with their bookstores and bookbinderies, butcher shops and restaurants, beeswax candle stores, dry-cleaning stores, grocery stores and vegetable stores, appliance stores and hardware stores—the signs in Yiddish and English . . . the gentiles gone now from behind the counters." Ironically, Reuven finds these Jews, "bearded and in skullcaps," disturbingly foreign (1). Despite the fact that the Hasidim, like Reuven, are Jews, that they share the same Torah, and that Reuven has been among people like them all his life, their presence feels "strange" to him; indeed, "everything about it was strange, faintly distorted and askew" (101). Their willed difference becomes, from the beginning, the source of enormous unease, nagging tension, and apprehension, all the more so for Reuven because they are all Jews bound by the "same distant origins . . . the same Torah" (183). Their shared history and identity frighten him in large part because the attitudes and dogmatic codes of conduct of the Hasidim bespeak an irreparable rupture in the lives of Reuven and his father. Walking through Williamsburg on Shabbat, surrounded by crowds of Hasidim en route to any of the number of synagogues that line the streets, Reuven finds himself "transported to a world I once thought had existed only in the small towns of Eastern Europe or in books about Jewish history. They were my own people, but we were as far apart from one another as we could possibly be and still call ourselves by the name 'Jew'" (238).

Indeed, the battle that will take place in this novel is not between Jew and gentile, but between warring factions of Jews who believe deeply and without equivocation in Judaism, in its history and traditions, in its rituals and collective identity, and in the value of its sacred text. It's a battle between Orthodoxy and change, traditionalism and modernity, faith and reason, the divine and the secular. The quarrel between the two groups focuses on the interpretation of ancient text and the location of textual meaning. And both are "fighting for what they believe in" with equal fervor and dedication (54). For Orthodox Jews such as Reuven Malter and his father and the more liberal Abraham Gordon, the locus of meaning is in humankind; for the ultra-Orthodox, the inviolate center is God. Rav Kalman and his ultra-Orthodox followers believe in a literal interpretation of the Bible. For them, the sanctity of the text and the survival of Judaism depend on an absolute belief in the revelation at Mount Sinai and on the belief that the "sacred texts were given by God to be *studied* by man, not to be rewritten by him" (235). Such texts are not to be tampered with and are not open to reinterpretation and revision.

For David Malter, the richness of the text derives in large part from the wealth of its interpretive possibilities, the ways in which the ancient writings are made accessible to contemporary human thought and action. Both he and Abraham Gordon look for ways to carry the sacred text into the modern world—the very world that the ultra-Orthodox reject. Gordon, professor of Jewish philosophy at the liberal Zechariah Frankel Seminary, whose books on philosophy and theology spark divisive and impassioned controversy, questions strict adherence to the Bible; these questions, he believes, open up ethical possibilities for Judaism. However, for the traditionalist Rav Kalman, such interpretative mobility threatens the fundamental principles of the faith. Gordon's scholarly books raise provocative questions that directly challenge a literal interpretation of the Bible and are thus seen by Rav Kalman and his followers as dangerously transgressive. Indeed, Reuven describes the books as "filled with blunt questions":

Do you believe the world was created in six days? Do you believe in the order of creation given in the Bible? . . . Do you believe in the biblical account of the Revelation at Sinai? Do you believe in miracles? Do you believe that God guides the destiny of every living creature? Do you believe that God talked, actually talked, in the manner described in the Bible? How is one to react to the findings of archeology and anthropology and biology and astronomy and physics? How is one to react to the discoveries of modern biblical scholarship? How might one not believe literally in the Bible and still remain a traditional Jew? (63)

Such lines of inquiry are seductive, especially for Reuven, who likes the questions better than he does the answers. Even Danny Saunders, something of "an enlightened Hasid, almost a Lubavitcher . . . not afraid of the twentieth century," can appreciate Abraham Gordon's scholarship if not his theology (181). As Reuven's father affirms, such questions pose "radical ideas" that make Gordon an "apostate" in the eyes of Rav Kalman and his followers (62). Gordon's work results in his excommunication (*cherem*); his books are banned and his writing considered, as is the man himself, a "danger" (112). And Reuven, Talmud student of Rav Kalman, becomes for Gordon "an ally in the enemy camp" (343).

Although considered blasphemously impertinent by Rav Kalman and other ultra-Orthodox thinkers, Abraham Gordon's questioning of scriptural dogma offers a way of bringing Judaism into the modern world, of reconciling scientific rationality with religious belief. One does not have to agree with Gordon's position to respect it, as David Malter suggests: "Abraham Gordon has achieved something that is remarkable. To develop a theology for those who can no longer believe literally in God and revelation and who still wish to remain observant and not abandon the tradition—that is a remarkable achievement" (87). Gordon refuses to participate in or concede to a perspective that reduces the world to a far too simplistic duality: "Are total belief or complete abandonment the only available choices, or is it possible to reinterpret ancient beliefs in a way that will make them relevant to the modern world and at the same time not cause one to abandon the tradition?" (63). Both Gordon and Rav Kalman want to preserve Judaism in the face of a changing world, but for Rav Kalman, Gordon's philosophical writings are a theological land mine. To save Judaism, Rav Kalman firmly believes that one has to make an unequivocal choice "for Torah" (157). In words that echo passages from *The Chosen*, Rav Kalman emphatically commands the young men who come to learn with him at his *shiur*, "A choice tells the world what is most important to a human being. When a man has a choice to make he chooses what is most important to him, and that choice tells the world what kind of a man he is" (147). It is, for him, the choice of the covenant, a choice made long ago by the first Abraham, the first Jew.

Ironically, it is his namesake, Abraham Gordon, who wants to reconceptualize the covenant and so reconceive "the promise" in America, to see American Judaism "become something an intelligent person would *have* to take seriously and be *unable* to laugh at and *want* to love" (280). Gordon's passionate attempts to ensure the life of Judaism in the contemporary world are rivaled only by Rav Kalman's single-minded efforts to save historical Judaism and his commitment to the never-ending and never-changing promise of the covenant. The questions insistently posed by Gordon raise difficult issues that are never completely resolved in the novel: What happens to theology when treated from the distance of academic scholarship? How does one measure religious devotion? Can religion coexist with the secular world? What does it mean to safeguard the Torah? Can one choose how to be a Jew? Ultimately, however, one question takes center stage: When does religious ideology become, dangerously, the expression of fear?

For Rav Kalman, survivor of the Holocaust, the secular world is a threat, and those who let the secular world in, such as Abraham Gordon, or those who challenge the Torah through modern methods of exegesis, such as David Malter, desecrate and endanger the faith. Rav Kalman, rigid, unbending, is an angry, desperate man whose rage is born of fear—fear of the demise of Judaism, of the abrogation of God, of the betrayal of those who died in the Holocaust because they were Jews. Uncompromising and intolerant, Rav Kalman believes in the strictures of the ancient, irrevocable Law, scripted on stone tablets. In the face of the secular world, "the bewildering American world into which he had suddenly been plunged," he can only react with increased outrage and inflexibility when his reading of the Talmud is challenged (322). Rav Kalman is an enormously complicated man, and he is brought to life by Potok in a realistic, compelling way. We, like Reuven Malter, initially are meant to dislike Rav Kalman and to find painfully distasteful his bullying of his students and his screed against David Malter and Abraham Gordon, whom we quickly come to view with considerable compassion and whose carefully measured and reasonable positions we respect.

Rav Kalman's rigidity is born of his direct knowledge and firsthand experience of the Nazi attempts to eradicate Judaism. Having witnessed the atrocities against the Jews, Rav Kalman fervently adheres to what he rightly perceives to be a vulnerable tradition, made all the more vulnerable, he believes, by attacks from within. And anything that questions the authority of sacred text is, in his dogmatic way of thinking, an attack. Potok explained this attitude in a 1976 interview with Harold Ribalow: "The way Reuven Malter studies Talmud . . . is threatening . . . because Reuven Malter takes a Talmudic text and makes it something fluid. That is terrifying to any fundamentalist mind, because the very basic notion of a fundamentalist mind is that the text is a given, it is fixed and our task is to understand it."[3] Having survived the concentration camps, Rav Kalman will bear witness to those who perished and to the letter of divine Hebraic Law, which he believes is increasingly at risk from explicit attempts to undermine it. In his religious zeal, however, he comes across as self-righteous and at times self-serving, as if he is determined to "mold Orthodoxy" to his own ends (*The Promise*, 240). In his attempts to keep the covenant untarnished, he is oppressive, intimidating, and egomaniacal. Reuven finds his actions intolerable; even attending Rav Kalman's Talmud class is "a suffocating experience," in which the students are forced to learn in an "atmosphere of oppressive tension" (107, 109). One is either "with him or against him . . . all or nothing" (189).

Rav Kalman has left one war only to engage in another, this one bearing the mark of an unreasonable and extreme, obsessive paranoia, as is made apparent in Reuven's bitterly resentful, satiric outburst to his friend Danny: "The enemy surrounds us. The evil forces of secularism are everywhere. Look under the bed before you say the Kriat Shma at night. Look under the bed before you pray the Shacharit Service in the morning. And while you're at it check the books on your desk and look in your typewriter and close the window because they come in with the wind. . . . We become like dead branches and last year's leaves and what the hell good are we for ourselves and the world in a mental ghetto" (141–42). To "open a window," metaphorically, is to let something dangerous in, but also to let something sacred and precious out. As Reuven's father fears, in Rav Kalman's dogmatic mission to defeat the secular world, he "turns away our greatest minds," for his fanaticism removes him from the contemporary American world that Abraham Gordon believes might revitalize Judaism (182). Both sides are desperately fighting for what they believe, but Rav Kalman is motivated by fear. Consequently, the theological sparring in the novel goes far beyond an intellectual disagreement among scholars. For anything that is motivated solely by fear diminishes the individual and makes him blind to the consequences of his actions. And young Michael Gordon, unarmed with the fortress of defenses that his father,

Abraham, and Rav Kalman have long cultivated, is the inadvertent casualty of this treacherous war.

When we first meet fourteen-year-old Michael, he is in the charge of his father's brother and his family, with whom he is staying while Abraham, accompanied by Michael's mother, is traveling in Europe and Israel, engaged in research. Joseph Gordon, his wife Sarah, and their daughter Rachel have left the city for their summer lakeside home not far from the resort area where Reuven and his father are renting a cottage. Reuven is as much enamored with Rachel Gordon, an English major at Brooklyn College, as he is fascinated by her infamous uncle. He accompanies Rachel and her younger cousin Michael to a county fair not far from their summer homes. More a traveling carnival than the advertised county fair, the rides and game booths are "bathed in a blaze of electric lights and neon signs . . . floodlights poking bright fingers into the black sky" (7). This electrified air creates a frenetic and not particularly welcoming atmosphere for Reuven and Rachel, who had anticipated a more leisurely country outing. But Michael, who was curiously quiet during their drive there, seems unusually animated by the carnival, and upon his insistence and against their better judgment, Reuven and Rachel agree to go on the rides. It's a decision that will prove perilous for Michael and will set in motion the sudden explosion of events that follow. Although the claustrophobic enclosure of the prologue rapidly gives way in this first chapter to the seemingly open-air expanse of a county fair, the initial relief at leaving Williamsburg behind is deceptive. The prologue's uneasy and ill-omened tone may be momentarily eclipsed by the anticipated pleasures of vacationing in upstate New York, but it revisits the subsequent scenes in increasingly disturbing ways.

The forbidding description of the carnival grounds sets the scene for Michael's unhinging. The carnival sits amid a "litter of pop bottles, ice-cream wrappers, soiled paper bags, popsicle sticks, beer cans, [and] discarded newspapers." Its booths are "small shanty-like affairs . . . operated by hard-voiced carnival people . . . [and] were scarred and blotched from travel" (10). Uninviting, cacophonous, "a thick din choked the air," Reuven says of the carnival sounds. "I heard gongs, bells, rifle shots from a nearby shooting gallery, the music of a calliope, the whooshing roar of the roller coaster, and a steady waterfall of human noise. It was as if all the noise of the world's wide night had descended upon this one stretch of lighted earth" (8). The carnival's strangely uninviting atmosphere is made all the more portentous by Michael's frenzied and distracted comportment. Indeed, the carnival itself comes to represent the out-of-control condition of the trio's lives. When, at Michael's stubborn urging, they board the roller coaster, the ride rapidly catapults them into a hellish panorama, as their car crests and then drops them "wildly into the night . . . downward on roaring wheels between lights that blurred into quivering lines." Out of control, the car "rose and fell and rose again and fell again. On the ground below, the carnival heaved and undulated like a garish blanket in a windstorm" (11). At the ride's crescendo just before its final plunge, amid the "screams and shouts from the other passengers," Michael, in a crazily daring and unpredictable instant, stands up in the car. This singular and ominous motion foreshadows the metaphorical fall he will suffer later, a descent into psychic despair.

It is interesting that both *The Chosen* and *The Promise* open in a seemingly innocuous setting that very quickly gives way to something sinister, something made all the more dangerous because its menace is initially nameless and cast in the frame of innocent and ordinary entertainment: in the first case, a baseball field, and in the second, carnival grounds. *The Chosen*, as we recall, begins with a baseball game played between two yeshiva teams—the yeshiva of Reuven Malter and the ultra-Orthodox yeshiva of Danny Saunders. The latter team makes for an incongruous sight on a baseball field, its members dressed in "white shirts, dark pants, white sweaters, and small black skullcaps."[4] The baseball field in *The Chosen* is replaced by carnival grounds in *The Promise*, but both are theaters for the dark drama that will unfold beyond the control of the novels' characters.

The baseball game and the carnival exist as narrative frames and as representative icons of Americana. Both function as cultural symbols of American leisure and mass-market entertainment. Both are characterized by crowds of participants and spectators joined in a common exuberance, in moments suspended in real time. Both are ersatz forms of the bucolic and thus of pleasurable distraction. But, for Potok, the freedom and entertainment that each one "sells" are deceptive. For both become sites of antagonism and unrestrained rage. In the baseball game in *The Chosen*, Danny intentionally hits Reuven with the ball that almost blinds him. Standing on the field, watching his rival Danny Saunders at bat, Reuven finds himself uprooted, displaced. The game "stopped being merely a game and became a war. The fun and excitement was out of it now" (*The Chosen*, 28). No longer a place of sport, the baseball field unexpectedly becomes the site of a contest that goes far beyond the field's confines. Competing factions become warring enemies, players square off as volatile rivals, and the field turns into hostile terrain. The young

Reuven ruefully admits, "I felt the anger begin to focus itself upon Danny Saunders, and suddenly it was not at all difficult for me to hate him" (28). This is a game in which the stakes are unpredictably high, as Danny steps up to bat, deliberately aiming for Reuven. He later acknowledges, "I really wanted to kill you" (67). The battleground staged in the theater of the baseball field is a place where emotions, otherwise held in check, are let loose and are somehow given license to get out of control. As such, the baseball game becomes an occasion for antagonistic transgression, a playing ground for the expression of deep-seated and barely articulated resentments and animosities.

The Promise presents an equally insidious occasion for discord and antipathy as the older Reuven Malter, accompanied by Rachel Gordon and her younger cousin Michael, approach the carnival gaming booths. Convinced by Michael to try their luck in an ostensibly simple game of chance, they find themselves defrauded, the victims of a swindler, a con man, who plays upon their most vulnerable misgivings. Here, the carnival is revealed to be an economically coercive mass-market enterprise of corruption under the guise of harmless entertainment; it is peopled with those both motivated by and manipulative of the desperate pursuit of happiness. The game that Reuven and the others are coerced into playing is simply a cover, not a game of chance or luck but a fakery and facade for the manipulation of the charlatan who runs it. And it is at this booth that Michael will lose considerably more than his money.

Reuven, Rachel, and Michael are taken in by the booth's owner, who opportunistically plays upon their assumed consanguinity. Having staked them out and overheard their interaction, the owner of the gambling booth identifies himself as a Jew. His tacit familiarity is only a ruse to entrap them. Speaking Yiddish, he shrewdly identities himself as a Russian Jewish émigré, counting on their naïveté and desperate desire to believe that their shared identity is a safeguard against deceit. The con man presumptively and accurately acts on the assumption that their common heritage as Jews will create among them an enclave in which they are no longer outsiders in the midst of the carnival. Reuven and Rachel feel alien there; they are aware of their difference. So it is with ease that the manipulative landsman takes them in with his self-serving camaraderie. Although he is, in fact, Jewish, he feigns solidarity, the status of an insider, and plays on—gambles on—the intimacy not only of recognition but also of fear. He moves in effortlessly and cheats them out of their money, knowing all along that he is impervious to their claims of theft. What he does not count on is Michael's excessive rage and uncontrolled hysteria upon finding himself the victim of such duplicity. It is indeed, as the ex-boxer Mr. Savo says in *The Chosen*, a "cockeyed world" (57). For here it is an ordinary carnival, its rides and booths drawing crowds of willing and eager participants, that, like the seemingly commonplace baseball game between two teams of boys in *The Chosen*, exposes that which is dark and reprehensible—the desire to win at another's expense.

The scene at the carnival gaming booth ironically parallels the situation that Reuven and his father, and Michael and his father, find themselves in outside the fairgrounds and in the seemingly protective safety of their lives at school and at work. In fact, the carnival is only a veiled simulacrum of the lives of postwar American Jews, who felt themselves to be marginalized as outsiders. One would thus expect a tacitly understood sense of safety in the shared identities of Jewish communities, such as Williamsburg, that flourished in America after the war. So it is all the more disturbing when one becomes an outsider among his or her own—when the enemy, as Michael so agitatedly sees it, is clothed as another Jew. Finally realizing that they have been cruelly duped by someone they trusted because of their shared identity and history, Michael, with "a strange dead look in his eyes," reacts with an unrestrained and excessive emotional outburst: "You're like all the others. . . . You're no different from the others. . . . You hate us" (*The Promise*, 29). He projects onto the con man his hatred and fear of those ultra-Orthodox Jews whose diatribe against his father's work is the source of such angst for him and for his family.

The "others" here, tragically, are not gentiles who are intolerant of the Jews' difference and turn on them with anti-Semitic malice. Rather, they are those Jews who, like Rav Kalman, create divisiveness within the Jewish community and thus pose a different kind of danger, as Potok sees it, to the future of Judaism. Rav Kalman's outrage is directed at Abraham Gordon's work, which he finds—like the Zechariah Frankel Seminary, where Gordon teaches—"unclean." His fear of the consequences of Gordon's writing leads him to an irrational and obsessive hold on a singular approach to the biblical texts that students study in his class. Rav Kalman's approach is intolerable for Reuven, who is genuinely devoted to studying Torah and grows "sick of the oppressive Eastern European ghetto atmosphere of his class, sick of his fanatic zeal for Torah" (*The Promise*, 155). Reuven finds the class to be suffocating, tyrannical, and certainly not conducive to learning. Not entirely unlike Rav Kalman, he reacts with anger toward the man who comes to represent, for him, irrational bigotry and narrow-mindedness, finding him, as Rav Kalman finds Abraham

Gordon, "detestable" (118). As Reuven will later come to recognize, there exists a palpable and unsettling difference between the two groups of Jews who inhabit the landscape of *The Promise*, Jews who share the same history and the same Torah but in whose presence even Reuven, a brilliant student of Talmud, is "an uncomfortable outsider" (238). Therefore, what the young and frightened Michael really sees in the con man at the carnival, and what explains the intensity of his agitated behavior and emotional outbursts, is the embodiment of his father's enemies and thus the personification of his own. Michael personalizes the attacks on his father—assumes them—because he is so helpless in the face of them, and as such it is Michael who tragically becomes the casualty of the war between his father and Rav Kalman.

The battle waged by Rav Kalman, fought in the very public forum of the academic scholarly world, is a war of words. As the dean of Hirsch University tells Reuven, Rav Kalman "was not of those who believed in going willingly to the crematoria. He was with the partisans and killed German soldiers for Torah. Now he defends it with words. . . . [It] is his right" (266). Aptly, then, in his utter helplessness, Michael responds to the attacks on his father with silence; his fear is so unbearable that he can no longer give it voice. His catatonia is a metaphor for silenced opinion, for censored expression. In the midst of the mounting battle between the Talmudic scholars, Michael's psychosis escalates. He refuses to participate therapeutically and suffers from delusional fantasies and increased paranoia. Having completely lost the ability to restrain himself, which was unstable to begin with, Michael is placed in a residential treatment center and enters a catatonic state. Treated by the young resident Danny Saunders, who curiously finds himself aligned with the liberal Abraham Gordon and his family in a complex web of relationships, Michael inadvertently becomes the conduit through whom the other characters collide. Ultimately, both Rav Kalman's fury toward the detractors of the Torah and Reuven's anger at the injustice that he so acutely feels are trumped by Michael's unbounded rage—a rage that terrifies him.

At the center of this compelling and deeply disturbing novel is the link between religious ideology and anger, as well as the way in which anger is generated by and simultaneously gives birth to uncontrollable fear. As we come to see, anger and fear diminish the characters. Michael pulls so far back into himself that he is reduced to the absence of self. And Rav Kalman is reduced to unintentional but equally isolating self-aggrandizing solipsism. Both characters unconsciously remove themselves from the potentially therapeutic, compassionate embrace of others. Rage finally defeats Rav Kalman, as it does the younger and thus more vulnerable Michael, who has had far less experience and time to secure his defenses against those he believes to be his adversaries. Furthermore, although both know what it means to suffer, Rav Kalman's immeasurable suffering, loss, and consequent helpless rage result in his own intellectual entrapment. Defending the Torah is, for Rav Kalman, a matter of life or death, but it's a battle that leaves him sadly diminished, "strangely small and a little forlorn" (169).

Finally, everything in the novel returns to the central fact of the Holocaust, the singular defining moment for Judaism in the twentieth century. As David Malter says of the sadly inevitable myopia of those who fled the concentration camps for America, "They know only the lives they led in Europe and the beliefs their families died for" (240). This horrific knowledge is the determining factor of their lives and, for Rav Kalman and others like him, has resulted in a bifurcation of the world into good and evil. As Malter explains to his resentful son, "When your world is destroyed and only a remnant is saved, then whatever is seen as a threat to that remnant becomes a hated enemy" (294). Although Potok designed *The Promise* around dualities, specifically two warring factions of Jews, his complex development of the characters militates against a simple resolution that places blame on Rav Kalman and those who would silence anyone who threatens their deep-seated beliefs. Potok is not asking that we value change over tradition, nor that we privilege a secular world over the divine. On the one hand, we, like Reuven, are deeply critical of Rav Kalman and his censorship of the ideas of others—ideas that are not intended to undermine the faith. On the other hand, we, like Reuven's father and Abraham Gordon, recognize that men like Rav Kalman are motivated by fear and consequently instill fear in others. Explaining the impetus for Rav Kalman's actions, Potok suggests that his suffering "leads, in turn, to his certainty. He says to himself, I cannot have gone through what I went through and have lost what I lost if it's all meaningless. . . . The alternative is to say that Hitler succeeded, that everybody really died for nothing."[5] We are asked to recognize the human capacity for suffering. Rav Kalman's anger and rigidity are born of anguish over his own and his people's immeasurable loss. The compassionate Abraham Gordon, whose damaged son will suffer all the more as a consequence of Rav Kalman's rabid attacks, expresses an empathetic understanding of the other man's trapped perspective on the world. In explaining Rav Kalman's actions to Reuven, he inadvertently acknowledges his own demanding and hard-won position:

"He is trying to save what is left of his world. I can't blame him. I wish it could be otherwise. . . . The concentration camps destroyed a lot more than European Jewry. They destroyed man's faith in himself. I cannot blame Rav Kalman for being suspicious of man and believing only in God. Why should anyone believe in man? There are going to be decades of chaos until we learn to believe again in man. . . . I have no one else I can believe in. . . . But I can understand your Rav Kalman." (*The Promise*, 302)

If Abraham Gordon can't "blame" Rav Kalman, then neither can we and, ultimately, neither can Reuven. It is through the giving of voice to the suffering of others that Reuven is able to understand, if not accept, Rav Kalman's relentless fundamentalism. It is likewise through Reuven's voice—the felt expression of his devotion to the Torah—that Rav Kalman comes to respect his obstinate student, for, as Rav Kalman observes, "It is impossible to print one's love for Torah. But one can hear it in a voice" (340). And so it is through the recognition of shared suffering that Potok provides some closure, although not a comforting resolution, to *The Promise*.

The claustrophobia and suffocation that Reuven feels as he traverses the streets of Williamsburg in the early pages of the novel are linked to the darkness of a world that, since the end of the war, he is only beginning to understand. But Reuven, in speaking to the self-punishing and silent Michael, makes a case for the necessity of giving voice to one's suffering and so fighting against those influences that would force silence upon others. In doing so, Reuven comes to recognize the unintentional and sad truth of Rav Kalman's suffering and, only somewhat incidentally, of Michael's: "People who are suffering sometimes take out their suffering on others" (352).

There may be no way to reconcile the two positions that fracture the lives of the characters in *The Promise*. However, Potok seems to make a case for the coexistence of the two worlds in the figure of Danny Saunders, who, in the end, marries the liberated, modern Rachel Gordon. Yet Danny does not leave behind the reassuring strictures of his faith, being "rooted deeply enough in one world to . . . be concerned only about the people of the other and not about their ideas" (257). At the novel's conclusion, Reuven receives his ordination and Michael begins to make progress toward functionality, but the real resolution, if it might be conceived as such, is in Reuven's realization that the "quarrels would continue" and that giving voice to one's compassionate embrace of Jewish history and tradition, in whatever competing forms, will help secure a future for Judaism—even if a contentious one. After all, argument has a long tradition in Judaism. In this way, *The Promise* advocates a future defined by the presence of an enduring ethical chorus of voices that the perpetrators of the Holocaust attempted to silence. Not unlike the rabbi and writer Chaim Potok, Reuven Malter—now "as much a guardian of the sacred Promise as Rav Kalman and the Hasidim"—will join voices with those who came before him and "try to learn something from the way Rav Kalman and the Hasidim had managed to survive and rebuild their world" (342). So, too, Potok's *promise* becomes a narrative of *tikkun olam*, attempting "to mold smoke and ashes into a new world" in which differences within Judaism can strengthen it against its antagonists without (342).

NOTES

1. Chaim Potok, *The Promise* (New York: Alfred A. Knopf, 1969; repr., New York: Anchor Books, 2005), 167. Subsequent citations to the 2005 edition will be given in the text.

2. S. Lillian Kremer, "An Interview with Chaim Potok," in *Conversations with Chaim Potok*, ed. Daniel Walden (Jackson: University Press of Mississippi, 2001), 38.

3. Harold Ribalow, "A Conversation with Chaim Potok," in Walden, *Conversations with Chaim Potok*, 15.

4. Chaim Potok, *The Chosen* (New York: Ballantine Books, 1967), 14. Subsequent citations to this edition will be given in the text.

5. Ribalow, "Conversation with Chaim Potok," 14.

DAEDALUS REDEEMED

Asher Lev's Journey from Rebellion to Rapprochement

S. Lillian Kremer

Some of the preeminent novelists of earlier centuries and of our time, including Henry James, Franz Kafka, Honoré de Balzac, Émile Zola, Philip Roth, Saul Bellow, and Bernard Malamud, have explored the aesthetic and ethical reaches of artists' lives and work. Often it is the troubled artist—misunderstood, unappreciated, and alienated from society—who has garnered the writers' attention. Chaim Potok, whose literary subject has consistently been "the interplay of the Jewish tradition with the secular twentieth-century," creates an artist-protagonist in two novels. In *My Name Is Asher Lev* and *The Gift of Asher Lev*, dramatic tension derives from a Hasidic Jew's effort to balance his devotion to modern art and to Hasidism, reflecting Potok's career-long interest in characters who "are at the very heart of their Judaism and at the same time . . . encountering elements at the very heart of the umbrella civilization."[1]

As our conversation during a 1981 interview at Potok's home turned to his place in the Jewish American literary canon, he confided that the strongest influences on his writing were not Jewish novelists but James Joyce and Flannery O'Connor, given the centrality of religious thought in their writing. Like the Catholicism in Joyce's fiction, the Judaism in Potok's is a force to be reckoned with rather than a subject of nostalgia or a source of exquisite exoticism. His Jews preserve the languages, traditions, and beliefs of Orthodox Judaism, even when they enter secular professions. They pray daily, guard the Sabbath, celebrate the holidays, and diligently study the sacred texts. Yet they also engage twentieth-century secular culture, whether it be modern psychology in *The Chosen* and *The Promise*, text criticism in *The Promise*, scientific Biblical criticism in *In the Beginning*, or atomic physics in *The Book of Lights*. So it is in the encounter with modern art in the Asher Lev narratives, particularly in the first, where the Joycean influence is manifest in the creation of a protagonist who introduces himself as the artist "about whom you have read in the newspapers and magazines, about whom you talk so much at your dinner affairs and cocktail parties, the notorious and legendary Lev of the *Brooklyn Crucifixion*."[2]

Potok, who painted a work entitled *Brooklyn Crucifixion* at the time he was writing the final chapters of *My Name Is Asher Lev*, casts the novel as defensive memoir. The protagonist, Asher Lev, examines his formative experiences to justify his work and explain how he became the infamous Hasidic painter of nudes and crucifixions. Like Joyce, whose *Portrait of the Artist as a Young Man* was a major influence in the construction of *My Name Is Asher Lev*, Potok integrates particular and universal meaning through religio-national perspectives. Joyce achieved this through Irish Catholic history and Greek mythology, and Potok through Jewish history and biblical analogy, as well as Joycean analogy. Each künstlerroman explores the young artist's state of mind and the collission of his unfolding attitudes with those of family and community. Youthful skirmishes and schoolhouse quarrels with prosaic and often boorish contemporaries herald the artist's alienation from his insular community. Each suffers recrimination: Joyce's Stephen Dedalus is accused of heresy by an English master and classmates for his poetic preferences, and Potok's Asher Lev is rebuked by his yeshiva teacher and classmates for defacing a sacred book with an unintentionally threatening portrait of the Hasidic spiritual leader. In a brief Job-like interrogation, the troubled young Asher struggles to understand God's purpose for his artistic talent:

> If You don't want me to use the gift, why did You give it to me?
> Or did it come to me from the Other Side? It was horrifying to think my gift may have been given to me by the source of evil and ugliness. How can evil and ugliness make a gift of beauty? (*AL*, 116)

In Asher's innocent, pained questioning, there is a suggestion of Job's lesson that suffering is a test of the devout believer. In another instance, Asher feels the judgmental gaze of the Rebbe upon him, "his dark eyes looking at me from below the fringe of his tallis that covered his head. . . . My face burned.

My heart beat fiercely" (141–42). Although educated in parochial schools and powerfully shaped by the religious and political beliefs of his community, each emerging artist eventually rejects complete acquiescence to the values that define his family and community. Each rebels. Each becomes an exile.

Joyce and Potok introduce their impressionable youngsters to community politics within the family setting—Stephen to the passionate complications of Irish ecclesiastic and civil politics in the argument that erupts at the Dedalus Christmas dinner, and Asher to the plight of Soviet Jewry and the Hasidic mission to rescue Russian Jews from communist persecution during family discussions. While Stephen has little interest in politics and maintains emotional distance from Irish nationalists, Asher identifies with the Jewish victims of the Stalinist purges. A Gulag survivor's reports of the Soviet murder of Jewish intellectuals and news of the fabricated Doctors' Plot to justify the murder of Jewish physicians inspire Asher's graphic representation of Jewish suffering in the land of ice and darkness and repeated drawings of the dead Stalin, "empty and hollow; . . . swollen and bloated . . . disfigured, ghoulish, [with] a horror of a face" (*AL*, 99). These youthful acts of artistic witness mark Asher's return to painting following his abstention to please his father, who, like Potok's father,[3] regards painting as frivolous. They also foreshadow his mature direction as an artist who responds to human suffering.

Although both books illumine a strained father-son relationship and the young artist's revolt against his biological father, the cause and manner of rebellion differ substantially. Stephen spurns his father's vanity and repudiates his ecclesiastic and political beliefs. However, aside from their disagreement about art, Asher respects his father, admiring his selfless devotion to Jewish survival, his efforts on behalf of Russian Jewry, and his facility for creating centers of learning and worship in post-Holocaust Europe. Despite the similarity in the young artists' rebellions—Stephen rejecting the priestly role his father intends for him and Asher refusing the dynastic emissarial role— the parallel is decidedly limited. Stephen's rebuff constitutes alienation from church and state. Asher remains a Hasid, adhering, in the main, to the principles and customs honored by his father and exercising great respect for his parents' efforts to enhance Jewish life. His departure from communal values resides solely in his choice of profession and his paintings that offend the community, specifically nudes that violate norms of modesty and crucifixions that serve as painful reminders of centuries of Christian anti-Semitic violence. In Potok's words, the conflict between Asher and his father is marked by "the different sense of the aesthetic nature of reality. The Jew's aesthetics are in the service of morality, the service of man and the service of the commandments. But the aesthetics of Asher Lev are just aesthetics for the sake of beauty itself, for the sake of enhancing the world so that it becomes a prettier place to live in."[4]

The novel's structural and thematic complexity is enriched by Potok's evocation of the mythic-method juxtaposition and balance of Greek myth and biblical analogies with Joycean allusion. He transforms the Joycean appropriation of the Daedalus-Icarus myth using dual Judaized character constructs who serve as Asher's mentors. Like the Greek artificer Daedalus, who freed himself and his son from imprisonment under a cruel tyrant, Asher's "mythic ancestor," who liberated his fellow Jews from Russian oppression and brought them to Torah, frees the guilt-ridden artist to paint subjects that reflect his moral concern for human suffering. The character of Jacob Kahn, modeled loosely after Jacques Lipchitz,[5] embodies the Daedalean artistic expertise and prepares his protégé for eventual exile with this mythic ancestor. At age thirteen—the age of moral majority in the Jewish life cycle—Asher becomes Kahn's pupil. Characteristic of Potok's idealized teachers, Kahn offers him far more than technical knowledge. He imbues their venture with significant ethical and aesthetic dimensions. More than a mere Daedalean artificer, Kahn, as his name implies, is a member of the Jewish priestly class. He acts as a moral guide to the young artist, whose allegoric surname evokes the Levite class, which is responsible for assisting priests in the sanctuary. Kahn not only teaches Asher the Impressionists' manner of representing light and the Abstract Expressionists' manner of treating volume and void, but also insists on Asher's religious authenticity, chastising the young man for concealing his earlocks because they violate his conception of the artist. Kahn objects to Asher's self-deception, claiming that it will falsify his art, and instructs his contrite pupil that "a man's painting either reflects his culture or is a comment upon it" (AL, 241). Paralleling the religious implication of the surnames is the filial relationship suggested in the characters' biblical first names. As the eighth son of the biblical patriarch, Asher was the child who received Jacob's blessing for prosperity and happiness.[6] Potok symbolically fuses the traditional priestly benediction with the patriarchal blessing, as Jacob Kahn blesses Asher Lev and predicts his artistic greatness.

Among the significant Joycean verbal echoes and image patterns that Potok uses to chart his protagonist's subjective response to his vocation are references to sea and light. In the conclusion to chapter 4 of A Portrait of the Artist, while walking along the seashore, Stephen experiences an epiphanic vision of a beautiful girl standing in the water and recognizes his true calling. With this baptismal image, Joyce links artistic beauty and Stephen's spiritual rebirth. Book 3 of *My Name Is Asher Lev*, set in Kahn's Provincetown summer retreat, also makes use of water imagery—suggestive of the Jewish ritual puri- fication bath—to link the artist's commitment to his vocation with religious fidelity. Water imagery is central to each artist's spiritual revelation and artis- tic commitment. The lovely girl standing in the sea awakens Stephen's sense of beauty, while Asher is moved by the wonder of creation as he watches boys and gulls diving and swimming in the sun-dappled sea. Having started the day traditionally in worship, wearing tefillin on the beach with "the waves and gulls audience to his prayer" (*AL*, 240), Asher emerges from the sea to rededicate himself to art. His afternoon dockside epiphany confirms the morning commitment. Although Stephen and Asher progress from shame and the humiliation of self-deception to spiritual renewal in scenes rich in purgative water imagery, the thematic implications of these seaside epipha- nies differ. Stephen concludes that he must deny the church and make art his religion, whereas Asher affirms both art and religion.

When young Asher violates halachic law or community values, his dreams are haunted by the mythic ancestor, who appears in recurrent noctur- nal visits like a prophet, chiding the boy for sins of omission and commission. However, as Asher grows from guilt-ridden child to assertive and successful young painter, the mythic ancestor undergoes a parallel metamorphosis from antagonist to advisor, recommending that Asher make human tragedy his subject. Asher associates his eventual exile, provoked by the *Brooklyn Cruci- fixions* (the crucifixion being the only aesthetic form in the Western tradition that suggests protracted suffering), with the mythic ancestor's travels to atone for the harm he had unwittingly facilitated while working for a corrupt Rus- sian nobleman. Asher comes to understand the dual nature of his artistic gift as "power to create and destroy. Power to bring pleasure and pain . . . the demonic and the divine at one and the same time." His petition for enlighten- ment is answered in the voice of the mythic ancestor, who invites Asher to journey with him and to "paint the anguish of all the world," but to do so by creating his own molds and play of forms (*AL*, 348).

The artist's need for balance between connection to and distance from community, conjoined with freedom of expression, is a dominant theme gen- erating dramatic tension in *A Portrait of the Artist* and in *My Name Is Asher Lev*. In lengthy conversations with college classmates, Stephen articulates his disinterest in the social and political problems of Ireland, delineates reasons for disregarding the demands of church and family, and defines his aesthetic principles. These conversations culminate in Stephen's oft-quoted exilic declaration of independence: "I will not serve that in which I no longer believe, whether it call itself my home, my fatherland, or my church."[7] Similarly, the younger Asher quotes an art historian whose rejection of parochial bias he approved: "Every great artist is a man who has freed himself from his family, his nation, his race. Every man who has shown the world the way to beauty, to true culture, has been a rebel, a 'universal' without patriotism, without home, who has found his people everywhere" (*AL*, 195). While this position reflects Stephen's concluding vision as he stands at the threshold of his writing career in *A Portrait of the Artist*, it represents Asher's early view, a judgment that will be modified under the tutelage of Kahn and the mythic ancestor. Kahn appears to speak for Potok when he advises the young artist to be faithful to his heritage, for he understands that Asher's art will be inauthentic if it erases his Hasidic values. Near the novel's conclusion, Asher cuts his earlocks, thereby symbolically demonstrating his capacity to free himself from externally imposed bonds and direction. In this liberating gesture, the young artist declares that his relationship with God will be of his own design, a voluntary bond of creative association rather than one prescribed by his father and his community. However, this act does not represent dissociation from Hasidism. The young Asher, imbued with Jewish historic memory, recognizes almost from the outset that one's past is part of one's future, especially for the artist.

During the 1981 interview, Potok told me that he intended to follow Asher Lev's career in a second novel. In 1990, nine years after this conversation and eighteen years after publishing *My Name Is Asher Lev*, Potok published his seventh novel, *The Gift of Asher Lev*, which presents a more nuanced view of the artist as witness. In the darker sequel, the reader meets Asher twenty years after he left the Brooklyn community in which he was raised. During his exile in France, he has found a balance between his religious beliefs and the imperatives of art. He is an observant member of the French Ladover community and a painter of international renown. At the novel's outset, we learn that Asher's work has long met with critical acclaim, but reviewers have faulted his most recent show as repetitious and the painter has fallen into a quiescent period.

Asher's controversial status within the Orthodox community remains unchanged, as evidenced both dramatically and reportorially. In a Parisian bookshop, Asher finds a book entitled *The Unorthodox Art of Asher Lev*, which quotes "a *Time* magazine critic who claimed that [Lev] was using [his] art to attack in a mean-spirited way the religious tradition in which [he] had been raised . . . and unconsciously detested." The criticism leads Asher to recall earlier charges: "Blasphemy. Perversions. Satanic sensuality. Deliberate dese-crations of the name of God."[8] Potok closes the scene with a rare instance of comic relief that punctuates the novel's serious treatment of the artist's rela-tion to a hostile society. The bookstore proprietor observes Asher perusing the book but does not recognize him; he informs the artist that he has heard a report that Lev converted to Christianity and that his father recited Kaddish for him. When Asher asks whether he has looked at the paintings, the philis-tine responds with a Yiddish expression of disgust: "Feh! Why would I want to see such paintings? They're a desecration of the name of God" (*GAL*, 199). Through the juxtaposition of misinformation and expletive with serious reli-gious objection, Potok suggests the complexity and intensity of the negative communal response to Asher's work, stemming specifically from his crucifix-ion paintings. The proprietor keeps the book in his shop because his wife, who operates the business, insists that Lev sells—and one must earn a living.

Potok's intent for the sequel, as stated in our 1981 conversation, was "to show how [Asher] . . . will make a serious first effort to depict the Holocaust in . . . Western art, which will probably ruin his career."[9] Five years later, Potok reiterated and elaborated this point in an interview with Elaine Kauvar, explaining, "In the next novel in which Asher Lev will appear, his 'play of forms' will have to do with how to attempt to render the Holocaust artisti-cally. . . . That's what Asher Lev is going to be preoccupied with."[10] But although the Holocaust is a decisive presence in Asher's life, it is absent from his paint-ing throughout most of the novel. Loyal to the charge of his mythic ancestor, he paints "the anguish of all the world" resulting from political and social outrages: the face of a student clubbed by the Parisian riot police, a terrorist on trial in Italy, a survivor of Hiroshima, an Indian woman on a reservation in South Dakota, a homeless black man in New York, and a legless man in his hovel in South Africa. Although Asher is now married to a Holocaust survi-vor whose family was murdered in the concentration and death camps, he has not engaged the central catastrophe of twentieth-century Jewry in his art. Veering from Potok's original intent, artistic representation of the Holocaust is peripheral to the novel's central concerns of religious commitment and the artistic life and process. As Marius Buning notes, "One important difference between [*My Name Is Asher Lev* and *The Gift of Asher Lev*] is that the earlier novel is more concerned with the psychology of the artist, whereas the later novel focuses more on the artistic process itself, offering a great deal of insight into such painterly problems as the use of color, space, forms and techniques, besides making us share in a good many discussions on art."[11] In *The Gift of Asher Lev*, the Holocaust is treated primarily in regard to the experience, memory, and trauma of Devorah, Asher's wife, and emerges as an artistic subject of his painting only at the end.

Returning to Brooklyn for his beloved uncle's funeral, Asher is once again plunged into communal and familial conflict. His artistic crisis is compounded by his uncle's decision that he, rather than his cousins, will take control of a formidable art collection and by the enigmatic demands of the community's spiritual leader. The word "gift," which signified the painter's artistic talent in the first novel, gradually assumes a new dynastic connotation as the sequel's plot evolves. Avrumel, Asher's young son, who is developing a strong bond with his grandfather, Aryeh, is the subject of the charismatic and childless Rebbe's enigmatic riddle: "Three will save us" (*GAL*, 20). Aryeh Lev will succeed the Rebbe on the condition that Avrumel will in turn succeed him. Just as the Rebbe had earlier found a mentor for the young Asher and counseled exile as conducive to his chosen profession, he now intervenes to foster the weary artist's reconciliation with the community and his artistic revitalization. He tells Asher, who begins to unravel the riddle, "Your answer may save us and return you to your work" (256). Reconciliation with family and community is achieved through Asher's capitulation to the Rebbe's wisdom. After much agonizing, Asher grasps the parallel between his artistic anointment by Jacob Kahn and the Rebbe's need for continuity. In the first narrative, Aryeh Lev would sacrifice his son's art and bind him to God's service. However, the paternal willingness to metaphorically play the Abrahamic role was not matched by Asher's filial assumption of the Isaac role. In the sequel, the roles reverse somewhat: Asher is a reluctant but accommodating Abraham, while Avrumel is a willing Isaac. In an automatic drawing entitled *The Binding of Isaac*, which depicts himself and Avrumel, Asher conveys his psychological torment and growing recognition that he will honor the Rebbe's request. In sharp contrast to his use of the crucifixion model to convey family tensions in the first novel, Asher now turns to a Jewish subject to render his moral dilemma, for in his words "the binding of Isaac is about a man who believes so deeply in the Master of the Universe that he is willing to sacrifice to Him his only son" (139). Signifying his acceptance of the Rebbe's request that Avrumel succeed Aryeh as a dynastic Hasidic Rebbe, Asher hands the child to his father and the Rebbe during a joyous holiday celebrating Torah learning. Not until this bequeathal of his son to the Brooklyn Ladover community is Asher able to resolve the bitter dispute over his uncle's modern art collection and return to painting with renewed vigor.

In 1978, Potok wrote that "the Jew sees all his contemporary history refracted through the ocean of blood that is the Holocaust," later reiterating that it is impossible "to think the world through Jewish eyes without having the blood-screen of the Holocaust in front of your eyes as part of the filtering."[12] The Shoah is therefore always in the background of his fictional universe, as I have explored elsewhere.[13] Aside from a short passage in *The Trope Teacher* cast as an American soldier's memory of a concentration camp liberation, Potok chooses to feature the catastrophic impact of the experience on survivors and American Jews rather than setting his works in the Holocaust-era landscape. The Holocaust enters the novel primarily in Devorah's voice, in the omniscient authorial account of the roundup of Jews in Paris, and in an account of a Hasidic child tutored by her father to sing "entre les bras de Jesus Christ" should she have to hide in the countryside with French peasants or fool Nazi soldiers. Despite his past omission of the Shoah from his European work portraying international suffering, Asher eventually turns to the specificity of Jewish twentieth-century calamity. That the Shoah has been a significant part of his sensibility is revealed in his incremental register and repetition of Devorah's history. Chased from her home as a four-year-old child during the 1942 roundup of Parisian Jews, she hid for several years in a sealed apartment—starving, suffering from scurvy and lice, and constantly fearful of denunciation—only to learn at the war's end that her parents had been murdered in the concentration camps. Early in the novel, Asher reflects that although he has "dreamed . . . the dream of Devorah's life in Paris during the war," he has never painted it because "it is not [his] life or [his] dream" (*GAL*, 59). There is nothing in Asher's painting addressing the Holocaust to this point, but Potok demonstrates that the catastrophe is a part of his identity, for Asher understands that "memories of the Holocaust often come unbidden to mind. They dwell in a realm of their own, and are not subject to the laws and whims of humankind" (251). Devorah's Holocaust trauma haunts Asher and is an intimate part of his reality. Not only does Asher absorb Devorah's story, but he learns the circumstances of her mother's death in a women's camp near Auschwitz before she does. He is burdened by the dilemma of whether to reveal or conceal the account of the murder of her mother and other Jewish women at the hands of German prisoners and guards incited by SS men to beat them for their amusement (250–51).

Reflective of the current discourse on the limits of Holocaust representation and Potok's doubts about "whether [he could] get the distance needed to handle it aesthetically,"[14] the novel's only direct dialogue on Holocaust art is between Asher and Devorah's cousin Max, who is a painter and was her childhood companion in the sealed Parisian apartment. Although Asher understands that Max "paints to conceal the terror of his tomb-time," he nevertheless believes that the survivor "should paint the darkness he feels, not the false light that he covers it with." During this exchange, Max bestows the subject upon Asher, encouraging him to paint the darkness, but Asher demurs, "I didn't live through it." Although Asher does not feel the freedom to paint the Holocaust at this stage, there is a foreshadowing in Max's counterargument: "We all lived through it, everyone; all of humanity lived through it" (*GAL*, 216). Referencing the painting that has been "a central element of [his own] life,"[15] Potok acknowledges that an artist may justly appropriate the Holocaust subject in Max's subsequent question: "Was Picasso in Guernica?" (216). The novel's concluding paragraph refers briefly to a fresh direction and energy in Asher's work, and to paintings that reveal "strange images in sealed rooms" (370); his work begins to flow. Thus, Asher adopts the role of many survivors in Potok's fiction by bearing witness and contributing to the regeneration of Judaism and Jewry through his active religious devotion and the dedication of his son to Jewish restoration. In the bequeathal of Avrumel for this purpose, Asher frees himself to interpret the Shoah and to experience a renaissance of his own artistic talent.

NOTES

1. S. Lillian Kremer, "An Interview with Chaim Potok, July 21, 1981," *Studies in American Jewish Literature* 4 (1985): 84–99, quote on 85. Reprinted in Daniel Walden, ed., *Conversations with Chaim Potok* (Jackson: University Press of Mississippi, 2001), 31–45.

2. Chaim Potok, *My Name Is Asher Lev* (Greenwitch, Conn.: Fawcett, 1972), 9. Subsequent citations to this edition will be given in the text and abbreviated as *AL*. In 1986, Potok described (to his thinking) the seminal importance of *A Portrait of the Artist as a Young Man*, claiming that he "absorbed whole components of that novel into the deepest recesses of [his] being." Elaine M. Kauvar, "An Interview with Chaim Potok," *Contemporary Literature* 27, no. 3 (1986): 291–317. Reprinted in Walden, *Conversations with Chaim Potok*, 63–87, quote on 66.

3. Potok wanted to become a painter at the age of ten, but both his father and his Talmudic teachers refused to permit him to pursue this interest because it was considered an idolatrous activity. It was only after the successful publication of *The Chosen* that Potok actually started painting.

4. Elaine Lindsay, "Chaim Potok," in Walden, *Conversations with Chaim Potok*, 29.

5. Chaim Potok, "The First Eighteen Years," *Studies in American Jewish Literature* 4 (1985): 101.

6. See Genesis 49:20, where Asher's portion is predicted. This is substantiated in Moses's blessing of the tribe of Asher in Deuteronomy 33:24.

7. James Joyce, *A Portrait of the Artist as a Young Man* (New York: Viking Press, 1967), 247.

8. Chaim Potok, *The Gift of Asher Lev* (New York: Alfred A. Knopf, 1990), 197. Subsequent citations to this edition will be given in the text and abbreviated as *GAL*.

9. Kremer, "Interview with Chaim Potok," 93.

10. Kauvar, "Interview with Chaim Potok," 76.

11. Marius Buning, "Chaim Potok," March 1995, http://potok.lasierra.edu/Potok.Buning.html.

12. Chaim Potok, *Wanderings: Chaim Potok's History of the Jews* (New York: Alfred A. Knopf, 1978), 398; Kremer, "Interview with Chaim Potok," 92.

13. Potok has generally treated the Shoah indirectly by introducing minor characters who are survivors. Potok's more sustained exploration and dramatic presentation of survivor syndrome appears in a little-known 1967 short story, "The Dark Place Inside," and in two late novellas, *The Trope Teacher* and *The Canal*, whose protagonists suffer the burden of repressed Holocaust memory. In the short story, an Israeli Holocaust survivor, Levi Abramovich, mourns the loss of four sons who "had walked the narrow corridor and tasted the smoky waters of poison gas in the shower house, together with their mother." Potok, "The Dark Place Inside," *Dimensions in American Judaism,* Fall 1967, 35.

For fuller discussion of Potok's treatment of the Holocaust, see S. Lillian Kremer, "The Holocaust and the Revival of Judaism and Jewish Civilization in the Fiction of Chaim Potok," in *Witness Through the Imagination: Jewish American Holocaust Literature* (Detroit: Wayne State University Press, 1989), 300–323, and S. Lillian Kremer, "Chaim Potok," in *Holocaust Literature: An Encyclopedia of Writers and Their Work,* ed. S. Lillian Kremer, vol. 2 (New York: Routledge, 2003), 954–60.

14. Kremer, "Interview with Chaim Potok," 92.

15. Kauvar, "Interview with Chaim Potok," 69.

DAVITA'S HARP

The Silence of Violence and the Limits of the Imagination

Susanne Klingenstein

Davita

Davita's Harp occupies an interesting place in Chaim Potok's oeuvre. Along with his nonfiction work *Theo Tobiasse: Artist in Exile* (1986), it marks the precise middle of his writing career. *Davita's Harp* appeared in 1985, eighteen years after Potok's first novel, *The Chosen*, catapulted the author to fame and seventeen years before his death in 2002. It is his sixth work of fiction and his only novel narrated by a woman and centered on two female protagonists. Six works of fiction followed *Davita's Harp*, among them three books for young adults, and with the exception of *The Gift of Asher Lev* (1990), they were not nearly as successful with readers as the six iconic works of fiction Potok had published between 1967 and 1985.

Potok himself may have felt that he was reaching a plateau with the publication of *Davita's Harp*—a plateau that turned out to be the zenith of his career as a fiction writer—because in 1986 he remarked in an interview with the literary scholar Elaine Kauvar, "What I am doing is setting the groundwork, and I am finished with that now. I have in my cast of characters a psychologist, Danny Saunders; a Talmudist, Reuven Malter; I also have a Bible scholar, David Lurie; an artist, Asher Lev; a mystic, Gershon Loran. Now I have a feminist writer; that's what Davita's going to be." Kauvar was surprised to learn that Potok regarded the six novels merely as groundwork for a more elaborate fictional edifice. She asked Potok whether he was planning a sequel to *Davita's Harp* and whether Reuven Malter, the narrator of *The Chosen*, was going to play a role in that sequel. Potok's reply revealed the energy and verve that generated his detailed plans for works still far in the future: "All of these people are going to be brought into the contemporary period, and the first one who will be brought into this part of the century will be Davita," Potok said. His novel had left Davita as a fourteen-year-old in 1942. "As a matter of fact," Potok continued, "she is going to be brought right into the eighties on a journey that she makes to the Soviet Union. That's the point to the whole Communist background in the first of the Davita novels."[1]

Unfortunately, Potok did not realize his plans, and very few of his central characters were brought into the second half of the twentieth century. The one sequel Potok did write was *The Gift of Asher Lev* (1990), in which he updated his readers on the life and fate of Asher Lev, the painter and Hasidic Jew in Parisian exile; this book came eighteen years (the numeric value of *chai*, the Hebrew word for "life") after the publication of the first Asher Lev novel in 1972. Ilana Davita Chandal also reappears in a later work as a full-grown adult but, disappointingly, not as a central protagonist or even a feminist writer. Rather, she is cast in a conventionally feminine role as a patient listener and inspiring muse. In Potok's last work of fiction, *Old Men at Midnight* (2001), a collection of three novellas, Davita largely serves as an empathic listener, unloosening the memories of three older men—a Holocaust survivor, a former Jewish KGB officer who defected from the Soviet Union via East Germany in 1955, and a professor of warfare. Davita inspires these men, who are nearing the midnight of their lives, to put their memories into words. Her function is that of spiritual or psychological healer. Thus, she is picking up the work (if not the mission) of her aunt Sarah Chandal in *Davita's Harp* rather than fulfilling her own destiny as a creative writer. Of the three novellas, only one, *The War Doctor*, actually has a direct connection to communism and the Soviet Union. In a set of stories mailed to Davita, a defector recounts his fate as a Jew under the rule of the Bolsheviks. He touches especially on the harrowing history of the Jewish Anti-Fascist Committee, which culminated in the rigged trial of fifteen Jewish intellectuals, all with stellar Bolshevik credentials, and the subsequent execution of fourteen of the defendants on August 12, 1952; among them were five brilliant Yiddish writers. The defector also alludes to the infamous Doctors' Plot of 1953, Stalin's last attempt at a pogrom against the Jews, aborted only because of his death on March 5, 1953.[2]

Potok's actual sequel to *Davita's Harp*—the book that undertakes a journey into the Soviet Union and explores in detail the lives of the Jews there—turned out not to be a novel at all but a work of nonfiction depicting the lives of Volodya and Masha Slepak, Russian Jews whom Potok met during his trip to Moscow in 1985. In his 1986 interview with Kauvar, Potok had pointed out that there was "another way to deal with reality that my new Davita novel will explore, and that is not to run away from reality by restructuring it through the imagination [this is Davita's technique of dealing with violence and injustice] but to sink into it and to reveal it with infinite detail."[3] It was Potok himself, not his heroine Davita, who decided not to run away from reality and not to render his narrative of the fate of the Jews under Bolshevism as a work of fiction.

In his passionate nonfiction work *The Gates of November: Chronicles of the Slepak Family* (1996), Potok manages to reveal scrupulously and "with infinite detail" the reality of the violent culture clashes not only between committed Jews and the Soviet regime but also between a father who continues to believe in the ideals of the Communist Party and a son who objects to the cruelty of the regime and becomes a refusenik.[4] Potok's decision not to filter this story through the feminist writer Davita but rather to present it directly in a nonfiction work was the right one. Although Jewish refuseniks and feminists have both fought for equality and basic social justice, the two issues—the oppression of the Jews in the Soviet Union and the oppression of women in Western culture—are not comparable. For Potok, the issue of the Russian Jews, the violent clash of two cultures, was more important than the feminist issue. And so it was that five years after the publication of *The Gates of November*, Davita reappeared not as an activist feminist writer but as a passive, silent recipient of the Jewish KGB officer's stories.

It is not unfair to conclude from Potok's *not* writing a proper sequel to *Davita's Harp*, with Davita as a fully matured adult and professional feminist writer (in the way we get to see Asher Lev in 1990 as a fully matured painter in Paris), as well as from Potok's use of her as a mere empathic listener, that he wasn't really interested in what she could do as a feminist writer.[5] The issue of female disenfranchisement and its remedy through female intellectual self-assertion, which Potok seems to raise consistently and in many facets in *Davita's Harp*, did not really interest him, or he would have pursued it and shown us how the male/female culture clash played out in Davita's adult life.

I am raising the issue of the novel's ending and missing continuation of Davita's story (and thus of Potok's seeming disinterest in the mature Davita) at the beginning of my reading of *Davita's Harp*, because it helps us determine the precise intellectual center of the novel. It is a long and varied narrative that touches on a broad spectrum of issues: intermarriage, the rise of fascism in Europe, the appeal of communism, the many aspects of violence, the abandonment of women and children by men with social or religious commitments, the subsequent aloneness of women, the power of the imagination, the function of metaphors, and the dual roles of will and serendipity in the shaping of one's life and destiny—to name only a few of the subjects Potok plays with in the novel. He gives the impression that he has done a great deal of thinking and wants to accomplish a lot.

However, one of the unintended consequences of so much baggage is that *Davita's Harp* lacks focus and a weighty intellectual center and seems always on the verge of falling apart. Contributing to this impression is the problem that, as protagonist, Davita is too young and too naive a thinker to hold the novel, with all its baggage, together. In addition, Potok seems much less interested and invested in her than in her mother, whose eventful life and concealed suffering give the novel emotional and historical heft. One is naturally tempted to think that Davita, an intelligent observer and narrator who draws conclusions for her own life from the events she observes, is the fictional presence Potok most cares about, since the entire narrative is filtered through her evolving self-consciousness. But in *Davita's Harp* the richer story line is that of the mother, who oscillates between her commitment to achieve social justice with the help of communism and her roots in an elitist, seemingly discriminatory observant Judaism. The desire to know more about the fate of this complex, energetic woman keeps the reader going. Her fate is much more compelling than the thoughts and potential future of a girl, depicted between the ages of eight and fourteen, whose experience of gender discrimination at the very end of the novel—Davita is denied the school prize at her yeshiva because she is a girl—sets her on the road of female self-assertion.

The real conceptual problem with *Davita's Harp* is that the novel itself diminishes our interest in Davita by featuring at its precise numerical center the brutal, premeditated destruction of the Basque town of Guernica by Franco's forces on April 26, 1937. This gruesome event also shatters the childhood happiness of the narrator, as Davita's father dies a horrific, unredeemably useless death during the attack. Recalling Potok's description of those scenes and their devastating consequences for the Chandal family, no reader can get worked up over the fact that Davita is denied a school prize at the end of eighth grade because she is a girl.[6] As upsetting and life-shaping events, the two occurrences (Guernica and the denial of the school prize) are simply not commensurate, yet Potok forces them into proximity and this diminishes our interest in his protagonist.

Potok conceived Davita less as a person than as a function: she is a vehicle for his exploration of the power of the imagination. In his interview with Elaine Kauvar, he argued,

> *Davita's Harp* is about the utilization of the human imagination as a way of coming to terms with unbearable reality. Every time Davita confronts something unbearable, she restructures it through the power of her imagination. Finally, at the end of the novel when she suffers this terrible indignity [when she is given two lesser prizes instead of the main school prize she deserves by merit], she restructures the graduation ceremony. . . . All the metaphors of her imagination are present in that last scene. . . . So you have this seesawing back-and-forth between reality that's unbearable and the imagination that tries to rethink reality. One of the people who has powerfully restructured reality in our time is Picasso, and the metaphor par excellence for that restructuring is [the 1937 painting] *Guernica*. Guernica is the prime example, the first example in modern Western civilization of the destruction of an entire civilian area solely for psychological purposes. It's a horror, isn't it?[7]

By putting Guernica at the novel's numerical center and Picasso's *Guernica* at the novel's thematic center—as an instance of transforming horror into art and thus making horror, if not comprehensible, at least assimilable to the human mind—Potok deprives Davita's own experiences of weight and thus decreases our interest in her. Thus, the center of *Davita's Harp* is occupied neither by Davita nor by her door harp, a witless little device that harmoniously registers people's comings and goings. Their significance is eclipsed by the destruction of Guernica and its transformation into a major work of twentieth-century art. Potok used to go see Picasso's mural "as one goes on a pilgrimage," and it became for him "the most significant achievement in this century of the redemptive power of the artist."[8] Any reading of the novel will have to take this fact into account.

The question is whether *Davita's Harp* was actually written around Guernica/*Guernica* or whether event and painting fortuitously fit into the communism-versus-Jewish-peoplehood theme that, in addition to the power of the imagination motif, forms the most persistent thematic strand in the novel. The key to the novel's elusive center seems to lie in the connection between Guernica and the mother's commitment to communism. What exactly is the link here? Once we have the link, we can get to the secret, unspeakable center of the novel, out of which everything radiates. The transformative power of the imagination is a secondary motif; we know that from the word "transformative." What does art transform? The thing it transforms constitutes the primary dark core of the novel. In order to get there, we need to look at Channah's life.

Channah

Potok has often made it clear that his main interest in writing his first six novels was to explore a "confrontation of ideas" and to depict "cultures in tension with one another," most notably the culture of "Western secular humanism" and the religious culture of observant Jews.[9] *Davita's Harp* is no exception, once we recognize that its central protagonist is not Davita but her mother, Channah. She is torn between her commitment to the Jews as a unique people with an ancient moral, though socially imperfect, religious culture and her commitment to the communist revolution—that is, to the creation of a world of material social justice based on the acceptance of the equality of all human beings.

The problem with recognizing Channah as the central character of the novel is that we do not know much about her and have no direct access to her thoughts. Our knowledge of her life derives from her scant autobiographical revelations to her daughter. Channah, who delivers long, persuasive speeches at rallies and party meetings, is almost mute about herself, about her former life in Europe, and about the memories that drive her to embark on the political path that becomes the center of her life. Very often, when her daughter touches on an emotionally difficult subject, Channah will cut the conversation short by moving from talk to action. Sentences such as these are almost a verbal tic with her: "We'll talk about it another time, Ilana. Are we done? Can I bring dessert?" (168; also 241); "My father was with the rebbe. Please, Ilana, let's not talk about it any more tonight. Are you done with supper? Then finish your homework" (312).[10] When Ilana is cruelly teased at public school and comes home to complain, her mother says, "Men can be like that sometimes." Ilana adds, "They are mean and evil," but her mother cuts her short without explanation: "Finish your lunch, Ilana." When Ilana persists, her mother completely kills the conversation: "Please finish your lunch, Ilana. Then you'll help me clean up and we'll take our walk" (201). As Ilana gets older and moves closer to discovering the experiential secret that forms the core of her mother's activism, Channah retreats even more fully into silence: "She was silent, lost in her darkness" (160); "She colored slightly and did not respond" (312); "I was quiet. We sat together a while in silence" (314).

The incessant repetition of this structure—question from Davita, nonanswer from Channah, and a request to *do* something—accomplishes two things. First, it builds up suspense and keeps the reader interested in the mother, because the reader wants to know why she doesn't talk. As is common in coming-of-age novels, the maturation of the child is correlated with the gradual understanding of a parent's "dark secret," usually sexual in nature. Second, the structure is a variant of a major theme in the novel—namely, the transformation of brutal reality either into social activism (by those who experienced brutality directly) or into art (by those who experience brutality indirectly, through the narrated experiences of others). The mother's reticence in her conversations with Davita leads the reader to suspect that something extraordinarily brutal happened to Channah as a child—a kind of Guernica in the life of the little girl—and we are led to understand that Channah's response to the brutality was to flee into an activism that would do away with the source of such suffering for all other little girls. So what happened?

Before we pursue this question, we need to see that as a character Channah is integrated into an orchestra of characters—three men and two other women—each of whom plays out the theme of transposing experience into (nonverbal) activism or (verbal) art in a different way. Together the six characters form a sophisticated composition (or textual web) of basic theme and variations stretching from the past into the future and across several cultures. The linchpin is Channah. She relates strongly both to the three main male characters (the observant Jew Ezra Dinn; her New England Episcopalian husband, Michael Chandal; and the secular German Jew Jakob Daw) and to the three main female characters (her sister-in-law, Sarah Chandal; Ezra's observant Jewish aunt, Mrs. Helfman; and her daughter, Ilana Davita).

The female web is less varied and less interesting. Sarah Chandal and Mrs. Helfman both channel their responses to reality into strong faith—Christianity and Judaism, respectively—and their response to social emergencies and severe distress is the same: they help. Mrs. Helfman's name contains the German word for helping (*helfen*), and she helps in the traditional Jewish maternal way of assisting those close to her. She provides shelter in her house (Potok's leitmotif for good shelter is the heat in Davita's room), takes Davita into her family when her mother goes off to communist rallies, brings hot food for the family when Channah is stressed, and provides companionship and an introduction to Jewish family life. Mrs. Helfman is warm and nurturing, but her interests are limited and do not extend beyond the narrow circle of her family and synagogue community.

Aunt Sarah's social interests are more catholic and inclusive, but her pursuit of the traditional Christian calling—to care for the sick and needy, whoever they may be—has also deprived her of a family. She follows in the path of Christ (*imitation dei*) as a female disciple. This requires celibacy because the dedication to *caritas* has to be total. Sarah is propelled to help people for the love of God (*amor dei*), in keeping with the traditional two-way street of loving God to be loved back. She describes her profession or calling as that of "a nurse for the Church and for our Lord Jesus Christ" (20).

Mrs. Helfman and Sarah Chandal are also book oriented. The key text for both is the Bible, of course, augmented by an oral tradition of stories and songs. Due to the catholic nature of Aunt Sarah's orientation and because of the strong Christian basis of the American self,[11] her arsenal of stories includes the basic American foundation myths (stories about Native Americans, Pilgrims, and pioneer women). Both women are treasure troves of the traditional lore of their cultures, but neither woman (unlike the men) is creative. The women *conserve* the knowledge of their cultures' foundation myths but do not creatively contribute to them; they do not make up new stories. Their way of responding to reality is by swinging into action and helping people. We can see how Channah Chandal fits this pattern. Her response to the yet unnamed social distress she experienced was to move into action, devoting her life to bringing about a world revolution that would radically change the living conditions of humanity. Like Mrs. Helfman and Aunt Sarah, Channah believes in redemption through good deeds.

The essential difference between Mrs. Helfman and Aunt Sarah is that the former has a family of her own and the latter does not. This means that despite her charitable work, Aunt Sarah spends a great deal of time alone, often in an isolated house at the seashore in Maine, which serves as a place of recuperation from severe emotional distress for both Channah and Davita. Thus, it is Aunt Sarah who first introduces the specifically female variant of the imagination theme.

We recall that Potok wants to illustrate the redemptive power of the imagination: the imagination can be used to transform and thus mitigate and make bearable brutal experiences. One of the basic difficult experiences for women is aloneness. Aunt Sarah first introduces this theme in her narratives about early America that she passes on to Davita: "In the chill darkness of my room [cold and darkness are both Potok metaphors for aloneness] I lay in my bed and listened to my Aunt Sarah from Maine telling me those stories about Pilgrims and Indians and lonely women who used their imagination to fight their loneliness" (19; also 246). Storytelling is a way to fight loneliness. However, you need a listener to tell the stories to. If you don't have that listener, then the storytelling becomes story writing. Here, then, is the portal to Davita's future as a writer. Although Davita has several friends, she is, essentially, a lonely child. She copes with the stresses in her life by thinking about the stories the adults are telling her; later on at the yeshiva, she will use structures acquired through these stories to write some of her essays.

The experience of loneliness also connects Davita strongly to Channah, for whom loneliness is a constant in life. Loneliness pervades the novel as a key experience. Female and male characters have bouts of loneliness—Michael Chandal in Spain, Sarah Chandal in her journeys to help the sick and needy, and Jakob Daw in his wanderings around Europe and in his final days in Marseille. But it is Davita and Channah who actually *suffer* from loneliness, especially after Michael Chandal leaves for Spain. His second tour of Spain, which he undertakes with Channah's consent and encouragement ("But I want Michael to go back" [168]) and which ends in his death at Guernica as he is trying to save a nun (a version of his sister Sarah), turns, for Davita, into parental abandonment. She voices deep-felt anger at her father for having abandoned her. In a crucial conversation, Davita displays the elemental selfishness that a nine-year-old child is still allowed. She asks Ezra Dinn about his own father:

> "Did your father also never stay at home?" I asked.
>
> He gave my mother a quick glance and looked back at me. "My father was home."
>
> "What did your father do?"
>
> "He owned a clothing factory."
>
> "Is he alive?"
>
> "No. He died when I was nineteen."
>
> "You had ten more years of your father than I did."
>
> The two of them glanced at each other and said nothing.
>
> "Did you hate your father for dying?"

He looked surprised. "No. I was angry. But I didn't hate him."

"Sometimes I think I hate my father."

"Ilana," my mother said softly.

"He didn't have to save that nun. He didn't even believe in religion. Why did he try to save that nun? . . . He shouldn't have." (263)

The issue of parental abandonment resonates deeply with Davita's mother. Several times in the course of the novel she mentions that her father was never home. One day, in January 1938, mother and daughter are taking a walk in Prospect Park. Davita asks whether her mother's father would have been angry if he knew his granddaughter was attending a yeshiva. A short conversation ensues, cut off, of course, by Channah, when Davita touches on core memories:

"I don't know how my father would feel about that, my mother said. "I don't know much about my father. He was almost never home. . . ."

"Was your mother very lonely because your father wasn't home?"

"Yes. So was I. My mother once told me that terrible mistakes are sometimes made in the name of loneliness. If not for my grandfather—"
She broke off, suddenly lost in some memory. (260)

Although there is a protective male (the grandfather), his caring presence cannot compensate for the absence of a protective father to the child and a sexually active husband for the mature woman.[12] The compensatory fulfillment of sexual desire elsewhere is hinted at in the "terrible mistakes" that are sometimes made by lonely women. The loneliness/abandonment theme links three generations of women (grandmother, mother, daughter) and connects them to the pioneer women of Aunt Sarah's story. For Channah, her mother's loneliness and her own abandonment as a child also correlate with religious commitment and the patriarchal organization of Judaism, because her father left the family to be with his Hasidic rebbe. This correlation (the father's religion becomes the child's abandonment) is Channah's main reason for leaving the elitist, discriminatory religious messianism of Hasidism for the secular universalist messianism of communism. But by pointing to the humanitarian failures of Soviet communism under Stalin during the 1930s and beyond, the novel argues that this was a foolish, shortsighted decision. Potok works hard to construct in Ezra Dinn an attractive, caring observant Jewish alternative to Hasidism that could cause Channah to reverse her decision.

The connection between the patriarchal (discriminatory) structure of Judaism and the attendant psychological (and, as we shall see, physical) suffering of women is firmly established in a key conversation. After Michael Chandal leaves for his first tour in Spain, Davita complains to her mother that she feels lonely:

> She said quietly, "We have to work hard, Ilana. That way most of the time we can forget the loneliness. I learned that from my mother."
> "Did your father go away, too?"
> "Yes. Often. . . . He was a member of a group of very religious Jews called Hasidim. He used to go away almost every Saturday and holiday to the city where the rebbe, the leader of the group, lived."
> "Your father went away? Why did he do that?"
> "He went to pray in the rebbe's synagogue with the others of the group."
> "He left you alone with your mother?"
> "Yes. Very often."
> "Your father didn't care?"
> "I suppose he didn't care enough. After all, we were only women. . . . My mother would keep very busy while my father was away. She ran a flour mill with my grandfather. But Shabbos was very hard. She couldn't find what to do because she couldn't work. It was very hard."
> "Were you angry at your father?"
> "Was I angry? Yes. I was angry."
> "I'm angry at Papa for going away."
> "Ilana, your father is a fine journalist and he'll be doing something very important in Spain, important for the world." (104–5)

Here, then, is the mother's *causa belli*, her reason for turning away from Judaism: she accuses her father of selfishness. In his infantile running off to pray with the rebbe, he leaves his family members to fend for themselves. The abandonment of women by men who spent their days studying and praying in study houses, synagogues, and Hasidic courts was an enormous social and economic problem for eighteenth- and nineteenth-century observant Jewish women in Eastern Europe.[13] Davita argues implicitly that her situation now is the same as her mother's was when she was a child. Channah holds that it is not: her father left the family to ensure his own spiritual well-being; Davita's father left his family for the greater good of mankind (symbolized by his attempt to save the nun). Thus, the novel's unresolved ethical issue is brought to a head: Whom do you care about first—your own kin, your near ones and dear ones, or mankind and the anonymous stranger (the nun), who might very well be someone else's aunt? Should you opt for helping people at home (like Mrs. Helfman and the immigration lawyer Ezra Dinn), or should you be catholic in your empathy and assist the stranger at the risk of causing pain to your own family? The novel does not answer this question explicitly. But in returning Channah to the fold of a Jewish family, Potok seems to opt for the narrow solution of caring for one's own kin and thus endorses a conservative point of view.

There are other consequences to the abandonment of women apart from emotional and economic suffering. In Channah's case, there is also cataclysmic physical trauma, and it is this experience that integrates her into the web of male characters (Michael Chandal, Jakob Daw, and Ezra Dinn) that counterpoises the web of female characters in the novel. An examination of the men, their dispositions, and their motivations will finally lead us to Guernica and *Guernica*, a civil war and a painting created by a man. When we examine Michael's biography, for example, we find that his motivation for "helping people" is as deeply rooted in a traumatic experience as Channah's, and that selfishness is an integral part of saintliness.

Guernica

If we begin our examination of the male characters in *Davita's Harp* by returning to Potok's main theme of the transformative power of the imagination, we realize quickly that Channah belongs as much to the male world as to the female world. As we have seen, the women in *Davita's Harp* respond to distress by swinging into action as caretakers. They provide food, shelter, nursing care, and companionship, and they tell stories; but they do not create verbal or pictorial artifacts. The men, in contrast, produce written works for specific audiences, works that are more or less effective: Jakob Daw writes literary stories, Michael Chandal writes news stories and political essays for the *New Masses*, a Marxist newspaper, and Ezra Dinn produces legal briefs on behalf of immigrants to America. Channah doesn't write and doesn't tell stories. She makes speeches, which is a hybrid of storytelling and persuasive writing. She also runs Sunday study sessions at her house in which the works of Karl Marx occupy the place of the Talmud in the male study sessions (*chevruta*) at yeshivot. As she moves back into the Jewish fold, she gives up both the speeches and the study sessions for social work with immigrants and eventually arrives at full-time Jewish motherhood. We note, then, that Potok reserves real writing for the men. He lays the groundwork for turning Davita into a writer in a later novel by having her write excellent interpretive essays at school, but, as we saw earlier, Potok lost interest in Davita as a (feminist) writer in later years.

It isn't intellectual activity, though, that ties Channah to the three men in her life. The deeper connections are based on childhood and youth in Europe (Ezra and Jakob) and the experience of trauma (Michael and Jakob). The triangle of men, each of whom is strongly bonded to Channah by love, is very deftly balanced.[14] Ezra and Jakob represent Jewish alternatives but not along the conventional Eastern European versus German Jewish lines, because the two men seem to have roots in both Eastern European Jewry (indicated by their ability to understand and speak Yiddish) and German Jewry. Jakob Daw writes in German, and one of Ezra's grandfathers, Isaac Dinn, was a "great rabbi in Germany" (116). Dinn is also supposedly "a town in southern Germany" (313).

Ezra is a first cousin of Channah (his mother is her aunt). He is, of course, aptly named. The biblical Ezra, a priestly scribe with a superb knowledge of Torah, led the Israelites from Babylonian exile back to Jerusalem in 459 BCE. He was particularly concerned with the looming identity crisis because the Jews had intermarried with non-Jews in Babylonia, and he reconstituted the Israelites as a people on the basis of the laws derived from the Torah. Thus, when Ezra Dinn or his son David tells Davita (several times) that "it's the law," we hear reverberations of the biblical Ezra. The American Ezra works as an immigration lawyer, which means that he uses his superb knowledge of American law to bring Jews (and non-Jews) to the Promised Land, which, in the 1930s, was America rather than the settlements in Palestine. Obviously, Ezra's long-term plan is to bring Channah back into the Jewish fold. He plays his hand well, giving the strong-willed Channah enough freedom to run out of options.

Jakob Daw is a more complicated and mysterious presence. It is clear that he is too weak and too shattered as a human being to be a viable romantic alternative to the energetic Michael Chandal and the courtly, well-adjusted, and effective Ezra Dinn. But he is charming and gracious in an old-fashioned Central European sort of way, cultivated especially by Vienna's bourgeoisie. He is essentially a tent dweller, like his biblical namesake, and a loner who writes enigmatic stories at night. These metaphoric concoctions made him famous in Europe, in part for being dense and difficult to interpret (although the examples Potok makes up are hermeneutically not particularly challenging). Daw's stories are hybrids of the extensive religious allegories created by Rabbi Nachman of Bratslav and the spare modernist parables of Franz Kafka. The stories of both men have proven fantastically difficult to decode and generated an enormous scholarly literature. Kafka, a native of Prague who wrote in German, is already dead at the time of *Davita's Harp* (he died in 1924). Nevertheless, we are strongly encouraged to think of Kafka as a model for Jakob Daw, not least because of his unusual last name, which is not exactly a German or even Eastern European Jewish name. If you take his last name together with the first syllable of his first name, you get "jac[k]daw" (*Corvus monedula*), which is what "Kafka" means in Czech. Daw appears in his own stories as a little black bird. Like Kafka, Jakob Daw is unlikely to marry, and he dies of a wasting illness (Kafka died of a form of tuberculosis) rather than being killed by the Nazis.

Daw is the only character in the novel who actually transforms a powerfully fierce and physically hurtful reality (culminating for him in the experience of being gassed as a soldier in World War I) into verbal works of art to make his memories psychologically manageable. Daw is Davita's most important model for what stories and language can do. His way of thinking gets her into trouble with the authorities at the yeshiva. When she arrives at a tricky phrase in a Torah verse, she thinks of "Jakob Daw writing this as a story" (348), which leads her to an unacceptable interpretation (namely, that the Torah was not written by God ahead of time but by a human writer at a time well into Jewish history). This interpretation had already been proposed by Abraham ben Meir Ibn Ezra (349),[15] a twelfth-century Jewish poet and commentator born in Spain, to whom Ezra Dinn traces his very distant ancestors. Introducing Ibn Ezra is a very neat move by Potok to show that there can be formidably knowledgeable Jewish intellectuals on either side of an issue.

The allusion to Ibn Ezra, even if it occurs only in the final pages of the novel, is also neat because it delivers a post-factum moral reason for Michael Chandal's having gone back to Spain. Ibn Ezra had to flee from Spain when the fundamentalist Muslim Almohads gained control of southern Spain in the 1140s and subsequently gave the country's *dhimmis* (Jews and Christians) the choice of death or conversion. In 1936, Francisco Franco, a Fascist in league with Hitler who had risen to power in Germany in 1933, was seen as a severe threat similar to that of the Almohads. Michael is driven by his desire to fight the Fascists in Spain—a concern that closely links him, Channah, and Jakob Daw.

Motivating that concern are their particular experiences of extraordinary physical violence, which changed the outlook and course of life of each of the three characters and unites them in ways that are much stronger than the ties of love. Daw experienced World War I in the trenches, was gassed in an attack, and became mentally unhinged (233). Michael witnessed the castration and lynching of Wesley Everest in Centralia, Washington, on Armistice Day in 1919. And Channah was raped as a child by Russian soldiers while hiding in the forest outside her village to escape from one of the pogroms the Russians indulged in during World War I. The Russian soldiers also killed her sister and her grandfather. These experiences of extreme violence, all connected directly or indirectly to the four-year orgy of violence that was World War I, are firmly locked up inside the characters.

None of the characters can talk directly about these experiences, because extreme violence renders them speechless. The mother's inability to talk to her daughter about her life or to address an emotionally difficult subject, which I pointed out earlier, is a consequence of her traumatization as a child. Each character dramatically changed his or her life as a consequence of living through violence. Thus, when Davita asks several times in the course of the novel whether a single event could change a person (177), the answer is obviously yes.

With the passing of years, the memory of trauma is translated into social activism. This is least clear in the case of Jakob Daw. However, in addition to translating his perception of reality (shaped by the horror of World War I) into enigmatic stories, he becomes a committed Communist (and Stalinist) and is willing to fight in the Spanish Civil War following communist party lines. Only when he witnesses the slaughter of noncommunist workers by Communists in Barcelona in the spring of 1937 (229) does he leave the Communist Party and turn against Stalinism. Deprived of his cause and deported from the United States, he finds refuge in Paris, withdraws into writing, and finally fades into death.

Michael Chandal is the scion of a wealthy family of Maine Yankees who made their money in lumber. His brother was badly wounded in World War I and died of his injuries after he was brought home (3–4); his sister Sarah compensates for the trauma by becoming a nurse "for our Lord Jesus Christ" (20). Michael's life is transformed in one moment on November 11, 1919, when he sees the hanging of Wesley Everest from the bridge across the Chehalis

River in Washington. The lynching of Everest, a member of the International Workers of the World (IWW, nicknamed Wobblies), by a mob of enraged American Legionnaires was the concluding event of the so-called Centralia Massacre. The conflict pitted all-American conservative types organized in the American Legion—many of them World War I veterans—against left-oriented workers organized in the IWW. The exact course of that day's bloody events is still contested.[16] Potok plays it safe by using as his source John Dos Passos's novel *Nineteen-Nineteen*, the second volume of his *U.S.A.* trilogy, published in 1932. Under the heading "Paul Bunyan," Dos Passos presents the IWW version of the events. Michael, whose "whole family is in the lumber industry" (177–78), is so shaken by what happened to the Wobblies in general, many of whom were lumberjacks, and to Wesley Everest in particular—his beating, castration, and brutal hanging by a mob—that he renounces his family, moves to New York, and begins to write about urban social misery for a leftist newspaper. He defies his family even further by marrying Channah, a Jewish immigrant who lives with her aunt and cousin Ezra in Brooklyn.

Michael and Channah are both so shaken by physical violence that they dedicate themselves to removing the social causes of such violence, which they locate in very different social phenomena. For Michael, the violence is caused by the exploitation of the working class; for Channah, it is caused by an alienating patriarchal religious system. Communism promises the ideal remedy for both phenomena: the abolition of exploitation through communal ownership of the means of production, the abolition of a religion based on strict distinctions between groups and its replacement by faith in a classless future and universal brotherhood, and the replacement of patriarchy by total equality of the sexes.

Channah very clearly connects her trauma to her father's absence, which resulted from his dedication to his Hasidic rebbe. Not only did his frequent long absences deprive her mother of companionship, connubial bliss, and economic security; when her father was home, she observed that the patriarchal attitudes of Orthodox Judaism "made a slave of my mother." When the Russian soldiers harassed the small town in which the family lived, Channah's father wasn't around to protect his family. "A father should protect his daughters, don't you think?" she asks Davita rhetorically. "A father should not leave that to a grandfather. My grandfather was an old man. He tried to help us, and a Russian soldier shot him. Then they left us in the forest and my mother and I came back to the town. It was my mother's idea that I go to Vienna" (268).

A lot is left out in that passage. The first thing to note is that Channah ascribes her family's helplessness directly to the lack of male protection. There is an absurdity to this, because the presence of one more Hasidic Jew standing guard over his family in his *peyes* and prayer shawl would hardly have stopped the Russian soldiers from doing what they wanted to do. So the question is whether one ought to read this accusation metaphorically and argue, as the scholar of Yiddish literature Ruth Wisse does, that Eastern European Jewry can be faulted for a deliberate cultivation of moral superiority in the face of real physical danger. Not having arms, not being strong, not being determined and prepared to defend one's kin and possessions physically was an invitation to be violated.[17] Is Potok here implicitly making a case for a strongly armed Israel?

In Channah's case, insult is added to injury. What the passage quoted above does not tell us is something we learn earlier: the grandfather was shot when he tried to prevent the rape of his two granddaughters. The older girl was raped and killed; Channah was "only" raped. The shame of the rape is not tolerable to Channah's father. So her mother suggests that she move to Vienna, a city that harbored many "fallen girls." Channah's father, instead of standing by her, acquiesces: "He was ashamed to have me in the house" (268). That is the final insult. We can see easily that only an observant Jew of a disposition as unrealistically angelic as Ezra Dinn's can possibly restore the good name of observant Judaism. Ezra Dinn is also one of the few characters in the novel without the experience of trauma. Thus, he is undamaged—whole and wholesome.

Of course, Channah never mentions the word "rape." She cannot speak about her trauma directly. The word she uses is "hurt," as in "They hurt me very badly, Ilana" (268). But we know that the trauma is rape because Potok uses the same phrasing to describe the rape of Teresa, a little Spanish girl from Madrid. Davita overhears someone say that Teresa was "raped," and she asks her mother what the word means. "It means to hurt someone very, very badly," Channah replies in a voice Davita "could barely hear" (83).

Thus, at the center of Michael's and Channah's traumatization are sexual violence and death: a man's castration and hanging, and a girl's rape and killing (the sister as alter ego). Potok sees these crimes, taking place in America and Central Europe, as identical. He makes this point in Davita's naive musing: "How could a single event like what happened in Centralia change a person so much? And what had changed my mother from an observant Jew to a Communist? I could not imagine events that could so change an individual" (177).

Of course not, because we say that these things are unimaginable. Trauma is caused by lived reality; only the experience of it makes it real. Channah makes this point late in the novel when she tells Davita, "We really can know only the people and things that touch us. Everything else is like words in a dictionary. We can learn them but they don't live deep inside us" (269). Only experience itself (not books or book learning) truly affects people. "Sometimes things happen to people and they change," Channah says (155).

When the Civil War breaks out in Spain, both Michael and Channah know that they must be engaged there because their own traumas are inflicted on others there every day—in lynchings, rapes, occupation, ethnic cleansing, and ideologically motivated violence. Hence, Channah urges Michael to leave for the war zone, even though this means inflicting on herself and Davita the loneliness she had observed and experienced in her own childhood, and even though for Michael it could potentially mean death. Channah and Michael ignore the warning shot of Michael's bad injury, which echoes the injury his brother suffered in World War I.

We have now arrived at the crux of the book: What, if anything, can the imagination do (1) to help people cope with traumas or (2) to help latecomers understand the suffering of victims? Early in the novel, Aunt Sarah explains that the pioneer women "used their imagination to fight their loneliness" (19). But loneliness is an affliction, not a trauma. When Davita encounters Teresa, who, like Jakob Daw, is mentally unhinged by the violence she endured, Davita wonders "how your imagination helped you if you were hurt that way" (100).

The novel is fair and does not suggest that the imagination can help traumatized people. Their primary reaction to physical pain is to scream. We hear the screams of Teresa, of Wesley Everest, and of Jakob Daw. The scream is followed by muteness, the inability to articulate pain. Indeed, we know from Holocaust survivors how long it takes to compose a narrative that organizes excruciating experiences. After the pain subsides, memory comes, and frequently the reaction to the secondary, remembered pain is to suppress the memory of one's own suffering, which means not talking about it (like Channah) and staying physically and socially active in an effort to override remembrance. Idleness allows painful thoughts to rise up. Michael and Channah become socially and politically active, which prevents them from being flooded with memories and from sinking into depression. An alternative is to transform the memory of trauma into art. Jakob Daw is an activist, but he also sits and writes his stories. They are shaped by his pain even though they do not deal directly with the memory of his experiences in the trenches of

World War I. Yet it is unclear whether writing helps Daw, because he still wakes up at night from his own screams.

When Potok talks about the "redemptive power of the artist,"[18] however, he does not refer to an artist saving himself from the torture of what he remembers. Rather, he is thinking of an artist processing a catastrophic event and making it accessible and tolerable to others through his art. His primary example of this process is the attack on Guernica and Picasso's painting *Guernica*. In his 1986 interview with Elaine Kauvar, he described this process precisely and called the artist's creative transformation of a historic event a powerful restructuring of reality, which then determines how other people see reality. When pushed further by Kauvar, he argued that this is why Orthodox Judaism shuns the visual artist: because it is he or she (a human individual, in any case) who determines how the world is perceived. For Potok, the artist who was most successful at transforming a horrific event into an object that people would go to see, and that then taught them the core truth about the event, was Picasso. "Picasso is the possibility of creating truth," he explained.[19] We are led to conclude, then, that Picasso's *Guernica* stands for the truth of the Guernica experience made available to those who weren't there. This transformation of event into art is at the center of *Davita's Harp* (as it was at the center of *My Name Is Asher Lev*). Let's see how Potok makes it work.

He places Michael's excruciating experience of Guernica at the numerical center of the novel—but it is a mute center, as Michael does not talk to us. We are not with him in Guernica for the attack on April 26, 1937, and we don't hear him narrate his experience of the violence. We learn about it from a distanced (outside) observer, a *New York Times* reporter (179–80). Later, there is another report from an eyewitness, a priest who survived the bombing of Guernica (186–88). It is only here that Potok presents his re-creation of the experience of Guernica, and he is modest enough to confine himself to a very small slice of it.

Two years after Michael's death in the attack, in the spring or early summer of 1939, Davita sees Picasso's *Guernica* in a New York art gallery (290–91). The painting pulls her into its vortex, making it possible for her to live through her father's experience but at such a safe distance that it does not shatter her. As she looks at the painting, she is also pulled into the allegorical world of Jakob Daw's stories. Thus, the two war zones come together in Davita's contemplation of Picasso's work. What is conveyed by the painting, then, is the truth of war: the horror of its brutality, the pain, the dying, the screaming. The painting is silent, of course, but the effect is one of great cacophonous noise. The advantage of seeing the painting is that the violence mediated through art does not destroy Davita, as the actual violence destroyed Jakob Daw and Michael.

I do not know if this is what Potok meant by the "redemptive power of art." One may legitimately question whether art is redemptive, as Chaim Potok argues. "The artist, in strange fashion, redeems the horror of reality through the power of his or her art," Potok said to Kauvar.[20] What does "redeem" mean here? Is the horror of Guernica lessened when we look at *Guernica*? Or do we learn something that makes us better people? If that was the intent, the painting failed, for we are not better people because of it. Potok never really explained what he meant by "redemptive power." However, it is certainly true that the horror becomes imaginable through the painting. It is reduced in size to an image that we can take in at one glance, and what is depicted is not so cruel that we have to look away in pain. Picasso presented metaphors of violence, disruption, and torture. Metaphors want to be figured out and thus invite contemplation, so we are tricked into thinking about Guernica and can do it in a nonthreatening way. While I am sure that the effect of the painting is quite different for people who have actually lived through war, it has certainly forced hundreds of thousands of people to think about what happened on that April day in 1937. And that is a good thing, even though it may not have prevented another Guernica from happening.

At one point, Davita talks to her cousin David Dinn about Lag B'Omer, the thirty-third day after Passover, which is celebrated by Jews with outings into nature to commemorate the cessation of a plague in Roman-occupied Palestine that wiped out twenty-four thousand students of Rabbi Akiba (certainly a metaphoric number). Davita wonders "if anyone will remember Guernica that long." David replies, "Jews would remember if it happened to them" (182). Observant Jews, who are dedicated to remembering, most decidedly transform traumatic history not into visual art but into poems (piyyutim), prayer, and ritual. Only recently have we begun to see great literary art in the book of Psalms and the book of Lamentations, in prayers such as the Akdamut and the Unetanneh Tokef, and in the medieval piyyutim. With those poetic texts the Jews pray for redemption, but they do not indulge in the illusion that the texts themselves are redemptive. With his theory of the redemptiveness of art, Potok put considerable distance between himself and rabbinic Judaism.

Chaim Potok's *Davita's Harp* is not a great work of art. It is not comparable in its artistic accomplishment to Picasso's *Guernica*. But it is a carefully conceived and skillfully executed novel that, like *Guernica*, has induced hundreds of thousands of readers to think about the political and ethnic violence of the first half of the twentieth century and challenged many of them to find a moral way to deal with this legacy. This is no mean achievement.

NOTES

1. Elaine M. Kauvar, "An Interview with Chaim Potok," in *Conversations with Chaim Potok*, ed. Daniel Walden (Jackson: University Press of Mississippi, 2001), 67.

2. Chaim Potok, *Old Men at Midnight* (New York: Alfred A. Knopf, 2001). See also Joshua Rubenstein and Vladimir P. Naumov, eds., *Stalin's Secret Pogrom: The Postwar Inquisition of the Jewish Anti-Fascist Committee* (New Haven: Yale University Press, 2001); Jonathan Brent and Joshua Rubenstein, *Stalin's Last Crime: The Plot Against the Jewish Doctors, 1948–1953* (New York: Harper-Collins, 2003); and, for a general history, Nora Levin, *Paradox of Survival: The Jews in the Soviet Union Since 1917*, 2 vols. (London: I. B. Tauris, 1990).

3. Kauvar, "Interview with Chaim Potok," 70.

4. Chaim Potok, *The Gates of November: Chronicles of the Slepak Family* (New York: Alfred A. Knopf, 1996).

5. In his interview with Elaine Kauvar, Potok actually pointed out that "each of [his main] characters, with the exception of Davita, is really, I suppose, a different aspect of myself and a reflection of my fundamental interests." Kauvar, "Interview with Chaim Potok," 78.

6. Potok reportedly based the discrimination against Davita on discrimination experienced by his wife, Adena Sarah Mosevitzky, at an Orthodox school when she was a girl. Cf. Eric Homberger, "Chaim Potok: A Writer Struggling with His Jewishness," *Guardian*, July 31, 2002, http://www.guardian.co.uk/news/2002/jul/31/guardianobituaries.boo ksobituaries.

7. Kauvar, "Interview with Chaim Potok," 69–70.

8. Ibid., 68, 70.

9. Chaim Potok, "On Being Proud of Uniqueness" (lecture, Southern College of Seventh-Day Adventists, Collegedale, Tennessee, March 20, 1986), available at http://potok.lasierra.edu/Potok .unique.html. See also Harold Ribalow, "A Conversation with Chaim Potok," in Walden, *Conversations with Chaim Potok*, 4–5.

10. Chaim Potok, *Davita's Harp* (New York: Alfred A. Knopf, 1985). Citations to this edition will be given in the text.

11. Sacvan Bercovitch, *The Puritan Origins of the American Self* (New Haven: Yale University Press, 1976).

12. Sexual deprivation is referred to when Channah and Davita enter their empty Brooklyn apartment. Channah has been reminiscing about attending Brooklyn College with Ezra Dinn but now murmurs, "Who can get used to this? After so many years together, to come home alone and go to bed alone, and wake up alone" (167). This image of loneliness recurs while Michael is in Spain. Channah talks to the window:

> She stood sharply outlined against the window—trim, thin-hipped, full-breasted, her head nearly touching the pane. She was speaking softly to the window, her lips almost to the glass. "You know what it is, don't you. You see through us the same way that we see through you. It's the loneliness. That's right. It's Mama waking to no husband on Shabbos and yom-tov. Yes, that's right. It's zaideh alone with us at the table. Yes, yes. It's the sounds in the darkness during the night, for which I need the strength of my man, and my man isn't here. It's pogroms that might come at any time. Yes, pogroms. Can anything be worse than the black plague of loneliness?" (155–56)

At times Potok doesn't quite trust that he has made his point clearly enough and adds little asides in which his characters explain how things are linked—in this case, loneliness, darkness, and night. In their strong connection and in the "black plague of loneliness," it's probably all right to hear a reference to the ninth plague (darkness) in Egypt, which ranks just before the terrifying slaughter of the firstborns, for darkness imposes loneliness and separation from others.

13. This is a major subtheme in Yiddish fiction, from Sholem Abramovitsh to Sholem Asch. It is presented in great detail in Asch's novel *Der tilim yid*. Published both in Yiddish and in English translation (under the title *Salvation*) in 1934, the book is exactly contemporary with the time period in which *Davita's Harp* was set.

14. Michael explains to Davita, "'The three of us were in love with your mother and she married me'" (140).

15. Baruch Spinoza, in his *Tractatus Theologico-Politicus* (1670), actually first inferred this reading from hints dropped by Ibn Ezra. But Spinoza had been excommunicated and thus cannot be named, because in the yeshiva his name would completely relegate Davita's conclusion of the non-divine/non-Mosaic authorship of the Torah to the domain of the unacceptable. For the exact location of Spinoza's remark about Ibn Ezra, see Benedict de Spinoza, *A Theologico-Political Treatise*, chap. 8, available at http://www.sacred-texts.com/phi/spinoza/treat/tpt12.htm.

16. See "The Centralia Massacre" on the University of Washington Libraries website at http://content.lib.washington.edu/iwwweb/read.html.

17. Ruth R. Wisse, *Schlemiel as Modern Hero* (Chicago: University of Chicago Press, 1971); Ruth R. Wisse, *Jews and Power* (New York: Schocken Books, 2007).

18. Kauvar, "Interview with Chaim Potok," 70.

19. Ibid., 69.

20. Ibid., 70.

THE BOOK OF LIGHTS
A Book of Choices

Sanford E. Marovitz

Two primary sources of illumination radiate at the center of *The Book of Lights*. One is mystical, drawn from the *Zohar*, or the *Book of Splendor*: "the Holy One," "eyn sof," "the Infinite," "the Supreme Cause."[1] The other is physical: the atom bomb, the "Death light."[2] All lights apart from those two sources in Chaim Potok's fifth novel, including the sun, are fiery emanations, symbols, reflections, or images of the radiant mystical core. Both primal sources of light dynamically affect the life of Gershon Loran, the protagonist and central consciousness of the novel, but they do so in completely different ways. The mystical light brings meaning to his life through his intense study of Kabbalah, and the atom bomb awakens him, albeit indirectly, to a new way of seeing the world around him; it transforms him, as it did Potok himself, by expanding his moral horizons.

Before either change can occur, however, Gershon must learn how to choose from multiple alternatives of which, for many years, he is only dimly aware despite his progressing education. The novel begins with this motif—*the need to choose*—yet Gershon cannot make the choice that will determine his future before the closing pages. In this respect, *The Book of Lights* is a bildungsroman that traces the hero's intellectual, moral, and psychological evolution from uncertainty and indirection to a stability worthy of his surname—Loran—which denotes a navigational system that enables travelers to find their way by determining their own position with reference to at least two

separate radio-signal stations. Ultimately, Gershon acquires a new way of seeing, being, and choosing with reference to signals from "the Author of light"
(*BL*, 225) and the "Death light."

His father gives him an early push in the right direction by insisting that
the seven-year-old boy learn to choose on a specific occasion. They are visiting the Statue of Liberty, and Gershon is told to decide whether they should
take the elevator or the stairs to the head of the statue. After choosing the
stairs and being carried up the last several flights, he gazes out admiringly
over the water toward the Brooklyn shoreline. Gershon's father praises the
"beautiful world" (*BL*, 4) out there but cautions the boy of his need to make
wise choices lest it hurt him. Potok emphasizes the dire effect of choosing
unwisely by abruptly revealing in the next three short paragraphs the death of
Gershon's parents in Palestine, the unfortunate loss to Jordan of the cemetery
in which they were buried, and the death of his adored cousin in the war with
Japan—all the result of poor choices. His parents foolishly went to a café after
being warned of the danger, and they were buried at a vulnerable site near
Jerusalem; his cousin volunteered to fly for the Army Air Force during the
war with Japan. All were poor choices.

When Gershon is about sixteen, living with his morose aunt and uncle in
a dismal ground-floor Brooklyn apartment, he lies sleeplessly on some nights,
terrified by the reality of sudden death in his family and neighborhood. At
such times in warm weather, he flees for relief to the roof of the building, as
he does on the night of August 5, 1945, when Hiroshima is being incinerated
on the other side of the globe, where it is the morning of August 6.[3] It is an
unusually clear night, and he can see "the vast heaven of stars . . . stretching
from one end of the city to the other" (*BL*, 6). The *Zohar* reveals that only the
Lord can count the seemingly numberless stars and name them all because
"'His understanding is without number.' . . . It is not without purpose that all
the stars shine and serve."[4] On this night their purpose seems to have been to
illumine the bringing forth of new life, for near Gershon a mongrel bitch is
giving birth to a litter of puppies, an act "which stir[s] him in a strange way; .
. . the birth and her body seem . . . filled with a singular radiance" (*BL*, 6–7)—
that is, *radiance* corresponding with the starlight over Brooklyn, versus *radia-
tion* from the almost simultaneous "Death light" over Hiroshima:

> Overhead the star-filled sky seemed to drop down upon him. He felt all
> caught up in the life of heaven and earth, in the mystery of creation, in
> the pain and inexhaustible glory of this single moment; . . . he reached

up and brushed his hand across the sky and felt, actually felt, the ach-
ingly exquisitely cool dry velvet touch of starry heaven upon his fingers.
. . . He cried a little and shivered in the chill night air.

. . . He never forgot that moment. He hoped it would return one day.
He felt he would be changed in some extraordinary way if it ever
returned. He began to wait for it. (7)

He does not wait in vain. Ultimately his rooftop experience (without the dog)
is replicated with great enhancement, and Gershon's long state of indecision
ends as his life's aim and purpose become clear.

Like most of Potok's young heroes, Gershon is brilliant and responsible
to others. He readily assists his aging aunt and uncle, who provide for him in
place of his parents. But as long as his aspirations remain unclear to him, he
cannot be truly responsible to himself. Usually at a loss as to what steps he
should take to progress, Gershon simply repeats time and again, "I don't
know" (BL, 12 passim) when asked about his plans for the immediate as well
as the distant future. Through most, if not all, of his career as a student, he
advances as fortune takes him. Although the early stages of his progress are
impeded by indecision, chance accommodates his uncertainties to his advantage, and, often without realizing it, he is seldom delayed for long.

For example, after graduating and receiving ordination from a yeshiva,
Gershon is uncertain where to turn next when a casual friend mentions that
he will apply for admission to Riverside, a non-Orthodox Hebrew seminary
in New York. Curiosity rather than commitment leads Gershon to apply there
also, and when his friend reneges, Gershon, having been admitted, registers
and remains at Riverside. Sharing the brilliance of Potok's other young heroes,
he attracts the attention of two distinguished scholars there even without
exhibiting the apparent passion for learning that characterizes their commitment. One of them, Professor Nathan Malkuson, an eminent Talmudist, calls
it *entheos,* "the feeling of possession by the divine," as he defines the Greek
term (BL, 19). In contrast, although equally illustrious, is Professor Jakob
Keter, who appears at the seminary during Gershon's second year there to
teach the history and texts of Kabbalah, Jewish mysticism. For Keter, Kabbalah is "the heart of Judaism, the soul, the core" (24). Keter (*keter:* Crown)
and Malkuson (*malkhut:* King) received their surnames from the first and last
of the ten *sefirot,* or aspects of God, in the early sixteenth-century mystical
system of Isaac Luria of Safed.[5] An expert in Kabbalah, Keter is also a theoretical physicist, mathematician, and secular Zionist. A man of imagination,

he becomes the primary model for Gershon, complemented by Malkuson, the man of reason. Visionary images of both appear to Gershon during his years at Riverside and afterward in Asia.

Fretting prematurely through his first year at the seminary over what he should do after he graduates and receives ordination as a rabbi, Gershon is awakened by Keter's classes on Kabbalah in his second year to a fascination completely new to him, one that leads him to extensive exploration and prob-ing of the texts far beyond the level of his classmates. Kabbalah texts are the principal textual source for *The Book of Lights*, in which light imagery of all kinds is rife, as Potok's first epigraph for the novel, from the *Zohar*, suggests: "See how many hidden causes there are . . . hidden from the comprehension of human beings. . . . There are lights upon lights, one more clear than another, each one dark by comparison with the one above it from which it receives its light. As for the Supreme Cause, all lights are dark in its presence."[6]

Because all light may be traced to the "Supreme Cause," all light is in itself good, according to Kabbalah, but powerful light, out of control and destruc-tive, creates evil. The explanation for this frightening irony may be seen in the origin of creation according to Isaac Luria. Greatly simplified, he believed that "the Holy of Holies" projected powerful lights with diminishing degrees of strength that were to be held in vessels and thus controlled, yet the lights were so potent that they broke the vessels and dispersed. They were then cap-tured as sparks by particles of judgment left behind when "the Holy One" withdrew into Himself from His ubiquitous Totality, a process called *Tzim-tzum*. According to Potok, the breakage was not supposed to occur. In Korea a visionary Keter reminds Gershon that "a terrible mistake [occurred] at the very beginning when even God lost control and the light spilled. A strange poetry of light" (*BL*, 242). In a 1982 interview, Potok reiterated to Leonard Rubinstein that "from the very beginning of things, this creator God did something fundamentally wrong. This is a very startling idea; . . . creation went awry from the very beginning."[7] However, Luria revealed that the error is correctable little by little. The sparks may be redeemed by human acts of benevolence; each *mitzvah* (prayer, good deed, and pious act) frees a bit of the divine light. In *The Book of Lights*, fires great and small represent this account of the transformation of lights in Kabbalah; uncontrolled they are evil and disastrous, whereas under control they are not.[8]

Although Keter immediately stimulates Gershon's interest in Kabbalah, and that interest rapidly gains strength, his goals for the future nonetheless remain unclear. He does not wish to become a pulpit rabbi, and he lacks the incentive to enter graduate school with the aim of moving into a teaching career after receiving his degree from Riverside. His choices remain open, but he cannot decide among them. Not even Keter's singular invitation to study with him for the doctorate motivates him to commit himself. Meanwhile chance appears to lead him to his destined end, as it brings him at a special time to the roof of his apartment building, then to Riverside, to Keter, and Kabbalah.

Similarly, it is not by choice but by chance that Arthur Leiden becomes his roommate during his years at the seminary. Arthur is there as a refugee from physics, a field in which he excels but has been driven from by his throbbing conscience, which makes him feel guilty over his father's role in developing the atomic bomb and the consequent destruction of two Japanese cities with tens of thousands of their inhabitants. Charles Leiden teaches physics at MIT, and his wife is a professor of art history at Radcliffe with a specialty in Oriental art (*BL*, 75); they are devoted to Arthur, as they were to his older brother, who was killed in the war. Arthur's parents are extremely wealthy, influential people who include among their friends and associates President Harry S. Truman as well as Albert Einstein ("Uncle Albert" to Arthur), Enrico Fermi, Leó Szilárd, and other eminent physicists who shared in creating the bomb; all but Truman are Jews like themselves.

Gershon first meets the Leidens when they accompany President Truman to the rare book room, where he is reading. On being informed that he is studying mysticism, Mr. Leiden tells him, "We have a mutual interest in light, then," which leads Mrs. Leiden to interject sarcastically, "Very different sorts of light" (*BL*, 72). After watching the Leidens drive away from the library with the president, Gershon sits for a few minutes on a nearby park bench and closes his eyes. Immediately he sees "a vast ball of white light flash across a desert night. An iron wall of wind and a tidal wave of fire. A black sky empty of stars." Part of this vision echoes Ezekiel 1:4, the starting point of *Merkavah* (or "throne") mysticism, the foundation of Kabbalah: "And I looked, and, behold, a stormy wind came out of the north, a great cloud, with a fire flashing up, so that a brightness was round about it; and out of the midst thereof as the colour of electrum, out of the midst of the fire."[9] This vision also makes Gershon recall a passage from the *Zohar* that refers to birds as representing angels healing the earth; then he sees and hears pigeons cooing (74). Although the "vast ball of white light" reminds Gershon of the *Zohar*, it also bears a strong likeness to the nuclear explosions of the bombs that Mr. Leiden was instrumental in creating. His reading interests broaden from Kabbalah to works on "the atom, atomic power, atomic bombs" (121), an extension induced, of course, by his learning about Arthur's family and their association with the nuclear bomb.

Informed shortly after the Leidens have left with President Truman that a prestigious new award endowed by Arthur's parents will be presented to him, Gershon hesitates to accept it. On being asked if he would agree to receive it, he responds first to the dean and then to the chancellor, "I don't know what to do," "I don't know," "I don't know" (BL, 78, 80–81). Of course, his parental aunt and uncle as well as Arthur urge him to accept the award, and he finally tells the dean that he is "proud" to receive it (82), yet he remains unsure of why he had been unable to decide (80, 81). Later, at the graduation ceremony, commencement speaker Albert Einstein states that theoretical physics, which led to the development of the bomb, was called by the Nazis "Jewish physics" (114). He explains that although the physicists' original intention in attempting to unlock nuclear energy was benign—to give "the gift of atomic power to a benevolent land, to America"—it resulted in catastrophic death and destruction, from which Arthur cannot free his mind. Einstein then praises the Leiden family, as they continue to grieve over the death of their eldest son, for "convert[ing] the ashes of its grief into a light of hope" (115) through the award they are funding.

Several weeks before Gershon leaves for Korea, Keter asks him why he stopped studying Talmud with Professor Malkuson. "I don't know," Gershon replies. "I ask myself often. I answer that I don't know. . . . I really don't know" (BL, 125). After studying for an additional year with Keter at Riverside, his indecisiveness has undergone no perceptible change. Unlike his girlfriend, Karen Levin, who has long been totally committed to earning her doctorate and moving into an academic career as soon as possible, allowing nothing—not even her intimate relationship with Gershon—to deter her, he has no such definitive goal, so any decision he must make regarding his future becomes a sticking point. "I wish I knew what I wanted," he tells Karen. "I wish I had your tenacity. Sometimes I think I'm afraid to make choices because whatever choices I make something will come along and blow them away" (41). He refers to himself as a "Zwischenmensch" in a dialogue with Karen,[10] where he tells her that he coined the word to describe himself as a "between-person. I don't belong anywhere. . . . Nowhere. I'm in-between" (121). Perhaps the fatal effect of poor choices on his parents and his cousin inhibit his own decisiveness, yet the examples of Karen and Keter should balance this fear.

Long aware of Karen's steadfastness in advancing her career, Gershon does not learn of Keter's timely decision to leave his native Germany about twenty years earlier until shortly before he himself departs for Korea. The kabbalist tells him of immigrating to Jerusalem probably in the early to mid-1930s when Jewish scientists were fleeing to England and the United States. He informs Gershon that he revisited Germany after the war and recalls, "I saw Dresden. In my darkest imaginings I could not envision such destruction. An ocean of fire from American fire bombs. Yet I felt no compassion for the Germans. And that distressed me. To think that Germany had succeeded in destroying a man's capacity to feel compassion toward human suffering. That is perhaps her greatest sin. No, I made no mistake when I left for Jerusalem. Those who remained, they made the mistake" (*BL*, 125). Leaving when he did was clearly a wise choice.

Not long after hearing this personal revelation, Gershon arrives in Korea during a snowy February to commence his fifteen months of service as an army chaplain. Shortly, he meets the Jewish chaplain stationed there, who blurts out, "My God! This is not a place for Jews!" (*BL*, 138). The next afternoon the chief of chaplains asks him to choose where he wishes to be stationed—in the relative comfort of Seoul or with an army division in the north. "'North,' he said, and was not sure why he said it" (139). Surprised, the chief chaplain sends him north. Two months later, when told he can transfer to Seoul if he requests it, Gershon "decided to remain in the battalion, . . . [but] . . . could not entirely explain why he chose to remain. Simply, he did not know" (160). To his credit, however, because of his intelligence and integrity, good fortune continues to be on his side in Korea. Typically showing more concern there for the welfare of his troops than himself, Gershon occasionally alienates his superior officers and suffers as a result but never regrets working on their behalf despite the possibility of being penalized for it. Although he knows what is best for the soldiers and persistently acts to help them, his self-knowledge is so inadequate that he rarely does more for himself than maintain his obligations to Orthodox Judaism and remain humane toward the Korean people, who are altogether foreign and largely incomprehensible to him. Nevertheless, he is very decisive when making demands of superior officers on behalf of the troops in his battalion, acquiring provisions for the Jewish holidays, receiving necessary materials to build a *succah*, and converting the Christian chapel into a synagogue. At one point he is transferred to a new unit after confronting a superior officer and insisting that the unsanitary and otherwise unhealthy conditions under which some of the men were laboring in the heat be corrected. He prevails but loses his post as a result, which angers him and the soldiers under his care.

For the first few months, Gershon shows no interest in the Korean people qua people, although he lives beside them in their own country: "He knew nothing about these people, had little desire to know" (*BL*, 162). The change in his apathetic attitude toward them appears immediately after his first visit to Japan in mid-June, about a decade after the atom bombs were dropped over Hiroshima and Nagasaki, but it is hinted at shortly before he leaves when he reads from the morning service, "Awake, arise, for your light has dawned! . . . The presence of the Lord has shone upon you" (157). When Gershon returns to his battalion after the visit, his Korean houseboy, Sammy Kim, tells him that his mother's grave was moved by orders of the army from a nearby hillside to an undesirable location. This news deeply affects Gershon, especially because he had seen her buried from a distance only a month before and asked Sammy about Korean customs regarding death and burial. "What a hell of a thing . . . to have to move your mother's grave," he mutters to Roger Tat, his Mormon assistant, but the generally helpful and considerate Roger is completely indifferent to it (174). Obviously, Gershon is not. Potok himself might have been moved by such an incident while serving in Korea; he told Elaine M. Kauvar in a 1986 interview that his "first novel has never been published; it became the paragraph or so in *The Book of Lights* which deals with moving the Korean grave."[11] Potok said in the same interview that "revelation is always attained linguistically . . . in the Jewish tradition," but this incident confirms he learned in Asia that it comes no less meaningfully from experience.

Gershon's awakening to Sammy Kim as a person, an individual human being like himself rather than merely a Korean servant, may be instigated by the thought of his own mother's grave in a cemetery desecrated by the Jordanians. No less important, however, is that his moral vision has expanded since his brief recent visit to Japan, where his attitude as both an American and a Jew begins to change. Memories of that first visit remain bright. For instance, he is astonished by the transcendent beauty of a geisha he sees there and the joyful singing and dancing of a group of men carrying "a large pagodalike edifice on poles," which reminds him of Jews carrying the Torah on Simchat Torah (*BL*, 172). Undoubtedly taken with the splendor of Japan itself, a country about which he had known nothing apart from its role in the war and its suffering from the bombs, Gershon is notably impressed with his altogether unexpected reactions to the sensitivity and spontaneity of the Japanese people.

He begins to see Asians anew as part of his own world rather than as some unfathomable distant realm of "others." This marks the beginning of Gershon's transformation by experience, as Potok's own stay in Korea with visits to Hong Kong and Japan marked the beginning of his.

Later, visiting Tokyo with John Meron, his roommate in Korea, he watches an elderly man with a long white beard praying before an altar; the beard "caught the soft lights of the candles and glints of the sunlight that came through the door of the shrine. In his hands he held a prayer book. His body swayed slowly back and forth . . . as he prayed. His eyes opened and closed behind rimless spectacles that flashed and flared with the lights of the candles and the sun" (*BL*, 261). Gershon asks John whether God is listening to the old man's prayer; John had not thought about it, and neither had he. But, Gershon wonders, if "He's not listening, why not? If He is listening, then—well, what are *we* all about?" (261–62). Near Mount Fuji, Gershon "abandon[s] himself to . . . this sacred mountain of Japan, this god. . . . He [feels] drawn to its majestic light-filled rise, its splendrous whiteness" (265–67). With such thoughts running through his mind, Gershon soon understands that he is "being taught the loveliness of God's world by a pagan land" (263). On his next visit with Arthur Leiden, who anxiously longs to see Kyoto and Hiroshima, Gershon is enchanted by everything he observes in Takamatsu: "How they [the Japanese] fused together nature and man! All one flow of world. No separations" (338–39).

In his introduction to *Wanderings*, Potok wrote that when he arrived in Korea he thought he was "prepared . . . for everything," but he soon learned that he was unprepared for "two encounters" there: "a vast complex of cultures perfectly at ease without Jews and Judaism, and a confrontation with the beautiful and horrible." He was "sundered" by "the loveliness and the suffering [he] saw in the lives of pagans," including his memory of the old man he had seen praying at a shrine, which he incorporated into *The Book of Lights*; this and other equally moving experiences of the pagan world "transformed" his "own Judaism," and he "spent the subsequent [two] decades in an evolving and reshaping of [his] faith."[12] Here Potok emphasizes the change that occurred in his Judaism while in Asia and after his return to the United States, but the transformation was more comprehensive than that, as is evident from his descriptions of Korea, Hong Kong, and particularly Japan in *The Book of Lights*. His hero's responses to Asia parallel his own.

Gershon is surprised during his first autumn abroad to learn that Arthur Leiden has just arrived in Korea. As far as Gershon knows, Arthur had joined the navy, but that did not work out for security reasons; he could not gain clearance for enlistment in the navy despite numerous requests to govern-ment officials by his influential parents. The impasse led Riverside to free him from a service obligation before he could receive ordination. Dissatisfied with being exceptional in that respect, Arthur has made a choice that stuns Ger-shon upon learning of it. He has volunteered to serve as a chaplain in Korea. His principal aim, however, as he makes clear to Gershon soon after they meet outside the chaplain's office, is to see Japan, especially Hiroshima and Kyoto. Still conscience-ridden over his father's contribution to creating the atom bomb, Arthur cannot rest until he visits the first city it destroyed and the one his mother saved.

Not until much later does Gershon learn that Arthur is driven obsessively to see Kyoto, which was initially chosen as the target of the first bomb but was saved from nuclear destruction because of his mother's influence. Mrs. Leiden, in her capacity as an expert in Oriental art, urged President Truman to spare Kyoto because of its invaluable and irreplaceable cultural structures and arti-facts. Consequently, Hiroshima was destroyed in its place. After being dis-charged, Gershon visits the Leidens and asks her about her part in Kyoto's salvation. Charles then reminds his wife, who has been unwilling to acknowl-edge her direct role in the final decision, "You helped save Kyoto and helped destroy Hiroshima." Elizabeth Leiden's former students were among the chief advisors on the selection of targets, and after consulting with her, they all advised against choosing Kyoto. Nearly as deeply pained by this time as Arthur, and heavily burdened over his role in creating the bomb, Charles reminds her once more, "You managed to slip a word to Harry Truman one evening. Hardly indirect, Elizabeth. Inadvertent, yes. It was our part in all the inadvertence that Arthur found unendurable. . . . Quite by chance you destroy a city, and quite by chance you save a city" (*BL*, 379–80). "The irony in all of this," he had men-tioned to Gershon a moment earlier, "is that you never visited the city of the real moral tragedy. Hiroshima is a moral stain, but Nagasaki was without doubt an act of utter cruelty. . . . Nagasaki turned my stomach. We were in the hands of the witless" (379). These lines and others pertaining to them near the end of the novel illuminate the source of Arthur's obsession with the bomb and his compulsion to see the two Japanese cities that the activities of his parents most affected. "Some turn deserts into cities," Arthur tells Gershon, and "others turn cities into deserts" (348). Not long after that, his obsession kills him.

With the major exception of Mrs. Leiden's influence in the bombing of one city and the saving of another, Potok did not stray far from history in describing how the final target was selected. Historically, the decision ultimately belonged to Henry Stimson, Truman's secretary of war at the time, as the narrative

accurately suggests. However, the officers and scientists on the Target Committee, chaired by General Leslie R. Groves, who was in command of the
entire atom bomb project, recommended Kyoto as their top choice for the
first bomb and again for the second. Stimson, who hated the idea of bombing
cities, vetoed their selection on both occasions. On being advised that Kyoto
was the "preferred target," he responded immediately, "'I don't want Kyoto
bombed.' And he went on to tell [his interviewer later] about its long history
as the cultural center of Japan, the former ancient capital, and a great many
reasons why he did not want to see it bombed."[13] When Stimson met again
with a group of nuclear physicists, he brought up the matter of Kyoto once
more, saying it "is a city that must not be bombed" and insisting that "the
objective was military damage . . . not civilian lives."[14] When pressed yet again
by General Groves, Stimson quickly replied that he had no reason to change
his decision; no one but the president could countermand it, which Truman
was clearly unwilling to do. In the novel, Charles Leiden acknowledges to
Gershon, who is on a short leave in New York to visit his hospitalized uncle,
"Not for a moment do I regret the work that we did on that bomb" (*BL*, 248).
According to Jonathan Soffer, Stimson, too, felt certain that the atom bomb
should be dropped over Japan, but "he vetoed the selection of the old imperial
capital of Kyoto as the first target, arguing that destruction of a major cultural
treasure would violate the norms of civilized behavior."[15] Exactly where
nuclear weapons fall on the gamut of "civilized behavior" in relation to "major
cultural treasure[s]" is one of the ambiguities that Gershon must struggle
with during and after his enlightening experience in Asia.

For Howard Morten, Gershon's assistant in Korea, no ambiguity exists
because he believes that the bomb probably saved his brother's life by elimi-
nating the likely need to invade Japan if it had not been dropped, an eventual-
ity that could have resulted in the loss of scores of thousands more American
and Japanese lives. "You know how many times my mother and father and I
have thanked Einstein and . . . all those who worked on that bomb?" he says.
"My father had a special prayer of thanks he made up for them the first Yom
Kippur after the war. I was a kid. I watched him cry . . . like a baby, my father,
as he thanked all those scientists for making the bomb and ending the war.
He even made up a prayer thanking President Truman" (*BL*, 229). Truman,
too, had a choice, of course, and there lies the kind of ambiguities among
which Gershon must navigate, preferably without hurting or alienating the
people close to him, including Howard and Arthur, who quietly seethes over
the gratitude expressed for Charles Leiden's work on the bomb (224). It is

unclear if Arthur is aware of his father's agonizing ambivalence over its use; if so, it has not fazed him.

Before crossing Kowloon Harbor to tour Hong Kong, Gershon offhandedly asks Arthur if he has noticed the attractiveness of the Chinese girls in their tight slit skirts, and his friend, surprised, asks in return if they have come to see Chinese girls. Gershon replies with another question: "Aren't they part of God's world?" Now it is Arthur's turn to respond with "I don't know. . . . Is Korea part of God's world?" "Definitely," Gershon answers, using a word he has rarely spoken before (*BL*, 292). His part in their brief dialogue reveals how broad his moral vision has become since his arrival in Asia, when he had no interest in the Korean people or their way of life; at that time he intended to serve his troops responsibly, study, observe the obligations of Orthodox Judaism, and leave when his term of duty was over. These commitments remain vital to him, but during his months abroad, his consciousness extends beyond them to include the lifestyle of a world heretofore alien to his own. Entering it has engendered what Potok calls "a core-to-core culture confrontation,"[16] in which the center of one culture meets the unlike center of another.

Before leaving for Japan, Gershon tells Arthur about his strange rooftop experience at sixteen and his way of relating it to the kabbalistic texts he studies, with their apparently heretical passages:

> Sometimes when I read those texts, I'm on the roof of that building again. I don't know why I feel that way. They say things in those books that no one dares to say anywhere else. I feel comfortable with those acceptable heresies: . . . creation as a vast error; the world broken and dense with evil; everything a bewildering puzzle; . . . I especially like the ambiguities. . . . You can't pin most of it down the way you can a passage of Talmud. I can live with ambiguity, I think, better than I can with certainty. Doubt is all that's left to us, Arthur. Doubt and desperate deeds. (*BL*, 308)

From such remarks, Arthur knows that Gershon is capable of living a more balanced life than he can himself, and he writes to his parents accordingly from Hiroshima that "the world . . . is a grayish sea of ambiguity, and we must learn to navigate it or be drowned" (378). Gershon has learned this, but Arthur never does. His letter home portends both his own death by drowning and Gershon's future amid life's lights and shadows.

Attracted rather than oblivious to ambiguity, Gershon opens himself to it and is transformed by it. He now wishes to explore the lifestyles of the countries he visits, whereas Arthur does not. Gershon cannot understand why, but Arthur's interest follows a single straight track; it aims only to see Japan. For Gershon, in contrast, the world "was a between-world. He wanted to look into it. . . . He wished to wander through this menaced and thriving world, this strange simultaneity of darkness and light" (*BL*, 293). With the help of two women to guide them, one in Hong Kong and the other in Japan, he and Arthur tour the region so that they can see at least that much of Asian culture, the best and worst of it, from the inside out, as explorers examining a new world. Arthur falls in love with Kyoto, the city his mother saved, and he becomes ill after leaving it for Osaka, Takamatsu, and finally Hiroshima, the city she had "inadvertently" left to be destroyed.

Toshie, the lovely geisha whom Gershon has hired to guide them in Japan, quickly cures Arthur with what he calls "Japanese chicken soup" (*BL*, 337). Then she relates her horrifying experience in the Tokyo firebombing, recalling it in an understated, nearly monosyllabic way that belies its fury and effects: "Give Jizo flowers to help children. . . . We had Jizo in Tokyo near our house. Jizo did not help in fire bombs. Children die. Fire was like ocean. Ashes and smoke like big storm. Air was on fire. All Jizos get burned" (339).[17] Yet only a short time later at the Peace Memorial in Hiroshima, Arthur almost dismisses that firebombing because of his obsessive focus on the death and destruction caused in and around Hiroshima by the atomic bomb. "We firebombed Tokyo, Arthur," Gershon reminds him. "No one feels guilty over that." "Why do people keep saying that?" Arthur asks in return. "They know damn well it isn't the same" (348). But, in fact, it was closer than he allows to being the same in its destructive effects, as the casualty figures indicate.

Beginning with Keter's recollection of seeing the burned remains of Dresden after the war, references to firebombing occur sporadically in *The Book of Lights*, although it receives much less attention than nuclear weapons, which seem to have minimized through awe the commensurate effect of incendiaries late in the war across both oceans. Keter does not exaggerate the horror of the Dresden bombing of February 13–14, 1945, which was estimated in 1946 to have killed about 300,000 people and burned up much of the city.[18] British bombers dropping incendiaries on Hamburg two years earlier, on July 27–28, 1943, are estimated to have killed approximately 45,000, mostly civilians,[19] although Horatio Bond's earlier estimate was 60,000 to 100,000 slain.[20] According to Bond, the Tokyo firebombing of March 9–10, 1945, left 84,000 people dead, and Rhodes's more recent figure is 100,000.[21] It must be noted that many more people, nearly all civilians, were badly burned or otherwise injured in these bombings, all of which—especially the air attacks on both countries early in 1945—undoubtedly reduced the duration of a long, abhorrent war.

Gershon attempts to placate Arthur by telling him that the nuclear bombs were initially expected to be used against Germany, but that makes no difference to him because he has heard it all before (*BL*, 348). Arthur then reveals that it is not only guilt over his father's share in creating the atom bomb that drives him to distraction, but also the prominent Jewish contribution to it. "I wish Jews hadn't been involved. Somehow there's something wrong in that," he says. Arthur cannot separate his soul's telling him that his father "helped kill nearly one hundred thousand people"; consequently, he hates Hiroshima because it cries out so much of death (348). At the Peace Memorial, Arthur recites in English the mourner's Kaddish in an attempt to expiate in some way his father's assumed guilt and therefore his own, for he as the son must carry the burden of his father's sin. As he utters these words of praise for God, Gershon ironically hears a low voice from inside the darkness of the open monument—a voice from the demonic realm, the *sitra akhra*, that Kabbalah identifies with evil. He has heard it several times before, not only in the Far East but as far back as Riverside (96).

He first becomes aware of this eerie phenomenon while working in the rare book room of the seminary's library when he envisions "death enter[ing] the room in the form of an impenetrable icy blackness" that spreads over everything, including the walls (*BL*, 49). The experience exposes him to the dark side of Kabbalah and its association with Gnosticism. Up to that point, darkness mainly evokes in his memory the night on his roof, when he undergoes a mystical communion under the star-filled heavens in response to the new life emerging almost within his grasp. But the "fetid" blackness that fills the rare book room where he sits seems "to him to be the angel of death" (49). In Tokyo with Arthur one night years later, Gershon hears the voice of a "ghostly messenger" from "the other side" a short time before twilight: "This was the hour he had learned to dread, the hour of questions. . . . He felt himself fearful and uncertain about most things, and never more so than at this hour when there hovered about him what he had come to call the four-o'clock-in-the-morning questions" (321). The seductive, provocative voice presses Gershon to reconsider his values, his aspirations, his relations to loved and admired figures in his past. It prods him to reassess "the truth" as he sees it and leads him to acknowledge that "truths [exist] in those words" from the mysterious voice. "How could truths emanate from such darkness?" he asks himself and listens as the sounds of temptation continue to urge his acceptance of its suggested "truths" until "the palest of lights" appears in the window and sends it back into the realm of shadows. "Only a light would drive it away" (321–25). It is this insidious rationalizing that returns to haunt him from the dim interior of the Peace Memorial as Arthur utters the Kaddish. The voice tempts him to relinquish his aim to study and build, encourages him to enter the "other side" instead and embrace its own dark truths, and promises to return because it "is in the nature of things" (352–53).

Soon after they return from Japan, Gershon's world is darkened by Arthur's death when his friend foolishly chooses to travel to Japan again immediately after his first visit. Arthur arranges to replace a new chaplain scheduled to go on retreat, and his plane crashes in a river when an engine explodes a minute after takeoff. The death of his closest and perhaps only real friend proves devastating to Gershon; he can fulfill his responsibilities and read from the *Zohar* and other kabbalistic texts, but he cannot pray, and he seems to have reverted to his former state of mind. "All the arduously mended pieces of his fragile world lay in shards everywhere around him," like the vessels shattered by the Holy One's primal light when the creation went wrong, "and he did not know what to do" (*BL*, 371). The darkness of a snow-laden winter in Korea complements Gershon's distraught frame of mind after Arthur's death is confirmed: "Deep shadows filled the dark room, darker than any darkness he had ever known before" (365). In this lightless room, Gershon anticipates hearing the silken, seductive voice from "the other side." But it does not return until months later. Before that occurs, the bright, scorching sun of May turns the earth brown, and the hill fires near the encampment start again, requiring great effort to keep them under control. These fires, like all unexpected fires, appear to be kabbalistic evidence of creation gone wrong. With the spring sun, shadows reappear amid the brightness, suggesting that Gershon, ever the "Zwischenmensch," is on the way to consolation and restoration, his army duty fulfilled, but his future is still undecided. He reverts to this self-assessment, comfortable among the ambiguities, knowing that "he ha[s] lived through a between-time with the army in Korea, . . . sorry that his time [t]here was over, [but] not sorry enough to want to extend it" (372).

After Gershon's discharge, the sibilant, imploring voice returns to haunt him again when he is prepared to encounter it, after his final visit with the Leidens and his last conversation with Professor Malkuson, whose concluding observation undoubtedly surprises him. Malkuson does not encourage Gershon to devote himself to Talmud and prayer, as he may have expected, but to continue studying Kabbalah to both help him overcome his sense of loss over Arthur's death and restore the *éntheos* that has dimmed because of it. Yet he also goes far beyond that when he stares directly at Gershon and acknowledges that what is ultimately important in the matter of faith "is not that there may be nothing. We have always acknowledged that as a possibility. What is important is that if indeed there is nothing, then we should be prepared to make something out of the only things we have left to use—ourselves" (*BL*, 383). This stunning existentialist concession draws no response from Gershon, but it is instrumental in helping him overcome the diminished voice from the *sitra akhra* during their final confrontation before he leaves for Israel. Gershon continues to gaze at Malkuson quietly until the Talmudist wishes him well and offers his help in the future should it be needed. Ironically, however, Malkuson's agnostic implication is not very different from what Keter says to Gershon before he leaves for Korea. "I cannot come to terms with our mortality," Keter tells him. "It is all one vast obscurity, one vast hopelessness. A veil. We know nothing, we can hope for nothing. Nothing" (126). Yet he inspires. As Gershon learns from both, the *mitzvah* lies in *doing*, not *hoping*.

Some weeks or months after his final interview with Malkuson, Gershon finds himself on his apartment roof again, but this time he undergoes a descent into self that brings him sanctification beyond the limited communion he had experienced on the rooftop long before. He easily dismisses the sibilant voice in the demon realm. Although he does not leave immediately after this mystical epiphany has enlightened him to begin working again with Keter, it clearly has brought him the sense of purpose he has sought, and he is well prepared to make his decisive choice at last. From the dismal, sunless ground-floor apartment of his aunt and uncle in Brooklyn, he ultimately arrives at Keter's garden in Jerusalem, where the "air was shaded by tall trees, through which streamed narrow pillars of light." A bird sings its angelic song from the branches above him while Gershon sits "in the light and shade" (*BL*, 389) of the garden. Like the *succah* he had made in Korea, which a then-visionary Keter had told him "conceals and reveals simultaneously, . . . hides the sun and lets in the sun simultaneously" (211), the pleached garden suggests the ambiguities that he works amid and thrives upon. Although he knows his choices will not always be clear and easy, Gershon has learned through study and experience how to make them; as Keter's prize student, then, he will likely do well for his mentor and himself as well as for all those he will serve in future years as a teacher and scholar.

NOTES

1. Gershom Scholem, ed., *Zohar: The Book of Splendor* (1949; repr., New York: Schocken Books, 1963), 27–28.

2. Chaim Potok, *The Book of Lights* (1981; repr., New York: Fawcett Crest/Ballantine, 1982), 110. Subsequent citations to this edition will be given in the text and abbreviated as *BL*.

3. The bomb was dropped on the morning of August 6 over Japan, which is across the international date line. Gershon learns about it in "his small sunless room" in New York the next morning over the radio (*BL*, 109), which would be about twelve hours later in Japan. His experience, then, must occur on the night of August 5 in New York, about twelve hours before he hears about Hiroshima, if it is simultaneous with the explosion, which I believe Potok implies it is. If his mystical experience occurs on the night of August 6 so as to be "the same day," it would be about twelve hours after the explosion, and much of Potok's powerful irony of simultaneity would be lost.

4. Scholem, *Zohar*, 100–101.

5. The names of the *sefirot* are probably in Aramaic. See Scholem's introduction to his selections from the *Zohar*; ibid., 10.

6. This quotation from the *Zohar* is one of two epigraphs that appear on an unnumbered page immediately preceding part 1 of *The Book of Lights*.

7. Leonard Rubinstein, "Odyssey Through Literature: An Interview with Chaim Potok on 'The Kabbalah,' in His Novel, *The Book of Lights*," in *Conversations with Chaim Potok*, ed. Daniel Walden (Jackson: University Press of Mississippi, 2001), 48.

8. For more information on the significance of Kabbalah to Potok's novel, see Sanford E. Marovitz, "Jewish Mysticism in the Shadow of the Bomb," *Studies in American Jewish Literature* 4 (1985): 62–83. For fuller exposition on Kabbalah, see Gershom Scholem, *Major Trends in Jewish Mysticism*, 3rd ed. (New York: Schocken Books, 1961), 156–286, esp. 205–86; Gershom Scholem, *Kabbalah* (New York: Quadrangle/New York Times Book Co., 1974); and David S. Ariel, *The Mystic Quest: An Introduction to Jewish Mysticism* (Northvale, N.J.: Jason Aronson, 1988).

9. Ezekiel 1:4, in *The Holy Scriptures According to the Masoretic Text* (Philadelphia: Jewish Publication Society of America, 1955), 716. For this earliest stage of Jewish mysticism, see Scholem, *Major Trends in Jewish Mysticism*, 42–79, and Ariel, *Mystic Quest*, 21.

10. Daniel Walden has addressed in detail the relevance of this term to Potok's life in a 1985 essay, where he refers to the author as a "Zwischenmensch." See Daniel Walden, "Chaim Potok, a Zwischenmensch ('Between-Person') Adrift in the Cultures," *Studies in American Jewish Literature* 4 (1985): 19–25.

11. Elaine M. Kauvar, "An Interview with Chaim Potok," in Walden, *Conversations with Chaim Potok*, 73.

12. Chaim Potok, *Wanderings: Chaim Potok's History of the Jews* (Philadelphia: Jewish Publication Society of America, 1978), xiv.

13. Richard Rhodes, *The Making of the Atomic Bomb* (New York: Simon and Schuster, 1986), 640.

14. Ibid., 648.

15. Jonathan Soffer, "Stimson, Henry L.," in *The Reader's Companion to American History*, ed. Eric Foner and John A. Garraty (Boston: Houghton Mifflin, 1991), 1033–34.

16. Walden, "Chaim Potok, a Zwischenmensch," 20.

17. Jizo is a guardian deity for children whose figure is seen in stone memorial statues all over Japan.

18. Horatio Bond, ed., *Fire and the Air War* (Boston: National Fire Protection Association, 1946; repr., Manhattan, Kans.: Military Affairs/Aerospace Historians, 1974), 83; Bond cites an article in the *New York Times* of January 2, 1946, as his source. In 1946 Bond was chief engineer of the National Fire Protection Association. See also Rhodes, *Making of the Atomic Bomb*, 593, 599. A more recent estimate of the number killed in the bombing of Dresden is "not more than 25,000 people"; "'Nation and World': 'Germany': 'Death Toll Disputed,'" *Akron Beacon Journal*, October 2, 2008, A4.

19. Rhodes, *Making of the Atomic Bomb*, 474.

20. Bond, *Fire and the Air War*, 81.

21. Ibid., 113; Rhodes, *Making of the Atomic Bomb*, 599.

HISTORY AND RESPONSIBILITY

An Assessment of Potok's "Non-Jewish" *I Am the Clay*

Nathan P. Devir

Introduction

I Am the Clay, a fictional account of the humanitarian crises unleashed by the chaos of the Korean War (1950–53), was both the first and last novel that Chaim Potok wrote. Potok started the original manuscript in 1956, when he was serving as a U.S. Army chaplain in Korea. The finished product, which differs considerably from the initial manuscript, was first published in Dutch translation by the Bzztôh publishing house in Holland in 1991; the English version of the novel appeared in print one year later, published by Alfred A. Knopf. During those thirty-five years, Potok struggled with rewrites, read copious amounts of material on Korean history and culture, and kept detailed notes on which he drew for the ultimate incarnation of the novel. It is therefore no exaggeration to state that the themes and ideas explored in the book occupied him all throughout his professional and intellectual trajectory.

Thirty-five years of labor and reflection, and yet *I Am the Clay* is the only one of Potok's novels that did not make the best-seller list. Scholarship on the book has also been lacking: to date, there are only two very short essays of literary criticism devoted to it.[1] Indeed, in spite of Potok's hopes that his readers would "let [him] lead them into new worlds"—that is to say, away from the ethnically specific niche around which his reputation as a writer had developed—*I Am the Clay* has found few devotees.[2] Understandably, some readers are unsure of what to make of a Potok novel about the shattered lives of Asian peasant farmers, not to mention of the novel's title, which many associate with the well-known Presbyterian hymn.[3] Moreover, the book contains no Jewish protagonist, no recognizable references to biblical, Talmudic, or kabbalistic sources, and, most significantly, no mention of the "core-to-core culture confrontation" (usually between Orthodox Judaism and Western secular humanism) that characterizes all of the author's other literary works.[4]

Because Potok achieved his fame as an author and an educator from the unlikely position of one who wrote, at least in the eyes of many, "from an insularly Jewish perspective that denies broader implications," the absence of Jewish motifs in his first and last novel should, in fact, give every interested reader pause.[5] In the pages that follow, I aim to provide the necessary background and context for understanding the lingering curiosity about this book by focusing on the following questions: What was the genesis of this work? What motivated Potok to return to his first novel, time and again, over the course of his career? Is there any symbolically Jewish component to the text that is not readily ascertainable? Finally, what is the place of *I Am the Clay* in the Potok canon? These are the questions to be addressed in this investigative essay.[6]

In the Beginning: Inspiration and Biographical Context

After receiving his rabbinical ordination from the Jewish Theological Seminary in 1954, Potok volunteered (in accordance with the expectations of the JTS) to serve in the U.S. Army Chaplain Corps. He was posted to South Korea, first to a combat medical battalion and then to a combat engineering battalion, both frontline units assigned to keep the peace in the aftermath of the Korean War. As Potok affirmed repeatedly in interviews and public lectures throughout his lifetime, the time he spent in Korea (1956–57), a place that he called "beautiful beyond all imagination," was a defining moment in his adult sense of self.[7] Experiencing Buddhist, animistic, and shamanistic spiritual practices in a country where Jews had hardly ever set foot, Potok was, for the first time in his life, forced to put into question his own ideas about faith and chosenness as they are articulated in the Jewish tradition. For instance, in an interview with Michael J. Cusick, Potok noted, "I know when I went to Korea I was a very coherent human being in the sense that I had a model of what I was—I had a map. I knew who I was as a Jew. I had been through Jewish Theological Seminary and was ordained. I knew who I was as a member of western culture.

And I knew who I was as an American. . . . My time in Asia utterly transformed me and left me with nothing but questions for which I'm still struggling to find answers."[8]

Among the seminal events that occurred for Potok during his time in the
chaplaincy was an incident involving the moving of Korean burial mounds
from a hill near the American military base. The base hospital needed to be
moved to an area more above ground, where the wounded would not have to
inhale the dust that was pervasive during the beginning of monsoon season.
The new location chosen for the hospital was an adjacent hill containing
many burial mounds. Consequently, the local Korean villagers were com-
pelled to transfer the graves of their deceased kin to another area. Potok witnessed the disturbing scene of these villagers moving their dead from the hill
and was struck by the moral conundrum of the incident. He thought, *what if
that were the grave of my mother?* Potok vowed to one day render in novelistic
form the event as it had taken place. Of this grim incident, Potok said, "I've
carried that image around with me all these years: elderly Koreans on a hill
digging up a grave. The notion of their having to move what I knew to be a
sacred site in order to make way for an American army unit struck me with
singular force and stayed with me."[9] Potok also made detailed sketches of traditional Korean burial customs and funeral rites, presumably from an actual
funeral that he witnessed (figs. 1a–b). (Since Potok did not know how to read
Classical Chinese, he must have copied the brushstrokes of the Chinese characters on the coffin that indicate the name of the deceased, "Sin Chŏngsun of
the Sin clan of P'yŏngsan.")[10] These scenes were to be the focal points around
which his first novel, *I Am the Clay*, would be structured.

Potok began writing the first draft of *I Am the Clay*, originally entitled "A
Cry of Stones," in 1956. As mentioned, the original manuscript differs considerably from the final (English) version published in 1992. Its plot more closely
resembles that of *The Book of Lights* (1981) than the published *I Am the Clay*
in that it focuses on the friendship between several American GIs stationed
on the Korean peninsula and their houseboy, a certain Sammy Kim. However, the kabbalistic and theodicic content of *The Book of Lights* is absent in
the original manuscript of *I Am the Clay*, since the latter story, as Potok confirms, is "entirely about Americans and Koreans. There [are] no Jews in it at
all."[11] In contrast to the final version of the novel, the plight of Korean refugees
who are being driven from their home villages does not make up the majority
of the narrative, although flashbacks to such times are provided throughout
the story. Instead, descriptions of the suffering caused by the war's aftermath

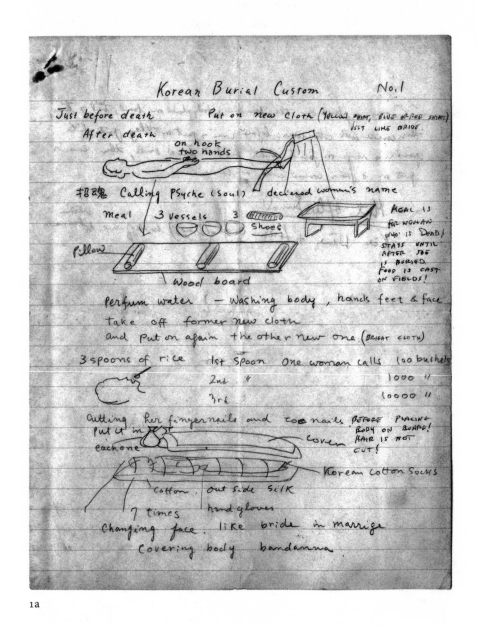

1a

Figs. 1a–b Korean burial customs recorded in Chaim Potok's notes. Located in Chaim Potok Papers, Rare Book and Manuscript Library, University of Pennsylvania, Philadelphia, box 100, folder 4614. Used with permission.

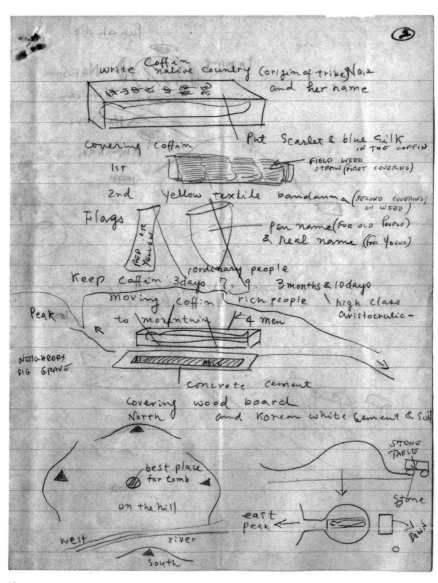

1b

constitute the major foci of the manuscript. The author in the original draft is listed as "Herman Potok, 1st Lt. Chaplain, 7th Medical Battalion."

Potok begins the manuscript with a dedication to the youth of Korea. Indicating that the Sammy Kim in the novel is a composite character based on several different people, he writes, "I knew many Sammy Kims during the long months I spent in Korea. Some were houseboys, some interpreters, others KATUSA [Korean Augmentation to the United States Army] personnel. To these Sammy Kims, in whose hands lies the future of their ravaged land, is this book dedicated."[12] The opening scene describes the young man, noticeably older than the unnamed boy of the later published version but existing in the same dire circumstances: "He was sixteen years old, and he lived in the village with an old man and his wife who were not his parents but who had found him in a drainage ditch one day near Seoul during the last great retreat and had taken him for themselves because they were childless."[13] The young man works as a houseboy for a major at the nearby American military base, and the elderly couple works a small plot of land in their village. The wife remembers vividly the horrors of the Japanese occupation of Korea (1910–45), including "the rape and the burning and the hills glowing red against the darkness in the nights."[14] However, her husband, who is older than she, can recall a time before the Japanese occupation when Korean soil was free of foreigners. He takes comfort in thinking of those early days, because now another alien presence, less evil than the Japanese although equally unwelcome, infringes upon what he considers his basic dignity. "It is an ugly world," he thinks. "We are clay now being molded into something new. It is no longer our land."[15]

For financial reasons, the old man approves of the boy's working in the American compound, but he does not initially believe in the possibility of true friendship with the occupying forces. His fears of the Americans corrupting Korean youth are realized when local women turn to prostitution and ruthless merchants take advantage of the village's traditional economic structure. These phenomena, coupled with American soldiers' outbursts of racism and public drunkenness, as well as the old man's own declining health, leave him bitter and hopeless. He understands why Li, the village carpenter, wishes to seek revenge on the occupiers for the deaths of his three children and the maiming of his now-mute wife, who were unintended victims of an American bombing raid. Yet, in time, the old man's opinion of the Americans will soften, and his main concern will be ensuring Sammy Kim's future education.

Most of the Americans and Koreans in the novel are depicted as judicious in their dealings with each other. This is in spite of the fact that the Americans express a real abhorrence of the living conditions under which they are forced to function in the war-torn country, and that the Koreans are resentful of the Americans' lack of respect for Korean custom and propriety. Potok highlights how select individuals from each side try to truly engage people from the other, such as when Sammy Kim invites a friend from the base to his village for a meal. The American soldier refuses, knowing that to set foot in a Korean home for the mere purpose of socializing would mean a severe court-martial. However, when Sammy is insulted with racial slurs by a frustrated enlisted man, this same friend duly warns the offending soldier, "You better stop going around acting like a goddamn conqueror."[16]

The major for whom Sammy Kim works is portrayed as a kind man, a weary thirty-eight-year-old who enjoys hearing the boy's calming "Good morning, sah" as the first utterance of the day. The major misses his own sons and tries to cope with that longing by helping the young Kim however he can, giving the boy extra meat rations for his adopted family and looking after him on the base. This goodwill is especially evident when the major authorizes two doctors from the battalion to journey through a fierce snowstorm in order to treat the boy's adopted mother, who is stricken with hemorrhagic fever. As expected, the doctors are too late to save her. She dies and is buried on a nearby hill, where "the dead slept in undisturbed peace, looking down from the hill to the village where life went on. The villagers believed it made the dead joyous to see their families happy and growing."[17] There are detailed descriptions of the preparation of her body for burial; these descriptions follow almost verbatim Potok's notes and drawings of traditional Korean burial practices.[18]

The scene involving the moved graves comes at the climax of the novel, as the symbolic culmination of the moral dilemmas caused by civil strife. (A similar scene appears briefly in *The Book of Lights*—the only published rendering of this image until the final publication of *I Am the Clay* in 1992.)[19] The villagers learn from the local prostitutes that the American army intends to move its base hospital to the hill where the burial mounds are. Sammy Kim receives confirmation of this from the major, who is powerless to stop the action. It is more important to save the lives of recovering American soldiers than to honor the customs of the land's inhabitants, the major realizes, although the situation grieves him endlessly.

The men of the village meet to decide on a course of action. The old man, now a weary widower, is resigned to the horrible idea that the graves will be moved. "We are clay," he says. "There is nothing else to be done." The carpenter,

Li, walks out of the meeting in a rage, threatening violence against the Americans. "I am not clay!" he screams. "I will not be molded!"[20] His resistance proves futile, and the end of the novel recounts the moving of the graves to another location. This agonizing upheaval of earth and flesh, in which the remains of the Korean ancestors are "molded" against their will, is the primary function of the metaphor of "clay" in the story. Unlike in the final version of the novel, the original manuscript's repeated references to clay are not qualified by biblical passages. Nor are there any allusions to the clay of the well-known Presbyterian hymn.

The Chaim Potok Papers at the University of Pennsylvania contain additional unpublished short works on similar themes from Potok's military stint in Korea, such as the short story "The Rejected Stone" (1957), which was rewritten in 1961 and renamed "The Journey to the Mountain." The plot of this story seems like a rough outline of the later *Book of Lights* and focuses on a Jewish chaplain—the first appearance of a Jewish character in Potok's literary work—by the name of Alan Steinberg. (Note the German meaning of the character's name, "stone mountain," which refers to both of the story's titles as well as to "A Cry of Stones," the original title given to *I Am the Clay*.)

Steinberg, like Potok, is a recent seminary graduate and an American military chaplain posted to a hunger- and poverty-stricken Korea, where, upon his arrival, he encounters "the sights of bowel movements along the banks of frozen streams, lines of hungry prostitutes outside the battalion area and the tracks of skillful thieves working silently in the snow-filled nights."[21] From the beginning, the man is wrecked with self-doubt about his ability to survive in such a place. He fears that his seminary training has not prepared him in any meaningful way for the experience: "This is a long way from Akiba and Meir, he thought dully, this time not without a little self-pity. This is a long way from quarrels over biblical emendations."[22]

In Korea, Steinberg is wrenched out of his familiar Jewish world and confronted for the first time with real-life death and decay. Shaken and revolted, the chaplain must question the stance of his Jewish God: Does this God feel the same for Koreans as he does for Jews? How should a Jew feel about the suffering of an unknown and completely different people, a people with whom Jews have no common points of reference? On one occasion, "he passed a dead Korean lying across a ditch by the road, and when he returned that night the body was still there, frozen, lying head up across the ditch, an old man in a pointed white beard and torn khaki coat. When he prayed the next morning and said, 'Thou sustainest the living with loving kindness, revivest the dead with great mercy,' there was the face of the dead Korean suddenly in front of him blurring away the words. 'That Korean, too?' he thought."[23] As in *The Book of Lights*, the chaplain comes to realize the rigidity of his fundamentalist Jewish upbringing through his encounter with the "other." The key moment in his adoption of a more inclusive, humanistic Jewish perspective occurs when he witnesses Shinto spiritualism while on furlough in Japan. The initial anguished queries of his time in Asia—such as "Almighty God, are these people also your creation?" and "Do I reserve compassion only for the sufferings of my own people?"—are answered for him upon his return to the battalion from Japan, when he is finally able to accept that chosenness does not mean religious exclusivism.[24] As noted above, "The Journey to the Mountain" shares other vignettes with *The Book of Lights*, such as references to the destruction of Hiroshima and Nagasaki by the atomic bomb, intimate encounters with Japanese women, and the friendship between enlisted men in Korea. The main concern, though, is the "journey" to self-discovery through the moral recognition of individuals and worlds dissimilar from one's own, which is, of course, part of the original premise of *I Am the Clay*.

Over three years, Potok revised *I Am the Clay* several times and finally submitted it for publication to two different literary presses in 1959 and in 1960. The novel was rejected by both houses for being too highbrow. Following these disappointments, he turned his attention to the story that would become his first published novel, *The Chosen* (1967), and its sequel, *The Promise* (1969). After the runaway success of these novels, Potok expressed relief that his "apprentice novel" had not been published, because, as he noted, "I wasn't quite sure how to handle [the material] then."[25] Moreover, by that time in his career, he was of the opinion that a novel with no Jews in it simply would not work, for himself as an author or for his audience, "because it was not situated anywhere along the line of continuity where I thought I was located in terms of what I had so far written and published and learned about writing."[26]

Nevertheless, the detailed notes in the Chaim Potok Papers show that the author worked on revising *I Am the Clay* consistently throughout the years, especially from 1973 to 1975, when he gathered additional materials, formed outlines, and read historical/ethnographic studies such as Charles Allen Clark's *Religions of Old Korea* (1961), Shannon McCune's *Korea, Land of Broken Calm* (1966), and Chun Shin-yong's *Korean Society* (1975). He also became acquainted with major works of modern Korean American literature. For example, he photocopied and filed away the notes that he had scribbled in the margins of Younghill Kang's 1931 classic *The Grass Roof*. Most significant in this prewriting phase, however, are indications that Potok wished to make the moral ambiguities that crop up in the wake of societal violence a major part of *I Am the Clay*'s thematic foundation. This intention can be seen in the fact that one of the major sociological readings included in the preparatory writing stages for *I Am the Clay* was political scientist and philosopher Vilfredo Pareto's "The Use of Force in Society," from his classic *The Mind and Society* (1935).

From "Apprentice Novel" to Last Novel

In the late 1970s and throughout the 1980s, Potok set about the task of finishing all of the novels in which he would attempt to work through, per the Freudian "talking cure," the major issues and concerns that occupied him as a Jew in the twentieth century. In the context of the "confrontation of ideas" and "cultures in tension with one another," which he felt were defining characteristics of our age, he formulated a strategy to address all of the ways in which traditional Judaism dealt with the vagaries, contradictions, and challenges of modern life.[27] In *The Chosen*, Potok tells the story of the Hasidic prodigy Danny Saunders, who encounters the world of Freudian thought, a system that looks at the world through the lens of pathology as opposed to the lens of religious doctrine and praxis. In *The Promise*, Potok explores what modern Judaism should do with regard to the phenomenon of scientific text criticism, which, in the novel, Reuven Malter agrees to apply solely to the study of Talmud. In *My Name Is Asher Lev* (1972), the problems are aesthetic and have to do with long-held notions about idolatry and iconicity. *In the Beginning* (1975) again takes up the issue of scientific text criticism of the Bible, but this time links it with the realization that many of this method's early proponents were violently anti-Semitic. The novel then explores the roots and consequences of European anti-Semitism, as well as the various mechanisms of Jewish defense that respond to that threat. *The Book of Lights*, originally entitled "American Labyrinth," uses mystical and kabbalistic sources to wrestle with the moral ambiguity of that ultimate symbol of modernity and its evils, the atomic bomb. *Davita's Harp* (1985) deals with what Potok calls "secular fundamentalism" (political ideologies such as communism, fascism, and so forth), as well as with the place of gender equality in modern religious movements.[28] Finally, *The Gift of Asher Lev* (1990) revisits Asher Lev, a celebrated painter, after a span of almost twenty years, drawing on the conflicts in his interpersonal relationships and emotional inner life in order to question which commitment will ultimately be stronger: the obligation to one's family or the commitment to one's personal calling. The answer provided at the novel's conclusion, when Asher symbolically offers up his son as the successor to the Ladover rebbe, is an ambiguous one in which the acutely painful core-to-core culture confrontation is ever present.[29]

As Adena Potok states in the interview included in this volume, Potok had, after *The Gift of Asher Lev*, more or less finished dealing with the "big questions" that he originally set about exploring in his novelistic work, specifically those of "the traditional mind encountering the modern world." After 1990, Potok would only write a few short stories (some of which never appeared in English), two books of nonfiction, several plays and screenplays, and children's stories. Potok considered working on what he called his "Jerusalem novel" and a third Asher Lev book, but apparently, after such a meticulous and successful run, the impetus was no longer there. "The first-person narratives in which I explored my early world are probably at an end," he admitted circa 1991, "unless I come upon strata of memory that are at present concealed from me."[30]

Around this time, Phil Muysson, Potok's Dutch publisher, asked the author whether he had anything in his "trunk" that remained unpublished. Potok mentioned his early "apprentice novel" but was noncommittal. Muysson asked to see *I Am the Clay* and, after having read it, was eager for Potok to revise it as his next novel. Initially, Potok was less than enthusiastic, but he was inspired to start working on the book again during the Iraqi invasion of Kuwait in 1990. The plight of the desperate Kuwaiti refugees moved him immensely and reminded him of all the displaced Koreans he had seen during the time of his military service. As he writes in the introduction to the Bzztôh edition, "The war in the Persian Gulf brought me back in memory to Korea . . . where I had felt on my flesh and in my soul the wretched remnants and consequences of war."[31] Potok wanted to capture that same desperation in the characters who would appear in the revised version of his first novel.

To that end, Potok constructed the opening scene of the published *I Am the Clay* with a chance encounter between an elderly couple and a young boy who are fleeing the chaos of the beginning stages of the Korean War. The old man and his wife (who will both remain unnamed throughout the novel) come upon Kim Sin Gyu, a wounded boy from another village, who is "blood-covered, barely breathing, lying face-up and unconscious in the snow in the bottom of the ditch."[32] The woman, whose only child died of disease in the first year of his life, immediately takes the boy out of the ditch and sets him on the makeshift cart into which she and her husband have thrown an improvised set of belongings. As they flee southward from the Chinese and the soldiers of the north, the old man vehemently disapproves of the boy's burdensome presence and quietly wishes for his demise.

> The old man then found himself gazing at something within him that he had never before seen. All knew of the unseen world beyond the everyday realm of appearances; but he had never thought there might be such a world inside himself: unexplored and cavernous. And because he could neither understand nor name it, he could not see which spirit or demon lurked within it, and that was for him the greatest fear and bewilderment of all.
>
> Still, he was certain he wanted the boy to die.[33]

As the story progresses, the elderly couple begins to realize that the boy possesses certain kinds of supernatural abilities, as he is somehow able to provide food, heal wounds, and unconsciously lead the three to shelter during the treacherous climb through the mountains in the dead of winter. Although still demonstrative in his hostility toward the boy, the old man understands the nature of his guardian function and accepts his presence as a temporary measure.

After a series of counteroffensives in the area of their refugee camp, the old man, the woman, and the boy are forced again to flee, only this time northward. Once more, it seems to the couple that the spiritual forces surrounding the boy protect them throughout the arduous journey back to their home village. When the Americans finally secure the southern sector of the country and Kim Sin Gyu, now healed, goes back to his community, he finds it razed to the ground. He returns to the village of the elderly couple, and they agree to take him in as their own while he goes to work in the nearby American compound.

The story ends with a meeting between the boy and a Jewish chaplain at the compound, "a troubled, dark-haired man in his mid-twenties [who] did not have a cross on his collar but a kind of arching double tablet."[34] The Jewish chaplain plays no major role in the story, appears only briefly at the end, and goes unnamed. Moreover, his Jewishness plays no part in the Koreans' perception of him. To them, he is simply a white foreigner like the others. We see this lack of perspective on his Jewish difference when the old woman hears from the boy about "a chaplain" at the American base. She immediately thinks back to the white Christian missionaries who taught songs to her mother:

> The woman seemed interested in the chaplain. "Does he sing?" she wanted to know.
>
> The boy said, "I have not heard him sing."
>
> "Tell me if he ever sings this song," she said and sang for him in her quavering voice *Have thine own way Lord have thine own way thou art the potter I am the clay.*
>
> The boy asked her what the words meant.
>
> "Once I knew," she said, embarrassed. "But I have forgotten. It is the language of the foreigners."[35]

In the final scene, after the woman's death and the forced transfer of her grave, the chaplain and the old man send the boy off to study in Seoul. The boy leaves with a jar full of earth from the grave of his surrogate mother. (It is from this scene that the title of the book in its Korean translation, *A Handful of Earth*, is taken.)

Reception of the Book

I Am the Clay was first published in Dutch translation in 1991. The book is dedicated to Phil Muysson, who encouraged the author to rework his first novel, as well as to Adena Potok, who was the novel's first reader. The fact that the book appeared in Dutch translation before it appeared in English is, in retrospect, not surprising. Since 1985, all of Potok's fiction had been published first in Holland, where he had a dedicated readership made up especially of Dutch Christians who understood his characters' struggles to reconcile tradition with modernity. (According to Muysson, Potok is such an important author in Holland that his books are still part of the required reading curriculum in Dutch high schools.)[36] The Bzztôh publishing house, which made Potok's books available to the Dutch-speaking populations of Holland and Belgium, was keen on using the author's paintings for the covers of his books—something to which the American publishers never agreed. This gesture thrilled the author. (For the cover of the Dutch translation of *I Am the Clay*, Bzztôh used a reproduction of the Potok painting *Wilderness of Sinai*.)

In 1992, the same year that *I Am the Clay* appeared in English, it also appeared in Korean, published by Younglim Cardinal. The reception in Korea was quite positive, as the following quotes demonstrate.[37] "[The novel features] some exaggerated interpretation of our traditions," stated the publication announcement for the translation, "but the author's attempt to understand our emotional life in depth is laudable."[38] In the opinion of literary critic Yu Han-gŏn, Potok's ability to tell the story from the Korean perspective was worthy of praise, since "the very Asian consciousness with which the author describes the character's inner life is remarkable." With respect to Potok's usage of indigenous motifs in the scenes involving religious rites, Yu echoed the minor criticism in the aforementioned announcement, pointing out that Potok "seems not to be able to discern whether it [the rite in question] is animism, shamanistic folk religion, or simple ancestor worship." But he commended Potok's incorporation of these motifs because "it is clear that he understands the strength of [these beliefs] and strives to recognize them."[39]

The positive reception of *I Am the Clay* in Korea was perhaps aided by two external factors. The first is that both *The Chosen* and *The Promise* had been popular in Korea for years, circulating in unofficial, pirated translations. (Korea joined the World Trade Organization in 1988, and it was almost impossible for publishing companies to navigate foreign literary copyright laws prior to that time.) In point of fact, *The Chosen* has been so well received that the South Korean magazine *Christianity Today Korea* recommends it as one of the must-read novels of the twentieth century. The second probable factor in the positive reaction to the book is that many South Koreans who grew up in the postwar period feel a deep affinity with the Jewish people due to their shared emphases on hard work, education, and family. In addition, there are obvious historical similarities between the two peoples—namely, near-constant domination and victimization by greater geopolitical powers.[40] During a United States Information Service trip to Korea in 1992, Potok expressed a deep appreciation of Koreans' warm reception of the novel.

Back in America, the reception of *I Am the Clay* later that same year was not as laudatory. As Adena Potok mentions in her interview, *Publishers Weekly*, *Kirkus*, the *Atlantic*, and the *Atlanta Journal-Constitution* gave excellent reviews of the book, but most reactions were lukewarm. Michael Stephens, writing for the *Washington Post*, said that the effect of *I Am the Clay* was "more that of a pumped-up fable than a full-blown novel."[41] In the review from the *Times Literary Supplement*, Bryan Cheyette wrote, "The synthesis of opposites is the basic pattern to which all of Potok's fiction conforms. But when applied to a world with which he has only a passing acquaintance, his didacticism is exposed as limited and anemic."[42] In *Book World*, J. Martin Holman disparaged what critics have referred to as Potok's "simplistic" writing style, commenting that "the diction [in the novel] brings to mind a conversation between Tonto and Tarzan." In spite of his objections to the diction and style, however, Holman voiced a largely positive response to the book overall, noting that its shortcomings did not, in his opinion, "do severe damage to the novel."[43]

For his part, Potok was disappointed by the reception of the book in the United States but remained steadfast in his belief that the novel was an important one. In an interview with David L. Vanderwerken, Potok said of the novel's detractors, "They're missing the essential nature of the story. The story is the important thing." Regarding the denigration of his writing style, he quipped, "British critics loved its style—and they invented the language."[44] Potok's retort to his critics recalls a similar statement made by the American naturalist author Frank Norris, whom Potok was fond of quoting on the subject of style. In his famous letter to Isaac F. Marcosson in 1899, Norris wrote, "Who cares for fine style! Tell your yarn and let your style go to the devil! We don't want literature, we want life."[45]

Conclusion: Locating *I Am the Clay* in the Potok Canon

As we have seen, Chaim Potok had much more than a "passing acquaintance" with Korea, as Cheyette's review incorrectly suggests. Moreover, the excerpts from the other two reviews given above—which are typical of most of the criticism of the novel with respect to its style, setting, and narrative technique—do not attempt to engage the thematic or ideological issues that Potok seeks to explore in *I Am the Clay*. In my view, these pervasive shortcomings in the critical discourse surrounding the novel not only betray a fundamentally flawed perspective on Potok's ontological stance and value hierarchy; they also imply readers' profound malaise with such a seemingly radical shift in subject matter. If, as S. Lillian Kremer has remarked, "the genesis and substance of every Potok novel until *I Am the Clay* is Jewish religious, historic, and cultural experience in a non-Judaic world," it seems, in retrospect, not at all surprising that this novel was greeted with less fanfare than the others.[46] After all, Potok's writing style did not change; only the situational context did. What's more, many of Potok's major philosophical concerns also remained the same. If one tries to pinpoint why audiences have neglected this particular Potok novel, the absence of attention to these issues is quite telling indeed.

The most powerful passage in *I Am the Clay* that deals with the afore-mentioned concerns is found in the portion of the novel focusing on the burial of one's kin. Per the haunting images that inspired Potok to start writing the book in 1956, the key scene in the 1992 edition has to do with the moving of the American hospital to the hill where Kim Sin Gyu's adoptive mother has recently been buried. Because the bodies of his parents and grandparents were left to rot in his ransacked village and consequently did not receive proper burial, the boy believes that their spirits, too, now occupy the grave of the old woman who cared for him until her death. He is horrified that the spirits of all of these people will now be offended by the forced transfer of their remains. When the boy attempts to persuade the chaplain to prevent the moving of the graves, "he saw the chaplain's face grow sad and dark, as though disturbed by a long-forgotten memory."[47] Clearly, the chaplain's reaction does not signal a common East-West motif involving geomancy, but rather a reference to the halachic argument over how to bury the scattered remains of millions of Jews slaughtered in the Nazi Holocaust.

Does this key passage mean that *I Am the Clay* should be read as a Holocaust allegory? Hardly. The chaplain's unspoken set of associations suggests instead that the attempt to bring meaning out of mindless death and suffering—including through reverence for the dead and through the careful documentation of such atrocities and their aftermaths (even in novelistic form)—will remain one of humanity's unending burdens. In fact, I am inclined to interpret Potok's comment that the story "is really about a woman" to mean that the old woman's sense of duty toward her fellow human beings (in this case toward a near-dead orphan who may very well hinder her own survival) is the novel's central ideological message.[48] In her interview in this volume, Adena Potok echoes this supposition, positing that the "Jewish" content of *I Am the Clay* is that, in Judaism, "there is the notion that God created all of mankind. And we're responsible for one another. We're responsible for one another in the smallest communities: our families. And, growing more and more broadly, we do have a responsibility for one another." In this sense, the novel is Jewish, for, as Potok has posited, the challenge for the Jews in a post-Holocaust world is to confront the atrocities of history in order to be a true "light unto the nations" and to "continue to exist . . . as witnesses to this darkest of human events and to the tenacity of the human spirit."[49] As Potok suggests, and as Isaiah 64:7 reminds us, this "human spirit" is not for Jews alone: "But now,

O LORD, Thou art our Father; we are the clay, and Thou our potter, and we all are the work of Thy hand."

What distracts many readers from an appropriate reading of *I Am the Clay* is that it seems out of place in the series of literary works for which Potok is well-known. And yet the overarching thematic concerns of Potok's first and last novel are not so different from those of his other books. Regimes change, the virtues of modernity collapse, and in the absence of a universally recognized covenant, we are in dire need of moral standards to guide us. Potok's worldview, according to which faith must coexist with an investigative, unwavering search for meaning, is therefore nowhere more prominent than in the inclusive, humanistic message of *I Am the Clay*. In that sense, it seems that Danny Saunders, Sammy Kim, and Kim Sin Gyu are not so different after all. By rejecting legacies of exclusivity, they all promote what Marius Buning has called an "affirmative" stance, in the same way that Potok has been called an "affirmative writer."[50] Moreover, they display a kind of integrated optimism that Potok himself says "is inherent in the Jewish idea of philosophical idealism."[51] Finally, they have violent confrontations with modernity that cut them off from familiar, clear-cut worlds. Humanized by their suffering, they charge ahead, painfully conscious of their past and cautiously optimistic about their future. Optimistic in spite of everything, because to be anything less, according to Potok, would be to give in to despair.

NOTES

1. J. Martin Holman, "A Voice from the Earth," and S. Lillian Kremer, "Encountering the Other," *Book World* 8 (August 1992): 303–7 and 315–25.

2. Wendy Herstein, "An Interview with Chaim Potok," *Book World* 8 (August 1992): 313.

3. Since the hymn does not appear in the original manuscript, Potok's original references to "clay" are most likely allusions to Isaiah 64:7 ("But now, O LORD, Thou art our Father; we are the clay, and Thou our potter, and we all are the work of Thy hand") and to Jeremiah 18:6 ("'O house of Israel, cannot I do with you as this potter?' saith the LORD. 'Behold, as the clay in the potter's hand, so are ye in My hand, O house of Israel'"). All English translations from the Hebrew Scriptures will follow the 1917 translation of the Jewish Publication Society. For the history of the hymn, see the explanation given with the musical score in Dana Mengel's *Have Your Own Way, Lord* (Nashville: Abingdon Press, 1996).

4. Potok frequently used the expression "core-to-core culture confrontation" to characterize the ways in which traditional cultures respond to the secular umbrella cultures in which they find themselves. For an explanation of this idea in the author's own words, see Chaim Potok, "Culture Confrontation in Urban America: A Writer's Beginnings," in *Literature and the Urban Experience: Essays on the City and Literature*, ed. Michael C. Jaye and Ann Chalmers Watts (New Brunswick: Rutgers University Press, 1981), 163.

5. Daphne Merkin, "Why Potok Is Popular," *Commentary* 61 (February 1976): 74.

6. Other clarifications and observations on *I Am the Clay* are found in my interview with Mrs. Adena Potok, the writer's widow, in chapter 13 of this volume. I would like to express my sincerest gratitude to Mrs. Potok for her time and insight concerning this and related subjects.

7. Marcia Zoslaw Siegal, "The Prime of Chaim Potok," in *Conversations with Chaim Potok*, ed. Daniel Walden (Jackson: University Press of Mississippi, 2001), 96.

8. Michael J. Cusick, "Giving Shape to Turmoil: A Conversation with Chaim Potok," in Walden, *Conversations with Chaim Potok*, 133.

9. Herstein, "Interview with Chaim Potok," 309.

10. Although the McCune-Reischauer system of romanization has been used to reproduce this name, other Korean names appearing in this document are spelled as given in Potok's text or, in the case of corporate names, as presented in company logos. With regard to Korean-language matters, I wish to thank Deberniere Torrey for her invaluable assistance in locating the relevant Korean materials for this article, as well as for translating the Chinese- and Korean-language quotations cited herein. All translations from these languages are hers.

11. Elaine M. Kauvar, "An Interview with Chaim Potok," *Contemporary Literature* 27, no. 3 (1986): 301.

12. Chaim Potok, "I Am the Clay," original manuscript, 1959, located in Chaim Potok Papers, Rare Book and Manuscript Library, University of Pennsylvania, Philadelphia, box 100, folder 4610. I received access to materials in the Chaim Potok Papers courtesy of the staff at the Rare Book and Manuscript Library. I am especially indebted to Donna Brandolisio, who processed the collection and was of invaluable assistance to me during the archival research process.

13. Ibid., 1.

14. Ibid., 5.

15. Ibid., 6.

16. Ibid., 22.

17. Ibid., 13.

18. Ibid., 73–77.

19. Chaim Potok, *The Book of Lights* (New York: Ballantine, 1981), 325.

20. Potok, "I Am the Clay," 84.

21. Chaim Potok, "The Journey to the Mountain," original manuscript, 1961, located in Chaim Potok Papers, box 139, folder 4780, p. 3.

22. Ibid., 5.

23. Ibid, 2. This passage is very similar to many comments Potok made about a scene that he witnessed while on furlough in Japan: "I remember standing in a Shinto shrine in a marketplace in Tokyo and seeing an old man there. He was in front of an idol of a female goddess, swaying back and forth like the Jews on Yom Kippur night in the little synagogue where I grew up. I remember asking myself if the God I prayed to every day was listening to *this* man's prayer? And if not, why not? I asked myself, 'Where are you ever going to see greater devotion in a moment of prayer?' And if the God that I prayed to *was* listening, then what were Judaism and Christianity all about?" Siegal, "Prime of Chaim Potok," 96.

24. Potok, "Journey to the Mountain," 10.

25. Harold Ribalow, "A Conversation with Chaim Potok," in Walden, *Conversations with Chaim Potok*, 8.

26. Herstein, "Interview with Chaim Potok," 310–11.

27. Chaim Potok, "On Being Proud of Uniqueness" (lecture, Southern College of Seventh-Day Adventists, Collegedale, Tennessee, March 20, 1986), available at http://potok.lasierra.edu/Potok .unique.html.

28. Ibid.

29. These observations about the ideological cruxes of each novel have been amply commented on in various media. My outline of them here, however (save the last one regarding *The Gift of Asher Lev*, which is my own), relies heavily on Potok's own comments about them as found in his lecture "On Being Proud of Uniqueness."

30. Chaim Potok, introduction written for the Dutch translation of *I Am the Clay*, located in Chaim Potok Papers, box 100, folder 4624, p. 6.

31. Ibid., 2.

32. Chaim Potok, *I Am the Clay* (New York: Alfred A. Knopf, 1992), 3.

33. Ibid., 58.

34. Ibid., 225.

35. Ibid., 219. The full text of the hymn (see Mengel, *Have Your Own Way, Lord*) is as follows:

Have Thine own way, Lord! Have Thine own way!
Thou art the Potter, I am the clay.
Mold me and make me after Thy will,
While I am waiting, yielded and still.

Have Thine own way, Lord! Have Thine own way!
Search me and try me, Master, today!
Whiter than snow, Lord, wash me just now,
As in Thy presence humbly I bow.

Have Thine own way, Lord! Have Thine own way!
Wounded and weary, help me, I pray!
Power, all power, surely is Thine!
Touch me and heal me, Savior divine.

Have Thine own way, Lord! Have Thine own way!
Hold o'er my being absolute sway!
Fill with Thy Spirit till all shall see
Christ only, always, living in me.

36. Personal communication with Phil Muysson, March 28, 2007.

37. All references here to reviews from Korea or from Korean publications mean those coming from South Korea (the Republic of Korea).

38. Publication announcement dated September 13, 1992, provided in an interview with Mr. Lee Seung-won, June 8, 2006. I would like to thank Mr. Lee, current president of the Younglim Cardinal publishing house, for his kind assistance in extending these insights, as well as for the detailed practical information he gave on the publication details of *I Am the Clay* in Korea.

39. Yu, Han-gŏn, "Hanguk-chŏk sanghwang-ui pŏminnyu-chŏk ihae" (A universalist understanding of the Korean situation), *Sŏp'yŏng Munhwa* (Book review culture) 8 (Winter 1992): 69.

40. Observations expressed in the interview with Lee Seung-won.

41. Michael Stephens, "The War as Koreans Say It," *Washington Post*, May 14, 1992.

42. Bryan Cheyette, book review, *Times Literary Supplement*, November 27, 1992.

43. Holman, "Voice from the Earth," 306.

44. David L. Vanderwerken, "A Visit with Chaim Potok," in Walden, *Conversations with Chaim Potok*, 172.

45. Quoted in Michael Davitt Bell, "The Revolt Against Style: Frank Norris," in *American Naturalism*, ed. Harold Bloom (New York: Chelsea House, 2004), 237.

46. S. Lillian Kremer, "Chaim Potok," in *Contemporary Jewish-American Novelists: A Bio-Critical Sourcebook*, ed. Joel Shatzky and Michael Taub (Westport, Conn.: Greenwood Press, 1997), 285.

47. Potok, *I Am the Clay*, 232.

48. Herstein, "Interview with Chaim Potok," 312. Interestingly enough, the Korean newspaper *Segye Ilbo* (World daily) notes that "the novel draws our attention . . . especially because it highlights the Korean archetype of the mother and maternal love." *Segye Ilbo*, August 31, 1992.

49. Chaim Potok, introduction to *Last Traces: The Lost Art of Auschwitz*, ed. Joseph P. Czarnecki (New York: Atheneum, 1989), xv.

50. Marius Buning, "Chaim Potok," March 1995, http://potok.lasierra.edu/Potok.Buning.html; Sanford Sternlicht, *Chaim Potok: A Critical Companion* (Westport, Conn.: Greenwood Press, 2000), 28.

51. Chaim Potok, "The State of Jewish Belief," *Commentary* 21, no. 8 (1966): 126.

LOOKING BACK

Memories of Potok

The essays in this part of the book reflect upon Chaim Potok's life and work from a more personal perspective. These are the remembrances of those who knew him—friends, fellow writers, and his wife, Adena Potok. The section opens with three eulogies delivered at a memorial service for Potok in December 2002; these essays were printed and distributed for that occasion and have been slightly edited for use here. The book closes with a 1982 speech in which Potok himself shared his personal experiences and insights as a writer.

CHOOSING THE CHOSEN

A Reappraisal of *The Chosen*

Hugh Nissenson

University of Pennsylvania
December 15, 2002

During the summer of 1973, just before the Yom Kippur War, Chaim Potok and I attended a conference of Israeli and American writers in Jerusalem. Late one afternoon, Chaim and I went for a cup of coffee at a café on King George Street. An old man, sipping a glass of tea alone at a table by the window, reminded me of Ernest Hemingway's story "A Clean, Well-Lighted Place." Chaim and I acknowledged to each other that Hemingway had had a formative influence on the development of our respective writing styles. Clarity and brevity of expression were our ideals.

In 1967, I had reviewed Chaim's first novel, *The Chosen*, for the Sunday book review section of the *New York Times*. It was a revelation to me. After all these years, I remember my response. Here was something different—a novel about Orthodox and Hasidic Jews living in Brooklyn toward the end of the Second World War that was written in a contemporary vernacular rather than in rhymes derived from Yiddish, like stories and novels of Bernard Malamud, for example.

Chaim's narrator, Reuven Malter, spoke in an authentic American voice. The novelist's first task is to find a voice appropriate to his story. Chaim dramatized a world about which I, a godless Jew with a minimal Jewish education, knew nothing. He peopled that world with characters that came alive on the page. The novelist's first task is to animate a cast of characters. I was impressed by *The Chosen*'s structure; each portion contributed to the effect of the whole. There wasn't a superfluous scene. The compelling narrative moved inexorably toward a classical Aristotelian climax, in which a recognition scene and an unexpected reversal of character occur. The novelist's first task is to make up a good story.

Three first tasks? The novelist has at least six first tasks, and they must more or less be accomplished simultaneously. They all require technical mastery of style, point of view, theme, structure, characterization, and plot. Chaim had technique; he was a craftsman. But that wasn't enough for him. He wanted to be considered an artist. Was he?

I recently reread *The Chosen* for the first time in thirty-five years. Well, Chaim was an artist. *The Chosen* is harmonious in all its parts. Reading it is an aesthetic pleasure; it's a well-wrought artifact. That book remains in the mind like the memory of actual experience. It gives the illusion of life.

Time has turned *The Chosen* into a historical novel. It captures that moment in the inner life of American Jews when they awakened to the nightmare of the Holocaust. The long shadows of gas chambers, sealed boxcars, and crematoria fall across the sunny streets of Williamsburg, where Reuven Malter and his friend Danny Saunders are growing up.

Cynthia Ozick recently reminded me that *The Chosen* has become a classic for young adults. "That way," she said, "lies immortality." Chaim pulled it off! His work lives after him.

A friend in New York teaches *The Chosen* to a junior high school class. The kids are not predominantly Jewish—there are several Muslims, some Episcopalians, one Jehovah's Witness. The kids are nuts about the novel. They talk about it outside of class. My friend says, "They relate to its depiction of the teenager's identity quest. They see that it's pertinent to their own lives."

Chaim's style is more derivative of Hemingway than I had recalled. The dialogue, particularly:

> "That ball could've killed me!" Schwartzie was saying. . . . "My God, did you see that ball?"
>
> "I saw it," Mr. Galanter said grimly.
>
> "That was too fast to stop, Mr. Galanter," I said in Schwartzie's defense. . . .
>
> "God, that ball could've killed me!" Schwartzie said again.

It's a catchy melody. Chaim and I belong to the disappearing generation of American novelists who learned to write from Hemingway. Our struggle with his influence forged our respective styles. We fell in love with the American language because of his prose. At that café in Jerusalem, Chaim and I discovered that Hemingway led us to read Mark Twain, who with Charles Dickens in the nineteenth century invented and perfected the genre of which *The Chosen* is a part: the first-person narrative of the coming of age of an adolescent male. *The Chosen* is a riff on *Huckleberry Finn*, like *Catcher in the Rye* and *A Separate Peace*. I wrote in that genre myself: my first novel, *My Own Ground*, is a chronicle of a Jewish boy growing up on the Lower East Side of New York in 1912.

The Chosen is a wonderful piece of Americana. It opens with the best-written baseball game in our literature. You all remember the scene: two teams of religious Jewish kids on a sandlot in Williamsburg; a hot summer day. Orthodox versus Hasidim; their payis fly, tzitzit dangle. A rabbi heads one of the teams: "A man disentangled himself from the black-and-white mass of players and took a step forward. He looked to be in his late twenties and wore a black suit, black shoes, and a black hat. He had a black beard, and he carried a book under one arm. He was obviously a rabbi, and I marveled that the yeshiva had placed a rabbi instead of an athletic coach over its team."

Chaim's deadpan style in his opening scene juxtaposes disparate details: a rabbi and an athletic coach, a Hasidic kid and his fastball, sports jargon and Yiddish. The effect is gently humorous. Chaim wrote with humor—not the first task of a novelist. Maybe it should be.

Chaim closely observed and recorded the details of physical experience. He sure could write baseball:

> The next pitch left Schwartzie's hand in a long, slow line, and before it was halfway to the plate I knew Danny Saunders would try for it. I knew it from the way his left foot came forward and the bat snapped back and his long, thin body began its swift pivot. I tensed, waiting for the sound of the bat against the ball, and when it came it sounded like a gunshot. For a wild fraction of a second I lost sight of the ball. Then I saw Schwartzie dive to the ground, and there was the ball coming through the air where his head had been and I tried for it but it was moving too fast, and I barely had my glove raised before it was in center field. It was caught on a bounce and thrown to Sidney Goldberg, but by that time Danny Saunders was standing solidly on my base and the yeshiva team was screaming with joy.

The scene moves like a shot. Chaim propels it with verbs of action: "snap," "pivot," "dive," "bounce." He makes mental images out of specific visual details: "I knew it from the way his left foot came forward and the bat snapped back and his long, thin body began its swift pivot."

That left foot brings the sequence into mental visual focus. The game continues. Reuven says, "I saw [the ball] coming at me, and there was nothing I could do. It hit the finger section of my glove, deflected off, smashed into the upper rim of the left lens of my glasses, glanced off my forehead, and knocked me down."

Once again, a specific detail—"the upper rim of the left lens of my glasses"—gives us the picture. Chaim was a talented painter. *The Chosen* is composed of thousands of vivid pictures made from words. Chaim's prose makes you see. Joseph Conrad says his only task as a novelist is to make the reader see. You visualize the whole ball game—and the accident that initiates the book's plot.

Two adolescent boys fall platonically in love, are parted, and reunited. Yes, Reuven and Danny are in love. They're not aware of it, but they are. Chaim subtly dramatizes the true nature of their relationship; he does it obliquely—by innuendo. After months apart, the kids come together; Danny speaks to Reuven, and Reuven says, "I felt a little shiver hearing his voice."

While rereading *The Chosen*, I was struck by its implicit homoeroticism. Women scarcely exist in this world. Neither does overt sexuality. The novel is a classic bildungsroman about budding intellectuals. Two brilliant male teenagers learn something of life and, as a result, assume adult identities—Reuven will become a rabbi, Danny a psychologist. But they've learned nothing about sex. They never think or speak about it. Their emergent sexuality is entirely sublimated into their respective intellectual pursuits.

I use the word "sublimate" advisedly. Chaim was a Freudian. Along with Hemingway, Freud was a crucial intellectual influence for many American writers of our generation. Freud was, to paraphrase Auden, our climate of opinion. Reuven and Danny sublimate their developmental homosexual attachment; they resolve to some extent their respective Oedipal conflicts. *The Chosen* is a kind of Freudian romance. Freud's books change Danny's life. He encounters in their pages one of the transformative discoveries of mankind: the existence of the Unconscious. The hidden workings of the Unconscious is a major theme of the novel. Danny's recognition of its power liberates him from his domineering father.

Danny's father, Reb Saunders, is a famous Hasidic rebbe—a holy tzaddik, a righteous man—who led his congregation out of Russian bondage to the Promised Land, America. Danny says of him, "Six million Jews have died. . . . He's—I think he's thinking of them. He's suffering for them."

The suffering rebbe deliberately inflicts suffering on his son "to make certain his soul would be the soul of a tzaddik no matter what he [does] with his life." The rebbe thinks something like this: Daniel—my beloved son! A Talmudic genius! But all mind! He needs a loving heart. The rebbe tells Reuven, "Better I should have had no son at all than to have a brilliant son who had no soul." He inflicts on Danny what his father inflicted on him as a child. He says,

> "When I was very young, my father, may he rest in peace, began to wake me in the middle of the night, just so I would cry. I was a child, but he would wake me and tell me stories of the destruction of Jerusalem and the sufferings of the people of Israel, and I would cry. . . . My father himself never talked to me, except when we studied together. He taught me with silence. . . . One learns of the pain of others by suffering one's own pain. . . . [Pain] destroys our self-pride, our arrogance, our indifference toward others."

The rebbe is rationalizing his father's cruelty—and his own toward Danny. Reb Saunders is, in fact, an unconscious sadist who compulsively abuses Danny the same way his father abused him. The rebbe's lack of self-awareness about his unconscious motivation enriches his characterization. Chaim's revelation of the rebbe's hidden depths gives him vivid verisimilitude. His complex character is Chaim's most memorable creation.

Reuven is initially repelled by Reb Saunders. Then fascinated by him. He's riveted by the rebbe's Talmudic disquisitions—his only communication with his son. These explications are brilliant set pieces:

> "Hear me now. Listen. How can we make our lives full? How can we fill our lives so that we are eighteen, chai, and not nine, not half chai? Rabbi Joshua son of Levi teaches us, 'Whoever does not labor in the Torah is said to be under the divine censure.' He is a nozuf, a person whom the Master of the Universe hates! A righteous man, a tzaddik, studies Torah, for it is written, 'For his delight is in the Torah of God, and over His

Torah doth he meditate day and night.' In gematriya, 'nozuf' comes out one hundred forty-three, and 'tzaddik' comes out two hundred and four. What is the difference between 'nozuf' and 'tzaddik'? Sixty-one. To whom does a tzaddik dedicate his life? To the Master of the Universe! La-el, to God! The word, 'La-el' in gematriya is sixty-one. It is a life dedicated to God that makes the difference between the nozuf and the tzaddik!"

Chaim is the only novelist I know who could have written that. He was an original. His textual explications in *The Chosen* are an innovative narrative element in the American novel.

The novel's intricate structure relies on the use of doubles—characters who are distorted mirror images of each other, related but disparate. Chaim's technique is reminiscent of Dostoevsky's *The Double*, Poe's "William Wilson," Twain's *Pudd'nhead Wilson* and *The Prince and the Pauper*, and Conrad's "The Secret Sharer." For a while, Reuven and Danny metaphorically exchange fathers, who become their new spiritual mentors. Mr. Malter introduces Danny to Freudian psychology; Reb Saunders teaches Reuven about gematria. The switch imparts a geometric symmetry to the complex structure of *The Chosen.*

The two fathers are ostensibly polar opposites, but both have been traumatized by the Holocaust and share a common, unquestioning faith in God and Torah. It is the pattern of their religious observances that differentiates them.

Isaac Bashevis Singer wrote in *The Slave*, "But now at least he understood his religion: its essence was the relation between man and his fellows." Judaism in *The Chosen* is dramatized by intense, ritualized human relationships: teachers and students, a tzaddik and his son, a rebbe and his congregation. They interact with each other according to Jewish law and tradition. They relate to God the same way. Reb Saunders's congregation rejoices in God's Torah but not in his world. Or in him. Saunders's Hasidim are not religious ecstatics; they pay lip service to Baal Shem's joyful mysticism but seem incapable of experiencing it. Reb Saunders's relationship to God is utterly submissive: "'How the world drinks our blood,' Reb Saunders said. 'How the world makes us suffer. It is the will of God. We must accept the will of God.'"

God never comes alive as a character in *The Chosen*. He is not felt as a presence in the fictive construct, as he is, for example, in *The Magician of Lublin* when he unexpectedly answers a sinner's prayer. Singer was a fantasist—and something of a mystic as well. Chaim was a naturalist; the eruption of the uncanny into everyday life is absent from his work. But, like Singer, Chaim was

a religious artist, and the essence of his religion was the relation between man
and his fellows.

Reb Saunders submits to God. Saunders's double, Mr. Malter—Reuven's
father—rebels against him. Malter teaches Talmud at an Orthodox high school.
He wears a yarmulke and upholds God and the Torah, but uses scientific exegesis in his study of the sacred texts. He's sympathetic to Reb Saunders's religious
fanaticism. Malter says, "The fanaticism of men like Reb Saunders kept us alive
for two thousand years of exile. If the Jews of Palestine have an ounce of that
same fanaticism and use it wisely, we will soon have a Jewish state."

Malter is a fanatic Zionist; he jeopardizes his health for the cause. When
he learns about the Holocaust, he renounces the immemorial religious messianic expectation of redemption for secular messianic nationalism. He wants
to force the end of exile by the use of force. He says, "I am tired of waiting [for
the Messiah]. Now is the time to bring the Messiah, not to wait for him."

Chaim created in Malter the archetypal Zionist of the postwar generation.
He promulgates a new secular faith: Jewish history culminates in the state of
Israel; Israel's creation through force of arms redeems Jewish history and
makes it all worthwhile. Malter keeps saying over and over that the creation of
Israel gives meaning to the death of the six million Jews: "We [are] a people
again, with our own land. We [are] a blessed generation."

In *The Chosen*, Chaim obliquely presents another transformative event in
Jewish history—the end of our exile.

Chaim was prescient. *The Chosen* was published in 1967. Remember that
Mr. Malter tells Reuven, "It is strange what is happening. . . . And it is exciting.
Jack [a businessman he knows] is on the Building Committee of his synagogue. Yes, he joined a synagogue. Not for himself, he told me. For his grandchildren. He is helping them put up a new building so his grandchildren can
go to a modern synagogue and have a good Jewish education. It is beginning
to happen everywhere in America. A religious renaissance, some call it." This
from a character who at the same time, because of the Holocaust, renounces
his belief in supernatural redemption.

In spite of everything, all the main characters—Malter, Saunders, Reuven,
and Danny—cling to traditional Judaism. Danny eventually accepts Freudian
psychology but rejects Freud's atheism. Reuven becomes a biblical scholar
who is willing to apply the methodology of modern textual criticism to the
Talmud but not to the divinely inspired Torah.

I once asked Chaim how he thought such a bifurcation was possible for
committed intellectuals. He said, "We do it all the same. We compartmentalize."

Chaim argued that most people separate their intellectual beliefs from their faith. They resist the attempt to synthesize them, and they're emotionally and intellectually satisfied by this compartmentalization.

Chaim's imputation of paradoxical beliefs to his characters humanizes them. They're unconsciously conflicted—like you and me. But *The Chosen* is a romance. Its characters' conscious and unconscious conflicts are easily and happily resolved. Danny's suffering sensitizes him to human suffering, as his father hoped it would. Its unintended consequence is to develop Danny's interest in psychology. In an Aristotelian reversal of character, Reb Saunders not only accepts but affirms Danny's decision to become a psychologist rather than take his hereditary place as tzaddik. His son will become tzaddik to the world. The rebbe asks Danny's forgiveness for his silence. Danny weeps. Reuven weeps with him. Silently. The motif of silence reverberates throughout *The Chosen*. It implicitly insinuates the silence of God during the Holocaust.

Just who are the "chosen"? The novel's title refers first to Danny, predestined by his father to take his place. And then to the Jewish people, who are conceived by Chaim to play an essential metaphysical role in human and cosmological history. The Jews and their Torah are to him the agents of redemption, the long-awaited transfiguration of mankind and the universe.

It's a tribute to Chaim's artistry that secular readers like myself suspend disbelief in his metaphysics and respond to the universal significance of the drama of two religious Jewish kids growing up in Williamsburg during a crucial time in Jewish history. We care about them—and all the major characters—as people.

However, I feel that their self-absorption in their closeness has become more problematic during the thirty-five years since *The Chosen* was written. Chaim was prescient to predict a Jewish religious revival. But he couldn't forsee that a number of Orthodox Jews, here and in Israel, would embrace a new belief that combines eschatological messianism and virulent Israeli nationalism. They have chosen themselves as redemptive agents, enjoined by God, to force an end to history and violently initiate the Messianic Age. These are religious Jews who have learned nothing from our history—nothing from the Sabbatean and Frankist scandals.

The Chosen evokes a more innocent time. It is fixed in our memory by Chaim's talent—his mastery of the novelist's craft, all those narrative elements that he simultaneously manipulated to achieve the unified effect of a work of art.

Chaim's death is an irrevocable loss to his loved ones, to his friends, and to American literature. But his work lives. Thirty-five years ago, I wrote in my review of *The Chosen* in the Sunday *Times*, "We rejoice, and even weep a little. . . . While Reuven talks, we listen because of the story he has to tell, and long afterward it remains in the mind and delights."

I stand by those words tonight.

Thank you.

CHAIM POTOK

A Zwischenmensch ("Between Person") in the Cultures

Daniel Walden

University of Pennsylvania
December 15, 2002

Born in 1929 in the Bronx, New York—his father, Benjamin Potok, a Belzer Hasid and his mother, Molly, a descendant of the Hasidic Ryzner dynasty—Chaim Tzvi grew up in an Orthodox Jewish family in an Orthodox Jewish neighborhood. Attending a cheder, a primary Jewish parochial school, his interest in and talent for painting came to the fore when one summer his yeshiva inexplicably hired an artist to give a course in painting to the children. That was his first step into the world of Western art. In his childhood, what Joyce was to Jesuits, painting was to Talmud. Deep into the study of Torah, and Talmud, he had begun that journey that would put his focus within the core of the Jewish tradition in confrontation with the world we all inhabit, the world of Western secular humanism. At the same time he was reading *Ivanhoe* and *Treasure Island* in his high school English subjects, he was browsing in the public library and came across Evelyn Waugh's *Brideshead Revisited*, an adult novel about upper-class British Catholics. He remembered asking himself, "What did he do to me? How do you do this kind of thing with words?" That's where his commitment to write began.

What Chaim Potok discovered as he was writing *The Chosen* (1967), his first published book, was a cultural dynamic, a "culture war." Within the overarching culture in which we all live is the culture we call Western human-ism—what Peter Gay calls "modern paganism"—and within that culture is a whole spectrum of subcultures. What happens is that these subcultures clash in a variety of ways with the overarching culture. What he seems to have stumbled across was a kind of core-to-core cultural confrontation.

To that point he had been committed to study. After reading *Brideshead Revisited* and soon afterward Joyce's *Portrait of the Artist as a Young Man*, a strange hunger arose to create worlds of his own out of words on paper, to tell stories. You have to understand, explained Potok, that Judaism is a text-oriented world; it is a word world. And to study is the central text of the tradition. It is a commandment. Not to study the text is a transgression. It was this that concerned the rabbi, the teacher of Talmud. He sensed that in some strange and unexpected fashion, Potok had made contact with a fundamental element from the general civilization in which we all live—with the world of Newton, Voltaire, Diderot, Rousseau, Nietzsche, and Freud. He had made contact with Western literature.

This powerful movement that the young Potok joined was part of a revolt of the modern contest against the grip of the emerging middle class, involv-ing those individuals using the story in order to act as a mouthpiece against the ordinary, the callousness, the hypocrisy, the games they witnessed every-where and felt they could no longer tolerate. He attempted to track one ele-ment of this confrontation; that is, ideas from the heart of one culture crashing up against ideas from the heart of another culture is what happens for indi-viduals caught in what he called a core-to-core confrontation—in his case, the rigidity of his Hasidic upbringing and Freudian psychoanalytic theory. For example, Reuven Malter, in *The Promise*, was in confrontation with the Jewishness that he still loved. For *In the Beginning*'s David Lurie, given his father's very militant Jewishness, all was in confrontation with a radical new way of looking at the central text of all Western traditions—the Bible. *The Book of Lights*, the most difficult of Potok's novels to read and fully grasp, the novel about the atomic bomb, dealt with one individual's confrontation with that core element of Western civilization and its effect on the world of Asia. *Davita's Harp*, a book about a young woman's struggles, was based in part on his wife's experiences in an Orthodox world.

But Potok was also concerned with images and metaphors. The central metaphor of *The Chosen* is "combat of various kinds," the central metaphor of *The Promise* is "people gambling and winning or losing," and the central met-aphor in *The Book of Lights* is "the mystery and the awe that some of us sense in the grittiness of reality." True, these metaphors are visual, which brings up the connection between metaphors, visualizing, and painting. Artists, to Potok, possessed the power to create metaphoric visions of reality, which is why Picasso's *Guernica* was a central element of his life. Picasso changed the way we look at the world; *Guernica* became the most significant achievement in this century of the redescriptive power of the artist. The fact is that an artist deals in images, and the Jewish tradition, embodied in the second command-ment, was against image making, because image making was part of ancient worship. All through the Middle Ages and into the Renaissance, Jewish law saw Christianity as essentially an idolatrous civilization. As a result there were no Jewish motifs in Western art, except for a few introduced by Rem-brandt and a few others. In the modern period, Christianity was replaced by secular humanism, all of the Christological elements became attenuated, and the Crucifixion, as a salvationist motif, became a motif for suffering and lost its salvationist tonality. But, he felt, in using this the artist was not violating Jewish law; what he was violating was an aesthetic line, for in the eyes of the Jews, the Orthodox Jew especially, the Crucifixion immediately triggers images of Jewish blood and the deicide charge.

Chaim Potok, a different kind, a new kind of Jewish writer, has written as a Jew and because he is a Jew. His version of the American Jew has never left the traditional Jewish community, although from age fourteen or so, growing up in the Bronx, New York, he began to understand that "the compression of urban existence, the living mix of peoples and cultures in my Bronx world, made possible for me a rich variety of cultural confrontations." This conflict between his traditional Jewish background and the echoing world he longed to embrace led to his perception of culture confrontation in urban America. As he put it in an interview, "In *The Chosen*, for example, the heart of the Jew-ish tradition, which is represented by the two boys, Danny and Reuven, that I write about, comes into contact with an element right from the heart of the umbrella civilization in which we all live today, with secular humanism." In short, having read Evelyn Waugh's *Brideshead Revisited* as a teenager and entered a new tradition, modern literature, he came to recognize that funda-mental to that new tradition "was a certain way of thinking the world; and basic to that was the binocular vision of the iconoclast, the individual who grows up inside inherited systems of value and, while growing, begins to recoil from the games, masks, and hypocrisies he sees all around him."

By the time he was eighteen or nineteen, young Potok had begun to experience what would later be called a core-to-core culture confrontation.

Significantly, all the disciplines he encountered that were alien, the exciting ideas, were from the core of Western culture; he and the people he came from were in the core of the subculture. In his case, having been formed by his very urban, very Jewish upbringing in the Bronx, but meeting with the umbrella culture, his urban and intellectual and literary wanderings produced a "Zwischenmensch," a "between person."

Basic to every Potok novel are two questions: (1) how to live as an observant Jew in a secular society, and (2) to what degree one can hold to the tradition of Orthodox separateness in a secular society. In *The Chosen* and *The Promise*, Danny Saunders and Reuven Malter symbolize the two poles within Orthodox Judaism, the Orthodox and Hasidic. At the same time, there is seen a confrontation between Western secular humanism and religious orthodoxy. In *My Name Is Asher Lev*, however, the realm of aesthetics is the subject of the book, a very different realm to navigate in the Jewish tradition. In *In the Beginning*, the confrontation is between the core of Judaism and modern Western anti-Semitism.

In *The Chosen*, set in the urban Crown Heights and Williamsburg sections of Brooklyn, a baseball game brings together Danny, son of the rebbe and thus heir to the Hasidic dynasty, and Reuven, son of a modern Orthodox Talmudic textual scholar. Reb Saunders, the tzaddik (the Hasidic sect's spiritual leader), believing that there is a danger that his gifted son's soul might be dominated by mind, communicates to him through silence; in this way he feels that he will foster the values of heart and soul. Mr. Malter, viewed by the Hasidim as one of the *mitnagdim* (a Jewish rational intellectual) who denies the basic Jewish religious tenets, and is thus one of the *apikorsim*, fuses the best of secular learning with the best in Talmudic scholarship. What cannot be predicted is that Danny will decide to become a psychologist while remaining an observant Jew, which means he is abdicating his role as the heir to his father's Hasidic leadership. Meanwhile, in a significant crossing pattern, Reuven decides to become a rabbi; from his point of view, such subjects as symbolic logic, math, and secular philosophy fuse the sacred and the secular. Each is combining two cultures. Each is reflecting his and Potok's own attempts as a "between person" to explicate the role of Judaism in a secular society.

In *The Chosen* and *The Promise*, Potok's emphasis is on Jewish scholarship and study in an Orthodox milieu in Brooklyn. Family, neighborhood, and synagogue are beautifully drawn; they are a necessary environment. True, physical poverty is present, but spiritually there is richness. Only from outside the ghetto do the influences impinge. Whether from the radio or the newspaper, or from friends or acquaintances, the news of World War II, the Holocaust, and the Senator Joseph McCarthy charges come through; from liberal and progressive Jews like Rachel Gordon (who learns to appreciate James Joyce at Brooklyn College), further cracks in Hasidism appear.

Probably as a direct result of his interest in the tensions of faith and scholarship in his first two books, Potok's third book, *My Name Is Asher Lev*, concentrates on the tensions between members of one Orthodox family and, in particular, on the possible aesthetic dimensions. Asher must become an artist, from within or without a society that doesn't recognize art for art's sake or its Western cultural (including Christian and pagan) antecedents. In his first-person identity as "the notorious and legendary Lev of the *Brooklyn Crucifixion*," as "a traitor, an apostate," he has to confront his father's duty and Jewish culture as a young man devoted to art, divorced from the history of his people. What reconciles him is suffering; he learns that his relatives, and millions of Jews, suffered because they were Jews. In this context, with signals coming from all sides, he uses the aesthetic model of the Crucifixion to depict his mother's suffering in the *Brooklyn Crucifixion* because he has no comparable aesthetic mold in his own religious tradition. The point, as Potok has explained, is that "for Asher Lev, the cross is the aesthetic motif for solitary, protracted torment." Potok believes that any artist functioning in the secular would who has used the cross "has emptied the cross of its Christological vicarious atonement content and uses it as a form only." Again, as in *The Chosen* and *The Promise*, a between person's concerns are demonstrated, except that this time the lessons of history are central.

In *In the Beginning*, Max Lurie, a Jew impressed into the Polish Army who realized he was not a full citizen, is the vehicle for David Lurie's story. At issue is anti-Semitism. Eddie Kulanski, for example, hates Jews with a "kind of mindless demonic rage"; "his hatred bore the breeding of a thousand years." At the end, having felt the suffering of the Holocaust, David, walking along the Hudson River, recognizes that the death camps have become a part of him. From the home and the yeshiva to Poland and the camps and back, from the isolated Orthodox and Hasidic ghettos of Williamsburg and Crown Heights, from Genesis's *berashith* ("in the beginning") to David's remembered prophetic bar mitzvah reading from Amos, Potok moves from despair to hope, to the restoration of the health of the people of Israel.

When he was a chaplain in Korea, Chaim Potok realized that his traditional Jewish education had not prepared him for a culture that did not know or care about Jews or Judaism, and it had not prepared him for a "confrontation with the beautiful and the horrible in the world of oriental human beings." In *Wanderings*, therefore, where the emphasis is on the influences of Egypt, Greece, Rome, Islam, Christianity, and modern secularism, he noted that the Jewish people were acculturated but not absorbed. As a witness to that process, as a part of that venture, Potok felt that "my people is now engaged in an attempt to create for itself a third civilization." What is needed is for Judaism "to rebuild its core from the treasures of our past, fuse it with the best in secularism, and create a new unity, and take seriously the meaning of the emancipation." As a rabbi, as a religious scholar, as a secular intellectual in the Western tradition, as an American, as a Zwischenmensch, and as a novelist, Chaim Potok was involved in the struggle to maintain the viability of Judaism as a living civilization.

In interview after interview, and especially in his books and articles, Chaim Potok tried to explain those events that transformed him and what resulted. When he read Waugh's *Brideshead Revisited*, he realized that challenging questions could be put down in words. When he served in Korea in 1956 for sixteen months, he understood that the world he had known was now relativized. When he saw Picasso's *Guernica*, he found a metaphor for life and suffering. In sum, he saw a continuing struggle between tradition and modernity, a struggle between Judaism for its own sake and Judaism in the wider world. What he as an individual was trying to achieve were his goals— that is, his sense of authenticity, his sense of self, vis-à-vis his place in community. The tension is what he was trying to explore in his books. As a writer, as a rabbi, as a teacher—in all three—he was trying to understand and explain the forces that exist and the culture confrontation that he saw as Judaism, traditional and modern, came into contact with the world we all know, the technologized, secular humanist, religiously driven societies of the second and now third millennium.

CHAIM POTOK AND THE QUESTION OF JEWISH WRITING

Jonathan Rosen

University of Pennsylvania
December 15, 2002

In the late 1980s, I was a graduate student in English literature at the University of California, Berkeley. My first summer there I took an intensive German course and made friends with a fellow student, a young man who was studying to be a priest. He had passed all his requirements for the priesthood except for his "final vows," which would seal his lifelong marriage to the church.

I didn't really have any Catholic friends, and none who were priests, and I had a lot of questions. Had his parents wanted him to become a priest? They had. Did he feel called to the priesthood? He did. What became of the consecrated wafer if it fell on the floor? He ate it. Most of all, I wondered how he could take the plunge into celibacy, especially since, whenever an attractive woman went by, which happened a lot at Berkeley, he would murmur, "Wow, look at her!"

Not long before meeting my friend, I had read and loved Thomas Merton's *The Seven Storey Mountain*, and the first day we met I mentioned the book, eager at last to have a real Catholic before me headed for the priesthood. Yes, of course he had read it, but he had very little interest in talking about it. The book *he* wanted to talk to *me* about was *The Chosen*.

The Chosen loomed very large in his religious life, and reading it had coincided with his call to the priesthood. I even felt in some strange way that he saw himself becoming a kind of tzaddik, as if to take the place vacated by Danny Saunders when he relinquishes his hereditary spot in the Hasidic dynasty in order to become a clinical psychologist. He had great admiration for Danny's father, the rebbe who raises his son in silence as a way of cultivating the boy's soul.

My friend seemed to feel that I should also have a fictional analogue in Potok's invented world. If I wasn't going to be Danny, I should at least be Reuven Malter, the rationalist proto-rabbinical student who first meets Danny when he gets smashed by a line drive leaping from the angry bat of the repressed young Hasid.

Despite the fact that I had not received a yeshiva upbringing, my friend often asked me questions that began, "What does the Talmud say about . . . ?" He had a hard time recognizing the sad disappointment of a lapsed Conservative Jew he had before him.

It would have been much easier for me if he had been obsessed with *Portnoy's Complaint*, published only two years after *The Chosen* and the same year as *The Promise*. But my friend had never read Philip Roth's novel, inspired— or so Roth has claimed—by the confession of an unhappy priest of his acquaintance.

I sometimes had the uncomfortable feeling that my failure to be either Danny or Reuven had theological implications. I had literally vacated my spot among "the chosen," and it was necessary for my Catholic friend to move in and take over the assignment, an unfortunate recapitulation of Jewish-Christian relations.

It was as if, through Chaim Potok, a challenge had been issued to my authenticity as a Jew. I resented my friend and I resented Chaim Potok for dogging me with Jewish questions I was not at the time in the mood to answer; neither was I educationally equipped to answer them.

I was not at Berkeley to study Talmud; I was there to study John Milton.

But, in a sense, *The Chosen*, and *The Promise*, and *My Name Is Asher Lev*— books I devoured in high school—had an enduring relevance I didn't really recognize at the time. At the time I told myself I was done with such books.

I grew up in a family where the fruits of secular knowledge were served for breakfast. But when I read *The Chosen* in high school, I wanted to *be* Danny Saunders, to be a prince of Jewish learning and righteousness, the heir to a living tradition that assimilation and the Holocaust had seemingly destroyed. My longing for that world may have been more intense because I knew it was already beyond my reach, but it was real nevertheless.

As I got older I came to feel that these books were not authentic American Jew novels—*those* were written by Saul Bellow and Philip Roth and Bernard Malamud and chronicled a very different set of struggles.

But I have come to understand that the world of Jewish learning that Chaim Potok placed at the center of his books gives those books an enduring relevance in the very place where I once felt they had the least to say to me when I was thinking of becoming a writer myself.

A strange thing started happening to me at Berkeley. Not only was it becoming impossible for me to settle for a definition of myself as an American that didn't involve a definition of myself as a Jew. I found I was growing increasingly bored with American Jewish writers who mistook Ellis Island for Mount Sinai and who saw the distance traveled from ethnic immigrant origins as the only journey worth recording.

I was growing more and more hungry for that other, older world that Jews once inhabited. By my second year at Berkeley, I decided, in addition to the German I was taking, to fill one of my language requirements with Biblical Hebrew.

The book I was planning to write my dissertation on, *Paradise Lost*, was, of course, all about tasting the forbidden fruit of knowledge and the consequences of that taste. *Paradise Lost* is *The Chosen* told about our first parents, who broke from that Ur shtetl known as the Garden of Eden, which we may only pine for because we do not live there.

But we do pine for it. Because it represents a time when we were whole, however much wholeness may be a human illusion.

One of the things about *The Chosen* I hadn't realized until rereading it recently is that it is in many ways a love story. Reuven and Danny are like Romeo and Juliet, except that instead of the Montagues and the Capulets, their families are Hasidic and *misnagid*, Zionist and anti-Zionist, Enlightenment and anti-Enlightenment. (Or perhaps it's better to liken them, as someone in the novel does, to David and Jonathan, and worth noting that David and Jonathan are perhaps the only friends in the Bible.)

Thinking about this love story component has made me realize how little Jewish American writing is in fact about love and friendship. I. B. Singer, if we count him as an American, is an exception. But for the others, it is by and large the solitary self, the individual consciousness, that they explore—and that American Jewish writers in general are exploring. Alexander Portnoy is full of longing, but it is a longing for freedom, an unspecified state that will liberate him *for* other people.

It seems to me that for love to be possible you need to acknowledge a certain incompleteness of the self. You have to relinquish some extreme form of American self-reliance. In a traditional world, of course, nobody goes it alone. But in a contemporary American world, at least in contemporary literature, that is not the case.

That's what makes the friendship, the love, of Danny and Reuven so memorable. They each long for something the other has, and they each lend the other an aspect of themselves.

Reading *The Chosen*, I also fell in love with Danny in some way and wanted what he had—even though he might have wanted what I had growing up. *The Chosen* awakened in me an unarticulated awareness of the part of myself that had traditional longings.

In one of the haunting and beautiful figures at the end of *The Chosen*, Danny cuts off his peias but still reaches up his hand to touch the place where the twist of hair had grown and that he had twirled when studying or speaking. I remember feeling that I too had phantom peios, as if, in some other life, I too had been a Hasid.

The Talmud teaches that all of us study Talmud in the womb and that, before birth, an angel touches us on the mouth and we forget it all. I've often thought of this as an explanation for why immigrant fiction retains its hold even when American Jews are no longer immigrants or even the grandchildren of immigrants. It's as if we ARE all immigrants—as if the womb were a kind of old-world shtetl where we studied all day, and we still have dim memories and longings for the old country. Sort of like Wordsworth saying that "not in utter nakedness or in entire forgetfulness but trailing clouds of glory do we come, from God who is our home."

One of many impressive things about *The Chosen* is that although it is a chronicle of escape, a story about throwing off traditional strictures, the world from which Danny Saunders is escaping is so richly evoked as to make it a world that those born on the outside long to return to. My friend, headed for the priesthood, had been more inspired by the Jewish world Danny leaves behind than by the Catholic certitude Thomas Merton finds.

The Chosen and *The Promise* are often described, dismissively, as simple books, but rereading them I am actually impressed by how subtle and complex they are. For example, although Danny leaves his post as tzaddik, he retains his calling as a righteous man. And although Reuven's father gives Danny secular books to read that are temporarily denounced by Danny's father as a corrupter of youth, he is ultimately thanked as the savior of his son's Jewish soul.

Reuven's father is the real hero of *The Chosen*. Without this model of devotion to tradition married to openness to the outside world, there would have been no place for Danny Saunders to go but out the window, metaphorically if not literally. In that sense, the real struggle in Chaim Potok's books, it seems to me, is to go not from faith to doubt, or from observance to nonobservance, or from piety to revolt, but to find a middle place.

This seems to me a great message for any Jewish writer, for any Jew, for any person whatever his religion. It is a deeply American message accepted by all Jews. For it makes belonging to modern life and religious life not an either/or proposition but something much subtler and more complicated. Which may explain why *The Chosen* is a book about leaving that nevertheless awakens a yearning for return. Just as it is a book about belonging that somehow sanctions flight.

My Catholic friend may have responded to this double message unconsciously. For years I assumed he loved the book because its depiction of religious devotion justified his own choice. But just a few years ago I reconnected with him and learned that he is now married with two children. I can't helping thinking that *The Chosen* somehow validated his own anticipated abandonment of his path, even as it appeared to sanction the opposite. No wonder he had no use for the absolution of *The Seven Storey Mountain*. Merton's only escape was death. Danny really does become a psychologist.

One of the things that I admire most about those early Potok novels is that they are about leaving a world without closing the door behind you. The education Potok gave himself in order to write about the world he left is a very rich model for any Jewish writer. Especially writers who might, as I once did, mistake the term "secular" for a philosophical choice when it is no more than a justification of ignorance.

Nathan Zuckerman, Philip Roth's fictional counterpart, decides to go back to medical school in *The Anatomy Lesson*, but it is impossible to imagine him attending rabbinical school or even taking a few classes that might deepen his understanding of the tradition he is so gripped by.

After dropping out of graduate school, I wound up working at the *Forward* newspaper. Once a paper for immigrants making their way into American life, it had become almost the opposite, a Jewish newspaper for Americans totally at home in America who were somehow immigrants inside their own culture, lost inside Judaism.

Many of the people who worked at the paper were people whose great grandparents had made the journey that Danny Saunders makes in *The Chosen*. But they were not satisfied with their easy world of freedom, and I believe they are representative of an entire generation of young Jews who are only now finding their voices as writers. The seat in the public library where Danny sat secretly devouring Freud is now, metaphorically, occupied by some hungry assimilated Jew reading *The Essential Talmud*.

It's been very interesting for me to realize how Chaim Potok and his books keep turning up in my life. Chaim Potok himself turned up, literally, at the *Forward*, where I had the pleasure of getting to know him a little because he would occasionally review books for the section I edited. I felt, in those assignments, a circle closing for me somehow.

But he kept turning up figuratively too.

Several years ago, I spent a semester as a writer in residence at Yeshiva University. Teaching writing at an Orthodox institution instantly brought Potok to mind. I recalled the fictional school where Danny and Reuven attended college in *The Chosen*—a place where Danny cannot find a Freud class—and where, in *The Promise*, Reuven battles with opponents of the critical method of Talmud study.

The atmosphere I encountered was very different from that world. But on the first day of class I had an informal conversation with my students about the role art and culture played at school.

I was told by several students who had tried to put together an arts festival for creative writing and the visual arts that they had included on their poster a reproduction of Andy Warhol's *Campbell's Soup Cans*. I found it a touching gesture toward an avant garde that, in reality, had passed into quaint cliché before most of them were born, and so I was surprised to learn that school authorities had ordered the removal of the posters. The reason, my students said, is that the soup can depicted something that wasn't kosher.

I was astonished and appalled, but I couldn't help feeling a certain thrill. Here was a world where art—like literature in the Soviet Union—was still subversive. And where the core values of one world still arrayed themselves against the core values of another. How lucky my students are, I thought jealously, to have a world from which to set themselves free, for a great deal of wonderful art often comes out of that struggle.

I also realized how hard-won Potok's fiction was and how my easy pronouncements about reconciliation are to some degree a projection onto a world I did not personally liberate myself from. I remember reading an interview with

Chaim Potok in which he stated that for the very Orthodox, a mediocre Jewish novel is a banal waste of time—and therefore something to be avoided—and a good Jewish novel is threatening—and therefore something to be avoided.

And yet it is possible to be the true product of a world and a rebel against it simultaneously. If Danny Saunders had not been so rigorously educated in the Talmud, would he have hungered as he did for learning of every kind? If he hadn't been schooled in silence, would he have wished to be a psychologist— a professional listener? This paradox, implicit in *The Chosen*, haunts Jewish culture, particularly in our own age when it is harder and harder to say what authentic Jewish culture is.

At the end of my semester at Yeshiva University, a student asked if he could stay late to talk to me. He looked distressed, although he often had an overburdened look—he was in the advanced Talmud track despite the fact that he was getting a degree in history, and was usually carting around what might have been the entire contents of the Cairo Geniza, along with the laptop on which he took notes during class. He was much admired for his learning by his fellow students.

He was my best student, as well as my *frummest*. The first assignment I gave the class was a standard in-class piece of writing: describe a burning house. He had written about the destruction of the Temple, or rather a replica of the Temple that he had made at camp and that his counselors had then burned for Tisha B'Av.

He had something very serious on his mind, and it seemed to make him extremely uncomfortable.

At last he came out with it.

I want to keep writing, he said. But I'm afraid that I'm trapped in the nineteenth century. I can't write about women in the right way. I can't write about sex. What kind of a writer can I be?

I tried to tell him that the struggle he was having was itself a good subject. But he wanted more than that.

I couldn't, of course, know the extent to which this was a personal struggle and the extent to which it was a literary problem.

So I made the only responsible suggestion I could.

"Read the novels of Chaim Potok," I said.

CHAIM POTOK

A Literary Biography

Adena Potok

Shortly after the child Chaim Potok configured letters into words, he became entranced with the world of books and read everything in English and Hebrew he could find. Yiddish was his mother tongue, but it remained for him an oral language. He began to make up stories, which usually took shape at the end of the day after all school and other obligations had been met. He often wrote them on the wall near his bed. Eventually they were painted over.

When he was ten years old, a down-at-the-heels drawing teacher appeared at the yeshiva (parochial elementary school) in the Bronx and offered drawing lessons to the vacationing students. (These were the dreaded polio summers.) Chaim was bitten by the art bug. He later moved on to cartooning, watercolor, and oils. The latter became too obvious to eye and nose, and he was required to empty his bedroom of the offensive materials, to the relief of his kid brother.

Meandering into the neighborhood library one spring day after exams when he was sixteen, he was grabbed by a book, a novel. It wasn't a read-it-in-school kind of novel, but a hand-reaching-out-and-pulling-him-into-it novel. The librarian advised him to give it fifty pages or so to get used to the prose of Evelyn Waugh's *Brideshead Revisited*. He was captivated. A new world! Then he read James Joyce's *A Portrait of the Artist as a Young Man*.

He committed to creating worlds on paper with words. He could write without bringing the attention of others to that enterprise. It was a "safe" activity.

He was the oldest of four children in an Orthodox Jewish family of Hasidic lineage. He was yeshiva educated, a shtiebel davener, a Torah reader. As a younger boy he was a trolley car chaser, a runner, a kind of kid who was not afraid of the neighborhood bullies who threw anti-Semitic slurs along with their punches. He performed well in school and shul (synagogue) and at his father's quizzes at the Shabbos table, while his younger sisters and brother waited their turns and their mother kvelled. There were frequent visits with the family's only relatives in the United States—his paternal aunt and uncle and four cousins. The rest of his parents' extended family were in Galician Poland. They later perished in the Holocaust.

His entire schooling, grade school through college, took place within the yeshiva world. In summers his parents allowed a camp environment, even a nonreligious one, outside the city for a few weeks as a rescue from the possibility of polio. In camp he learned to swim, row, even sail a bit. He was there, among people not of his community, for health reasons alone. His world was that of Orthodox Jewry.

Books introduced him to other worlds. Books took him out of his narrow confines. Books were his Star Trek. In books he discovered new, different ways of thinking, of acting, of walking through the world. In books people led independent lives. In books people experienced and expressed frustration, rebellions, temptations, travel outside of their small worlds of origin. In a very real sense, books gave him a taste of life as it could be lived. A part of him ached to join the "alien" world he saw around him—its art, its outside people, its characters who came alive on the stage. A part of him yearned to go wherever his feet would take him; much of him held him anchored to the milieu he knew. It was comfortable; it was familiar.

What would it be to fly off?

During his senior year in college, he overheard a conversation between two students. They were speaking in Yiddish. Translated, they were saying,

"Have you heard? Steinberg died."
"Really? Now they're punishing him for his books!"

He was an English major and an avid reader, and he had never heard of this author. He headed for the card catalog in the college library. When he

didn't find Steinberg there, he consulted with the librarian. The response—
"We don't have his books here"—was followed by a frown and an admonition
not to pursue "such writing."

How do we keep the ALIEN out? He began to feel the sense of being an
alien. He felt himself identifying with the rebellious Catholic heroes of *Brideshead Revisited* and *A Portrait of the Artist as a Young Man*. He was becoming
suspicious of the thinking that kept the works of Milton Steinberg out of the
college library, and he was revolted by the hostile comments of fellow students
toward a writer. For his books! Was this the fate that awaited him? Did he have
to leave the world of Jewish learning to pursue his dream? On the other hand,
all the contemporary Jewish writers dismissed Jewish tradition and religion.
Was that the model for his work? He would create a new model! But to do that
he needed to learn Jewish history, philosophy, storytelling, poetry.

His cousin had married a student at the Jewish Theological Seminary,
and they lived not far from Yeshiva College. During a visit to their apartment,
he saw the "forbidden" text on a bookshelf. After a free-ranging conversation,
he realized that here was an opportunity to learn in depth and breadth a rich
reading of Jewish civilization. He applied to the seminary, was accepted, and
pursued higher Jewish studies. One year after graduation/ordination, he
enlisted in the U.S. Army as a chaplain. Eight months later, he was in the
northern reaches of South Korea as a division chaplain to combat medics and
combat engineers.

Most of the troops were not Jews.

While on leave in Japan some months later, he saw an elderly Japanese
gentleman in front of a Shinto shrine. The man held a slender, worn book and
swayed back and forth as he prayed, reminding him of the Orthodox shtiebel
back in the Bronx. But this was a man in prayer to a pagan idol. Didn't the
Torah consider paganism an abomination? How could it be? Here, in front of
his eyes, was an example of religious devotion. Was not the Almighty paying
heed? And, if not, why not? He had more questions than he could answer at
the moment. It would take a lifetime.

His extraordinary contribution to literature is how he explored the mys-
teries of living simultaneously deep within Jewish civilization and Western
secular humanism—two cultures—as they sometimes overlapped and sometimes were in uncompromising confrontation. The world of fiction was, for
him, the area of creativity in which his characters could explore, unfettered,
within family and community, their conflicting loyalties and values. The
beauty as well as the angst of his work lay in the terrain of truths discovered

and in conflict, often with no clear and unequivocal choice. The specific Jewish conflicts he painted not only presented the Jewish world to the outside. They also resonated exquisitely in the minds and lives of people throughout the world living in similar conflicts. He made connections, as with the Navajo lad in Utah who thanked him for modeling how to live simultaneously in two worlds.

In a 1986 interview on *Fresh Air* with Terry Gross, he opined that there are various truths that inform human experience and belief: "How do you come to terms with a system of ideas that seems to be hostile to your system of ideas, but has answers to questions, and the answers are absent in your system of ideas? What do you do when you fall in love with opposites? The best way you can encounter the world is by taking from it the best that it has to offer you, enriching yourself as a result, and then giving that combination back to the world. That constant mixture of fruitful elements is really what human civilization ought to be about." And then he said, "[The notion of] 'What I am is better than what you are' is an infantilistic notion of the human being, and one that we had better learn to outgrow as quickly as possible. Because if we keep that up we're not going to be around much longer to brag about our own particular way of seeing the world."

He saw with an open eye.

CHAIM POTOK IS NO LONGER WITH US, BUT HIS LESSONS REMAIN

Jane Eisner

The Forward
February 26, 2010

On February 17, Chaim Potok, the novelist, scholar, painter and playwright whom I was privileged to call a dear friend, would have turned 80 years old. In the spring of 2002, he and I sat down for a series of interviews in the book-lined library of his home near Philadelphia. My Tuesdays with Chaim, we used to call these weekly sessions.

By then, brain cancer had noticeably affected his speech and thought patterns. His wife, Adena, would gently pick up a phrase or complete an idea when the flow of words and memories hit a sudden block. But these conversations, published in the Sunday magazine of *The Philadelphia Inquirer* in June 2002, the month before he died, also allowed Chaim to lay claim to his legacy. Even if the words were expressed more simply than they might have been in the past, the focus was more intense, as if he was trying to drive home a point.

One of the things we spoke about was the challenge of confronting modernity through the prism of tradition. This was the essence of Chaim's contribution to the world of literature: the tug-of-war, as he called it, that he

This essay is an adaptation of remarks delivered by Jane Eisner at a reception celebrating the arrival of the Chaim Potok Papers at the University of Pennsylvania Libraries. It is reprinted from the *Forward* with permission.

so brilliantly evoked through his characters Danny Saunders and Asher Lev and Ilana Davita Chandal—the struggle to reconcile deep faith and fidelity to ancestral ritual with the pulsing challenges of modern life. He asked the questions that others dare not ask, not out of disrespect or arrogance, but with an almost sweet and trusting belief that honest inquiry would eventually land us all in a better place.

Today, we need the right vocabulary for that discourse. Instead, I fear that the discourse is becoming ever more reductive and coarse, and that we, as a community, are becoming ever more illiterate. Not just in the matter of knowing language and text in the way that Chaim believed was so essential, but in our ability to bridge different worlds. Reuven Malter and Danny Saunders learned how to speak to each other, to listen and understand. So must other Jews with divided loyalties and conflicting passions.

Chaim used to lament what was lost in the Shoah, beyond the straightforward accounting of the six-million Jews and millions of others who perished. What was also lost was a generation in Eastern Europe raised with a rich grounding in Jewish text and culture, scholars who could encounter new ways of thinking and grapple with them from a position of knowledge and confidence, unafraid that one would diminish the other.

As he once said: "I think that people who were in possession of the tools to move into modernity are gone."

So what would it take for us to re-possess those tools today? This is not just a question of figuring out how the Hasid in one part of Brooklyn speaks to the hipster in another part of Brooklyn, although that would be a bridge worth building. I see a deeper impasse.

We live in a time when Jewish discourse seems to revolve not around God and Torah and Talmud, except in some religious circles, but instead around the State of Israel. It has become our new theology, our new self-definition. To the degree that Jews reference Israel at all, feel a strong attachment to it—and that number is dangerously shrinking, especially among the young—it seems to be in the polarized fashion of either being for or against whatever policies are promulgated by the current government in Jerusalem. The behaviors that once defined Jewishness—observance of laws, attendance at synagogue, study of text, creation of family, expressions of concern for the less fortunate—are not as relevant in many quarters. What seems to count more, from the left or from the right, is where you stand on Israel.

I have to believe that Chaim would cringe at the simplistic and divisive nature of this discourse, and would rail against its ugly turns. I won't pretend to know whether his politics would have been more hawk or dove, AIPAC or J Street—that's not important. I do know he believed in learning about and embracing a variety of thought and culture. "I am open to all people and to all means of expression," he once told me.

I wonder if the polarization of our discourse isn't rooted in a heavily laden anxiety about our future. Of course, this existential worry is buried deep in the Jewish psyche. My kids and I used to repeat the old joke that most Jewish holidays can be described in nine words: "They tried to kill us. We won. Let's eat."

But if you believe that the *only* way Israel will survive is through a hard-line defense policy that brooks no dissent . . . or if you believe that the *only* way Israel will survive is to accommodate its neighbors, no matter how unwilling or unable they may be to compromise . . . then, in either case, it's just a short step to say that whoever is on the other side is inherently danger-ous, an enemy of the Jewish people, and must be stopped.

And within that construct, if the person on the other side is a righteous person who adheres to Jewish practice and values, but happens to disagree with you on Israel policy, it often makes no difference. One thing trumps all.

What's missing here, first and foremost, is the kindness and compassion we are instructed to show other Jews, no matter what their beliefs or dress code or voting habits. But what's also missing is confidence—the assurance that the tradition will be able to beat back the assault. Chaim struggled with our tradition as much as anyone did, but that struggle grew out of enormous reverence for its vitality and ability to adapt to new challenges.

The bickering nature of our discourse today reflects a kind of fundamen-talist outlook that Chaim would have deplored. It also reflects a lack of belief in ourselves, as Jews, to meet 21st-century challenges with the same passion and flexibility that we have displayed in centuries past.

One of my favorite scenes in Chaim's work is at the conclusion of *The Gift of Asher Lev*, that magnificently woven scene at Simchat Torah, when Asher Lev—who had to distance himself from his ultra-Orthodox community to become a painter of world renown—is temporarily back in the exuberant but complicated fold and sees his beloved son Avrumel designated the heir appar-ent to the great rebbe. The father's choice will not infringe upon the son's destiny. Two worlds are bridged, with sacrifice, but also with understanding.

ADENA POTOK ON *I AM THE CLAY*

Nathan P. Devir

Adena Potok kindly met with me in Merion, Pennsylvania, on March 8, 2005, to discuss her late husband, Chaim Potok, and his novel I Am the Clay. *This text is the result.*

NATHAN DEVIR: Mrs. Potok, your husband edited or was the author of a significant number of books, reviews, articles, and essays. The corpus of critical material on his writing is highly diverse. And yet, aside from mostly lukewarm reviews, there has not been much attention given to *I Am the Clay*. Why do you think this is so?

ADENA POTOK: I think part of the reason is that when Chaim first came on the scene as a novelist, he broke ground in a very radical way. Before him, there had not been a Jewish American writer who wrote from the depths of the Jewish world, with no apologies. He didn't romanticize; he didn't castigate. He presented. He presented a world, and it caught on. He was the most surprised that *The Chosen* took off in the way that it did and developed such an audience. But, of course, the longer we were around and listened to people, we realized that it was not the exoticism of the Jewish world that captured them, although they did learn about it from the story. It was the story that did it. It was fathers and sons, it was friendship, it was silence—and we all live with different kinds of silence. So, with each book that he wrote—and he did have a plan in mind, to develop conflicts that were deeper and deeper within the Jewish world, that were more radical—he started with different ways of looking at Jewish history, and God's place in it. In *The Chosen*, he went to the different ways of reading the Talmud, and then eventually to different ways of reading the Bible, the Torah, which was *In the Beginning*. And then he had a plan of [writing about] how art impacts the universe of culture and the Jewish world, and then of course *The Book of Lights*, the mysticism of it. He really went into another universe in *I Am the Clay*. And maybe I'm being very cynical, but that's okay. I think maybe the publishing world said, "This is not where he is, this is not Potok," instead of welcoming not only the nuances but the other view of life from a broader world, and how much it had to offer. I don't know. I really don't know the reason for their not promoting it, except that it didn't fit their view of Chaim Potok.

ND: Who was supposed to be categorized as distinctly "Jewish American."

AP: I think so.

ND: And how did he respond to this lack of enthusiasm?

AP: Kind of a fatalistic shrug [as if to say], "That's the way they're doing it." There's a very interesting vignette I'd like to put before you: he was invited by the United States Information Service to Eastern Asia—Japan and Korea, essentially—in the fall of 1992, or in the beginning of 1993, to speak to various groups up and down the islands of Japan, down to Okinawa, and then to Korea, various cities in Korea, and then to wind up in the dedication, or the rededication, of the U.S. Cultural Center in Seoul. In the interim, there had been interests expressed in publishing this book in the Korean language. And it was done. In fact, the publisher didn't like the translation, and so people said, well, you give it a try, you know English, you know Korean, so he did a chapter and they loved it. So then they said, why don't you do the entire translation? Well, he did. The evening of the dedication of the library, somebody read a section of it in Korean and a section of it in English. Then a poet with whom we had met that morning—we had met with a whole group of poets and writers, kind of like a Korean PEN, we had a wonderful time with them over coffee—one poet, who was magnificently articulate, got up in response to the reading. I thought, "Okay, we're gonna hear what it feels like to a Korean artist," and I braced myself. And she got up and said, "How did you do it?

How did you capture our rhythms? Our language, our souls?" Even now, I'm moved. And she had read it not only in the Korean translation but in the English, because she was at least bilingual. So it was very well received in the country that is depicted in the book, but I'm not happy with the way in which the publishing world greeted this, although it got some beautiful responses on the part of reviewers: *Publishers Weekly, Kirkus*, and a few others, the *Atlantic*, the *Atlanta Journal-Constitution*, some extraordinary reviews. But the publishing world, I think, made a big mistake. Every time I see a picture in the newspaper—because that's still where I get my news from—of refugees, the Kurds in Turkey, to more current shifting of populations, whether it's Africa or Iraq, or wherever it is, I say, "Why isn't this book out there again?" But . . . that's a long answer to a short question.

ND: What about the lack of scholarly attention?

AP: Well, it was well regarded, but not enough. I think that the publisher could have done much better. You see, I can understand why the business end of books, the publishing world, would make its decisions. I can criticize it, but I can understand it. But why wouldn't scholars want to pick this up, even more so than the other ones? Once you start with 1, 2, 3, there's a genre, there's a pattern, but aha! Here's something that is outside that pattern. How much more intriguing is that! You picked that up.

ND: Well, theoretically it should be more intriguing, but perhaps a lot of scholars are not sure what to do with it, especially if it falls outside of their own conception of Potok's work. I also wonder if it has to do with what several reviewers have termed a "condescending" or "elitist" attitude toward the Korean characters in the novel, especially toward the old man and woman, who have no names and whose speech is "simplistic." For example, in his book *Chaim Potok: A Critical Companion*, Sanford Sternlicht writes,

> A somewhat negative aspect of *I Am the Clay* in this post-colonial era is that Kim is rescued from illiteracy and poverty by a Western outsider, an army chaplain, a superior person from the sophisticated, developed world. This smacks of paternalism associated with missionaries and colonialism. Although they came as liberators, the Americans keep themselves separate, expect the Koreans to learn English while they seem not to attempt [to learn] Korean, and generally behave as over-

lords. Readers in the developing world today read *I Am the Clay* quite differently than do most Americans or Europeans.[1]

What is your reaction to this criticism?

AP: Well, most of the Koreans that we met valued his contribution. A few were resentful. One person asked, "How could you, a stranger, dare to come into our culture and write our story?" His answer was, "I wrote it as I saw it. I could not write it as a Korean." There's one way to look at it: you stole our story and wrote it. Like a journalist once asked me after *Davita's Harp* was written, "How did you feel about his writing your story?" We own our stories and we don't own our stories. If we tell them, we don't own them the way we did before we told them. As soon as we tell something, it becomes the property of the hearer, or the see-er, or the "tell-ee," as opposed to only the teller. Our vision of it is our vision of it. So if I were to write my story, I would not write it the way Chaim wrote Davita's story. Similarly, there have been renditions of the war, and its affects and devastation, written by Koreans; the American market hasn't gotten them, to my knowledge. And going back to your first question, maybe this was a Jewish story in the sense that it was the Jewish observance, or the *Jew's observation*, of what happened in another land, to another people, that maybe sounded echoes from Jewish history. We were in fact exiled from our land a long time ago, then came back, then were exiles again, over centuries; it didn't happen within months, as it did with the Korean people. But a writer's imagination either collapses stuff or expands it, or both.

ND: Well, if he did somehow deviate from his Jewish American themes, is there anything concretely Jewish to be found in *I Am the Clay*?

AP: To the extent that in the Jewish religion, or *weltanschauung*, in a larger sense, there is the notion that God created all of mankind. And we're responsible for one another. We're responsible for one another in the smallest communities: our families. And, growing more and more broadly, we do have a responsibility for one another. It's interesting, there are two versions of a pair of comments in the Talmud: "He who saves a single soul is as if he saves the entire world," and "He who destroys a single soul is as if he destroys the entire world." There is one version that says, "He who saves or destroys a single soul in the *Jewish* world is as if he destroys the entire world." It's interesting that in the Talmud, there is a more parochial vision of life, and a much more universal vision of life of the world. So, in that sense, I think that this is a reflection of a Jewish outlook: we're responsible for one another. In that sense, yes, there's something Jewish about it. In another sense, it's a universal book, but it's universal in a particular framework. You can't really write a novel that's universal. You can't write a story about universal people. You write a story about very particular people with particular quirks, particular outlooks, particular backgrounds, and from that, one could be able to extrapolate to others. Chaim was fond of quoting Joyce, who had been asked, "Mr. Joyce, why do you only write about Dublin? It's not a very large city at that." And he is reputed to have responded, "Well, I write about Dublin because if you can get to the heart of Dublin, you can get to the heart of every city in the world." And Chaim said the same thing about himself. You write from the particular to the universal.

ND: Okay, thank you. Something else: apart from the first dedication to Phil Muysson, the Dutch publisher, the book is also dedicated to you, who "read it first." I am wondering if you might be able to shed some light on the story of this novel's creation. Some say that it is a rewriting of Chaim Potok's first book about Korea that was never published, while others say that *I Am the Clay* is a different book entirely. Which is it?

AP: When he was in Korea, he was in a medical battalion at first—a combat medical battalion—and then a combat engineers' battalion. This was in February 1956 through June 1957, when he mustered out. During the first year, I think it was spring of '56, spring or maybe early fall, he came into the Officers' Mess one day, and he noticed some people—through the window you could see the mounds, the burial mounds of a village right nearby—and he saw some people working at it, and he asked, "What's going on?" The answer was, "We're moving the battalion hospital to that hill, so people are going to have to move the graves." His parents were still alive at the time, so he said to himself, "What if that were my mother's grave?" He said the idea just dropped into his insides and stayed there. The reason they moved the battalion is because the hospital was on a main road, and in those days there was no paving yet, it was a dirt road, and in the winter monsoons it splashed mud; as it got dryer and dryer, it kicked up mounds and mounds of dust and powdery earth, and that wasn't so good for people who were being treated. It wasn't good for anybody, but especially for the people who had wounds and were in the hospital, so they moved it. Subsequently, he did write a first novel about two officers in the American army in a medical battalion, a major and a captain, and their "houseboy," whose mother's grave was being moved. It was a very spare novel. I loved it. It was greeted by various publishers as a masterpiece, but totally uncommercial. It never saw the light of day. I was disappointed, but he treated it as his apprentice novel. That vignette appears later in *I Am the Clay*.

ND: That novel was written when? In the sixties?

AP: He started it in Korea, in the mid-fifties, and then stopped, and then we were married in '58. He had told me about it. So, soon after the honeymoon, I said, "Let me see it, let me read it!" And I did, and I got to the end of what he had written and I said, "Where's the rest?" So he did complete it. In '59 we came back to the East Coast, to Philadelphia, actually, and he completed the novel in '60 or '61, and then an agent picked it up and absolutely fell in love with it.

ND: Did it have a title?

AP: *I Am the Clay*. [*Laughs*] It's about this woman who is part of the earth, who has become part of the clay, whose body is now going to be moved.

ND: So the title is derived from that, and not from the Christian hymn that she sings?

AP: Actually, that phrase can be found also in the Yom Kippur service.

ND: It's from Isaiah 64, right?

AP: I believe so. There's a whole litany of addressing God from a very human perspective—that we are the material and you are the creator, we are the glass and you are the fashioner of glass, we are the copper and you are the smelter, we are the clay and you are the potter, we are stone and you are the sculptor. That's where it really came from. But he needed to think, "How is this woman going to hear about it?" She's not going to come into contact with a *machzor* [a prayer book for the High Holy Days] or with Isaiah, especially. It's much more likely that she will come into contact with it through one of the many

Christian chaplains, or soldiers, than with Jewish ones. And certainly the Jewish ones wouldn't be reciting something from the High Holiday liturgy.

ND: Right. That's where the hymn comes in, then.

AP: Yes, originally. Then he talked to friends who were Christian and asked them how commonly it was used. That's where that came in.

ND: Why didn't he try to pursue this novel after he had published *The Chosen* in 1967?

AP: You mean the original one?

ND: Yes.

AP: That's not the same one. This is a totally different book, because by that time he had focused on the journey of this chaplain whom he had alluded to at the end of the novel. Also an allusion was laid to a Jewish chaplain in the original *I Am the Clay*, where the boy goes off and he meets the chaplain. Every time he sat down to write this novel with the chaplain, he had to figure out who was the boy who *became* the chaplain. So he went back to the beginnings. He started with Reuven, then continued with Reuven, then David Lurie, and then later on Gershon Loran, and Arthur Leiden, so he had a whole vision, and he also had one foot firmly planted in art, the notion of art. He had to give up graphic art, fine art, because as a kid, he was growing up in a small apartment in the Bronx, and he and his brother shared a room, his two sisters shared a room, and his parents shared another room, you know, where was he gonna do it? He started to draw, then he started to paint, then the oils and the turpentine . . . well, it didn't go too well. So that got shut down, and he turned to cartooning, and then started to write. He always wondered, "What would it be like if I had continued painting? Where would it have taken me?" He kept reading about painting as well, in addition to just loving it and seeing it, and he realized that the syntax of Western art presents the Crucifixion as the ultimate language of solitary suffering. And what would happen if he, an Orthodox Jew, had continued on this road, in painting? He would have had to come up against the Crucifixion, because every painter worth his salt has done a crucifixion, has done a Madonna and Child, etc. It's the syntax of Western art. What circumstance would allow an Orthodox Jew to paint it? It was just in his head, rattling around, and eventually, the story of Asher Lev began to form. So he finished up, or developed those various threads the way he wanted to with *My Name Is Asher Lev* and *The Gift of Asher Lev*. He had in mind a final book, but did not live to do that. And when the first war broke out in Iraq, after Saddam had invaded Kuwait, he just turned his head again to a different locale. He remembered the idea of the story and the wrenching—you know, war is wrenching—and he came back to that. He had pretty much worked this thread through, of the traditional mind encountering the modern world.

ND: And so, in a sense, *The Book of Lights* can also be traced back to his original work on Korea?

AP: Yes, in that sense, but instead of focusing on the doctors—the original book on Korea had a chaplain, but just peripherally, at the very end, when the houseboy went off to study, as this young kid does later on, and meets the chaplain—what he did was then he got to his chaplaincy. He did go through an incident of having lost a friend in a plane crash, not another chaplain but a young man in the battalion who was particularly sensitive and had issues he needed to discuss with a chaplain. And then fate, this awful thing, happened. You know, with any writer there are seeds of reality in his work.

ND: So, are the figures in *I Am the Clay* modeled on specific individuals? Most notably, did Kim really exist?

AP: He had a houseboy in Korea. A young Korean came and stubbed the fire, I mean, got the kerosene stove working. They would not use it overnight—there had been a fire, and so the commanding officer said at 11:00 P.M., I think, that the fires had to be put out. So they froze. They had as much on them as they could just to keep warm. Someone came in and shined their shoes and made the beds, stuff like that, for the officers. So he knew somebody, a young boy who spoke some English, and he was interested in what his interests were. From what I recall, he was not connected with the moving of the graves, the boy in real life. But he knew people whose graves were being moved. I think he came from another village, and so his grandparents were buried elsewhere, and his parents were still alive. But the idea just really stayed with him.

ND: How about the journey of the old man and woman, the story of their flight?

AP: The flight as refugees from the North Koreans—this he knew happened. He came later, he came to Korea in '56. The war was over in '53. But the lore, all lore is based in reality—the lore of the war was current, there was such destruction in the country, that's what was prevalent. And people talked about it, about the movement of the population being pushed south, and then pushed north, as the allied forces moved up, and then back again with counteroffensives. His was a very sensitive soul and mind, very observant. Very imaginative. I think any sensitive mind thinks about suffering, because you can't help it, you're not there, and you thank God for the comfort of not being there. But what if? Also, Chaim was a relative of those killed in the Holocaust. My father-in-law had a sister here and her husband and family; my mother-in-law had a cousin here—"here" being the United States—and his wife and family. Everybody else in their families was annihilated in the Shoah. There were other people in the community who had similar experiences of having suffered, even at a distance. You can either turn it off, or turn off from it, or you become sensitive to other people's suffering, and that's what happened here.

ND: Your husband was once quoted as saying, "For thinking people, Jew or non-Jew, I don't think it is possible to think the world anymore in this century without thinking the Holocaust."[2] Should these statements also apply to our allegorical reading of *I Am the Clay*?

AP: I don't know if he saw in Korea [things that reminded him of] the Holocaust, but he saw, felt, a kinship with the people who were suffering. I think that's more accurate. The Holocaust was its own universe. He called it "a black hole in history." Not only a black hole for the Jews, but a black hole for civilization, which maybe one day we'll gather and understand, or be able to put into some historical context. This was another example of savagery. In that sense, yeah. People were in the way. They weren't even considered people. In the Holocaust the Nazis went after a nation to annihilate them, but in Korea the nation was in the way. So it's like when you take a broom and you sweep out rubbish. They didn't go after them to kill them, but they were in the way. That's not important for the person that's being swept aside. Whether he's being purposely swept aside or nonchalantly swept aside, he's swept aside, he's killed. The community is dead; it's destroyed. So yes, in that sense, [he felt] kinship with the suffering.

ND: What about the notion of spiritualism in the book? There is a lot of talk about the boy's magic powers, his ability to bring good. Is that any particular reference to something you know of?

AP: Well, just that he was intrigued by this whole notion. If you recall, in *In the Beginning*, there is a woman in the building whom David Lurie's mother calls in for incantations, to help protect David against illness, and he was intrigued by that. On the one hand, Chaim was a very rational, intellectual man. On the other hand, his parents were both from Hasidic backgrounds. His father was clean shaven, and his mother did not wear a *sheidel*, a head covering, but they still stemmed from Hasidic families, and were very proud of it, and had melodies and so on from that world. And there is a sense of mysticism in the Hasidic world, no doubt about it. Or whether it was just his own sensibility . . . the mystery of life intrigued him. I think that's what made him write to begin with. That stuff you see is not all that's there, and I would venture to say—although it's probably a truism, it almost has no meaning, it's so obvious and true—that all writers are impelled by looking underneath the surface, or around the point of focus, to see what else is infringing: what's underneath, what's above, what's behind, what came before, what came after, what could be. All of that. And that was part of him. You mix the essential wonder and imagination of a writer with the mysticism inherent in religion altogether, and with the additional mysticism of the Hasidic Orthodox world, the believing world altogether, and the Hasidic *kneitch*, or wrinkle, in Orthodoxy, in religious life. I don't like to use the word "Orthodoxy" because it's too confining. The way I'm using it now, I'm talking about the Hasidic world, and most Hasidim are essentially Orthodox. There's a Hasidic influence more than in the Orthodox world. But that's where he got it from. Sorry he's not here to tell you.

ND: I wish he were.

AP: Yes, me too.

ND: Mrs. Potok, the following quote is from Albert Camus's *The Myth of Sisyphus*. I'd like to read a portion, if you wouldn't mind: "Unconscious, secret calls, invitations from all the faces, they are the necessary reverse and price of victory. There is no sun without shadow, and it is essential to know the night.

The absurd man says yes and his efforts will henceforth be unceasing."[3] You must recognize the line that says, "There is no sun without shadow, and it is essential to know the night," which is the quote that appears at the beginning of *I Am the Clay*. On the surface this seems a bit strange: Why would an ordained rabbi affiliate himself with existentialism, a movement that is decidedly atheist in nature? Did your husband have a particular affinity for Albert Camus, or for the existentialists in general?

AP: Oh, yes. I don't know if this is commonly known, but he pursued a doctorate in philosophy, in secular philosophy. I think all of us, when we were in college, right after World War II, were swept up, or were at least intrigued by the notion of existentialism because the world was so shattered. We were all looking for meaning, interpretation, not exactly explanation, because you can't explain a phenomenon as gigantic—both in scope and depth of the degradation—as the war, in so many of its aspects and fields of fighting. So, that is a combination of an "existential interest in existentialism," if I can put it that way. And, his interest in philosophy. He was very deeply interested in how we think.

ND: Who were the philosophers he worked on mainly for his doctorate?

AP: His thesis was on Solomon Maimon, who was a bridge, a counter to Hegel, and he was originally a Polish Jew who, I think when he was about fifteen, left his town and went to Berlin and Heidelberg to study. He was interested in epistemology. And this was Chaim's thesis: "The Epistemology of Solomon Maimon." But he was very taken with Aristotelian and Socratic thought, the classical philosophers. He enjoyed reading Buber. He himself, I think, was an interesting blend of the classical patterns of thinking. And when it doesn't work, okay, so how do you explain? What streams of thought can be brought into play to explain the phenomena that you see around us? Is that enough of an answer?

ND: Sure. Actually, I think I recall in a lecture that Chaim Potok gave, he said that there can be much meaning in nothingness. Does that sound familiar?

AP: I think he was saying that in order to survive with intellectual honesty—I don't know if "honesty" is the word—to survive with our intellect intact, we have to be able to extrapolate something out of nothingness, otherwise we fall into that hole. Nihilism was never an option for Chaim. One had to find it somehow. "Extract" was the term he used. That's the most apt. You not only find it; you look for it. Like extracting the final threads from a load that had been mined, or that had suffered an explosion, or an implosion, rather.

ND: Mrs. Potok, thank you so much for your willingness to respond to these questions.

AP: You're welcome. Let me ask you something, may I?

ND: Please.

AP: What drew you to *I Am the Clay*?

ND: Well, the main reason is that it's one that I hadn't read before. Once I had, I realized that this one doesn't fall into the accepted categories as the others do. And I think that it's quite daring for somebody to write outside of his own culture, and to do it so well.

AP: You know, now that we're talking, I'd love to think that maybe it's the ugly duckling! [*Laughs*] They will see that it's a swan!

ND: I certainly hope so!

AP: I'm deeply pleased, in addition to being touched, that you are bringing a scholar's eye to the book. It deserves it. It's so rich. And, specifically, *dafka*, because it's *yotzei dofen* [outside of the pattern]. Things that are outside the pattern are always interesting.

ND: Thank you. I agree.

NOTES

1. Sanford Sternlicht, *Chaim Potok: A Critical Companion* (Westport, Conn.: Greenwood Press, 2000), 143.

2. S. Lillian Kremer, "An Interview with Chaim Potok, July 21, 1981," *Studies in American Jewish Literature* 4 (1985): 91–92.

3. Albert Camus, *The Myth of Sisyphus and Other Essays*, trans. Justin O'Brien (New York: Vintage, 1955), 91.

CHAIM POTOK

My Life as a Writer

Chaim Potok

Schwab Auditorium, Pennsylvania State University
October 18, 1982

Thank you very much for the kind invitation to be with you here this evening. I'm especially grateful to the very nice people who hosted me at dinner this evening.

Let me try to use the very brief time that we have together to tell you something about the background of the books that I have thus far written. Try to present to you the invisible scaffolding that holds the books together. The scaffolding that you're really not supposed to discern as you read the books. You need not have read the books in order to follow what I'm going to try to present to you this evening.

I'm going to start in a place very distant from the setting of the early novels. It isn't so much a matter of scratching your left ear with the right hand, as much as it is an effort on my part to present to you how it came about that I worked out the basic model with which I do the exploring that I do as a writer. The triggering for the model was very far from the Brooklyn world in which the early novels are set. Early in February 1957, before many of you were born, I stood in Hiroshima at the blast site of the atomic bomb. I was, as you heard from the introduction, a chaplain at the time with the frontline engineer combat battalion in Korea. I had been in Korea for about a year before the time that I journeyed to Hiroshima, and all the time in Korea I had felt myself drawn to that site, had felt somehow the horror of it, the awe of it, and knew that I would one day end up there. It was for me, and for the friend that accompanied me there, a long and very arduous journey. We went via Hong Kong and Cairo back to northern Japan and down through Japan across the sea to Hiroshima, in those days a lengthy journey indeed. I remember standing in front of the monument to peace, on what was then a bare, sandy, clean-swept area. A park, it is now green. I remember standing there, and remembering how I felt as a teenager, about the age of many of you here, when I heard for the first time about the dropping of the bomb. Very glad, truth to tell, that that bomb had been dropped because I knew somehow the war would be over. That was my initial response, and then frightened, feeling somehow that our species had turned a corner in its development, and nothing would ever be the same for us again. I stood there as a confused set of feelings came through me. What did it mean to me, that moment? Why was I there? What did it mean to me as an American? As a participant in Western civilization? I could not understand. I went back to my battalion and was haunted by that moment for all the remaining months I spent in Korea. Returned home, the haunting would not dissipate. That experience in Hiroshima, and a number of other experiences that I had during the months that I spent in Korea, continued to resonate inside me. And I began to explore that experience with the world of Asia, and the only way that I knew to do anything, I had trained myself from the time I was a young teenager to see the world through the medium of fiction, storytelling, a certain way of giving configuration, shape, to the way we think of the world as human beings. I began to explore that long encounter with the world of Asia through the medium of storytelling, and slowly, through writing, and the writing took years and years, a model began to develop. A model of activity in which every one of us is engaged today whether we are aware of it or not, and for the most part we are unaware of it, it is so integral to our lives. What I would like to do is share that model with you. All the books that I have thus far written have utilized this model, and all the books have been an attempt to lead up to and explore that moment in Hiroshima, and that long, dark night of the soul that I experienced in the months that I spent in Asia. Here is the model.

It will come as no surprise to any of you, I suspect, at this point in time to learn that we live inside a general or umbrella civilization. A civilization that I alluded to in the seminar this afternoon. Generally known as Western secular humanism, it has many names—let's call it that tonight. It's Western because for the most part it really pertains, I think, only to our side of the planet. The Eastern side of the planet has some measure of overlap with our side, but at the hearts of things, I think the two sides of the planet really think the world structures reality in ways quite different, one from the other. It's secular because in its most essential nature this civilization that we have established for ourselves on this side of the planet, a civilization that's only about three hundred years old, has its beginnings with Voltaire and the philosophers. This civilization really makes no appeal to the supernatural. We will do it alone or it will not get done. Sure, in moments of high terror, and profound joy, we will fill our churches and synagogues with prayer, but those moments really don't begin to approximate the kind of relationship members of our species had to the supernatural three hundred, four hundred, five hundred, a thousand or more years ago.

Some years back there was a very bad drought on the East Coast of the United States, and after a long period of time, indeed, people filled their churches and synagogues, prayed for rain, and at the same time we were seeding the clouds. Indeed, the rains came one day, and I remember a cartoon in the *New Yorker* magazine—two clerics looking out of their church window at the pouring rain, one of them asking the other, "I wonder if it's us or them." We will do it alone, we say to ourselves. Or it just will not get done. You're in a university; you know how you handle knowledge here. You take the enormous spectrum of knowledge, you break it down further in coming decades. Each of those disciplines is still in a state of flux, and they will certainly be broken down further in coming decades. Along each of those disciplines are the frontiers trying to come up with sensible questions. Models are made; the truth is sought for. Models are shipped back to the classrooms or the laboratories for further intersubjective testing. Those models are what I call tentative hypotheses, temporary truths, impermanent absolutes. No truths anymore in Western civilization. No truths with capital T's, as we hunger to explore and tame the knowledge of the universe. Tentative truths, truths that operate only as long as it takes for them to really work. The minute they don't work, the model is either subsumed beneath a broader model or thrown out the window, altered. Knowledge constantly pouring in along the peripheries of all models. We live in a kind of quicksand-ish universe today. No certainty anymore beneath our feet as we walk, and we're not quite used to this kind of situation as a species. We don't quite know how to handle it yet, and we're trying very hard to get used to it. Secularism—many, many kinds of aspects to this secularist world in which we live.

It isn't my point to overemphasize for you the essential nature of Western secular humanism. You know it very well; you are in its generating plant. Universities are power plants of this civilization. It is, and I think you must admit this, a civilization beset with many difficulties at this point in time. Individuals like George Steiner and others will call it a civilization really in its final stages. We're in a post-cultural civilization, whatever that might mean, but with all those problems one must admit that this civilization is still in a seminal phase of creativity. It is spinning off, year after year, brilliant windows into reality. Insights into the way we live that literally alter the eyes by means of which we structure our lives. Inside this civilization, part of its fiber, I would say, is an enormous spectrum of other kinds of civilizations, smaller civilizations, less seminal civilizations, civilizations with specific ways of seeing the world. One might say frozen ways of seeing the world, older ways of seeing the world. Sometimes these cultures rub up against one another; enormous tension is created. All of the time, all of these civilizations in one way or another rub up against elements of the umbrella that I'm talking about, which is up there somewhere, and we're down here looking at it. We are that civilization. We are its students, its teachers, its doctors, its lawyers, its entrepreneurs, its research scientists, its mathematicians, its writers. We will go through our lives, almost all of us here, giving the best creativity that we have, the best energies that we have to give to that umbrella civilization. We breathe its air, and we give it our thoughts and our dreams. These frictions, these rub-ups of cultures, sometimes go awry, as they did here in the states in the sixties and seventies, and you have blood in the streets. It is a tenuous umbrella; it is a constant becoming. There is no being yet insofar as we can perceive this civilization. It is a civilization in constant development. Some of these rub-ups begin between the settled or beginning mini-civilizations that we find all around us, and flux umbrella civilizations generate a certain kind of result, sometimes. It is the tension between a subculture and the umbrella culture that I'm trying to explore. A tension of a certain kind. And what I would like to do now is get off this very lofty plateau of deep philosophical abstraction and do what a writer really ought to do. I want to tell you what I'm talking about by telling you a story, and in the telling of the story you will understand concretely, rather than abstractly, what I mean by confrontation of brother culture, subcultures, tensions, responses, and so on.

It will come, I think, as no big surprise to you that in my own particular subculture this business of being a writer occupies no point of any significance whatsoever. Of all the things I might have done with my life, writing stories? In the edifice of things Jewish, writing stories is somewhere in the basement. Scholarship—that's the measure of an individual in the Jewish tradition, especially Talmudic scholarship, though these days Jews will settle for a professorship in a university. But writing stories? I love to tell the story of when *My Name Is Asher Lev* was published, that my mother tells me all the time how proud she is of what I've done with my life. She's a very Orthodox lady, eighty-two years old. She told me when *My Name Is Asher Lev* was published that she was down in Miami Beach, and when people were buying the book in the bookstores they discovered there was a Potok around. So they hunted her up, they found her on her beach chair, and asked her to sign their copies of the book. So she sat there on her beach chair, signing, "Molly Potok, mother of the author Chaim Potok." For the longest time I thought the story would be apocryphal, the kind of tale a mother might tell her son who, from time to time, doubts the essential integrity of the enterprise to which he's dedicated his life. One evening, for a reason not altogether clear to me, I told that story during a lecture at a synagogue group, and when I was done, and people were filing out, a little old lady came over to me with a copy of *My Name Is Asher Lev*, and sure enough there was my mother's signature. And she asked me to sign under it "Chaim Potok, son of the mother, Molly Potok." Really I must tell you there are times when I'm alone in the room with my mother, when I catch her looking at me out of the corner of her eye, and I have this feeling that she really doesn't begin to understand what it is I'm trying to do with my life, with this business of writing stories, and it isn't too difficult for me at such moments to remember her reaction to me when I was about fourteen and a half, fifteen years old, and I told her that I thought I would spend my life writing stories. "You want to write stories, darling? That's very nice. You'll be a brain surgeon, and on the side you'll write stories." I do love to tell those stories, particularly that last line to my mother. I'm sure it finds echoes in your own lives.

How'd I come to the business of writing stories from a tradition that regards the writing of stories at best as a frivolity, and at worst as a menace? The tale I'm about to recount to you is a tale of culture confrontation of a certain kind. I was about fourteen and a half, or fifteen years old. It was at the end of a high school term for me; I was done with my exams, and I knew that I would have time on my hands in the following week, and in my world, time on one's hands meant time to read. And I decided to take a crack for the first time at a really tough adult novel. I had never read a difficult adult novel before. I read the kinds of things that we used to read in my day in English Lit classes—*Treasure Island, Ivanhoe. Catcher in the Rye* had not been written as yet. So I did what any of us did in those days when we wanted a book; I went down to the public library in the neighborhood. I browsed around for a long time, took down from the shelf a book, a title which intrigued me. Professor Walden reminded me that I couldn't even pronounce the name of the author. I took the book over to the librarian, and asked the librarian, "Is *Brideshead Revisited* by Evelyn Waugh serious adult fiction?" I used to tell this story in the past, and when I mentioned *Brideshead Revisited* I invariably would get glassy stares from much of the audience. Now, of course, most everyone knows what I'm talking about as a result of the television series. The librarian looked at me and said, "*Brideshead Revisited* by Evelyn Waugh is very serious adult fiction." I said, "Evelyn Waugh, is she really a good writer?" She said, "*He* is a very good writer." Nobody in my world named Evelyn was a he. That's one of the reasons, I think, why I constantly pay for that minor sin by the way people pronounced my name in the United States, from Ohio west: Chaim (sounds like "chain" with an *m*).

The librarian had been tracking my reading and knew that I was about to make an intergalactic leap in literature. And she urged me to be very patient with this book—it's a different kind of reading from the reading you've done before. You're entering a world about which you know nothing. You owe that kind of experience fifty, seventy-five, a hundred pages of investing before you make a decision about whether to go on or not. You can't just start with page one and by page three decide that you've had it with a book of this kind. I'm forever grateful to that librarian for that bit of advice. I took the book home. *Brideshead Revisited* is a novel about an upper-class British Catholic family of the decades prior to the Second World War. It's a novel about the strange personality and unwavering faith of the mother of that family, the wavering faith of the daughter of that family, and the disintegrating faith and personality of the boy in the family. Now, I was a yeshiva student. I attended at that time a Jewish parochial high school in New York City—very, very Orthodox, very fundamentalist. I would get up about six thirty every morning. I'd get dressed. I'd pray the morning service. I'd have breakfast. I'd hop a bus. I'd be in school about a quarter of nine. From nine to twelve or so, we studied our sacred subjects, which in my school consisted of Talmud. From about twelve fifteen, twelve thirty till two or so, we studied the Talmud with the rabbi. First part of the day was preparation. The next part of the day after the Talmud was for secular subjects. I'd leave school about five or six, get home, have supper, do my homework, go to sleep. If I was lucky, I caught the radio program called

The Lone Ranger once or twice a week. If I was really lucky, I made it to a symphony on WQXR, and if I made it to *Gang Busters*, and *The Green Hornet*, it was a messianic week for me. That was the way I lived my life. Up in the morning, school all day, home, supper, homework, sleep, up in the morning, day after day, week after week, month after month. You can imagine that I knew a great deal about upper-class British Catholics. I will never forget the effect that this book had on me. I tell this story very often, mostly as a kind of debt of gratitude I'm paying back to Evelyn Waugh. If there's some sort of heaven or hell that writers end up in, he must be a very astonished chap to realize the effect that he had upon this little boy from New York. But the business of writing books, and the aspects of writing. I tell this story to pay back a debt to a man who affected my life, every day of my life. It took me quite a while to get into that book. Once I was inside the book, I found myself so profoundly engrossed in that world and in the people of that world that I completely lost track of the world in which I was actually living. I remember walking the streets lost in awe at the tenacious faith of the mother of that family in the face of such terrible adversity. I remember my Talmud teacher snapping me awake in class; he thought I'd fallen asleep. I was sitting there with my eyes closed wondering about the fate of the daughter of that family. Asking myself, "Will she remain a Catholic, won't she remain a Catholic?" I remember trying to fall asleep at night, lost in the horror of the disintegration of the being of the boy in that family. I lived more deeply inside the world of that book than I lived inside my own world for the length of time it took me to read that book.

I remember finishing it. It was in the living room of our apartment in New York. Finishing it, closing it, looking down at it, and experiencing an overwhelming sense of bereavement. These people were gone for me now. And then experiencing an overwhelming sense of astonishment. What had he done to me, Evelyn Waugh? The whole thing had only been a story. How do you take words and, utilizing the faculty of one individual's imagination, so fuse words and imagination onto empty sheets of paper that out of that fusion comes a world more real to the reader than the world in which the reader is actually living, his or her day-to-day life? What power there is in that creativity! That was the beginning of it for me, the beginning of this strange commitment to write stories. I don't understand the why of it to this day. We can talk about the where of it, the when of it, the what of it, but the why of it I leave to psychoanalysts, who also need to earn a living. And everything that I read in fiction from that point on, even frivolous fiction, had as its fundamental purpose to teach me how to create worlds out of words on paper.

I began to read, and I began to write. You didn't do anything of an extra-curricular nature for too long a period of time in my tight little New York Jewish world before someone in authority discovered what it was that you were doing. So one afternoon as we were filing out of Talmud class, my Talmud teacher called me over to him, and when we were alone he said to me, speaking in Yiddish, he said, "What is this I hear?" So being a very good Jewish boy, I answered his question with a question. I said, "What do you mean, what is it that you hear?" He said, "I hear you want to be a writer." I said, "Yes." He said, "What is it that you want to write?" And I said, "Stories." And he was horrified. "Stories! Stories!" My god, wasn't it enough that we had to spend every afternoon of the school day involved in secular studies in order for the school to be licensed by the state of New York? I had to add to that yet? And in the evenings and on weekends write stories? There is in the Jewish tradition a category of behavior called study, study of texts. It is one of the fundamental tenets of the Jewish tradition. Judaism is a text-oriented tradition. Study is right at the spinal cord of the tradition, and clearly I was going to violate it. This particular tenet troubled him, but he was more troubled by something even more significant than that. And this is to the point of my words to you this evening. He sensed—and he was from an Eastern European tradition, a very perceptive and intuitive gentleman, this Talmud teacher—he sensed that I had somehow made contact with an element from the umbrella civilization in which all of us live our lives today. And as far as he was concerned any element from that umbrella civilization was inimical to, adversary to, what he took to be the essential nature of the Jewish tradition, especially the literature of that umbrella civilization. And he tried very hard to dissuade me from this strange love affair that I was experiencing with this alien goddess known or called serious fiction. He could not.

That was the beginning, truth to tell, of rather uncomfortable years that I had in school, with this teacher, and other teachers, though there were some who tried very hard to understand what I was trying to do. It turned out in the end he was right. This teacher of Talmud was absolutely right. What do you do if you want to become a writer? There's not a mystery attached to writing, although people have tended to romanticize it. You read and you write. You read and you write. You read and you write. You read the great masters of creative, serious literature, your teachers. You read and you write, and you enter a long tunnel of apprenticeships. You never know if there's an end to that tunnel. If there is an end, you never know if you'll ever get there. You send stories out to magazines, they come back with letters from editors, and all that means is that your apprenticeship isn't over. You read and you write, teachers encourage you, English teachers, friends, and the years go by. And you discover as the years go by what we call modern literature, serious modern literature, beginning with the epistolary novels of Richardson in England about three hundred or so years ago. And you discover, too, that fundamental to that tradition is a certain way of looking at the world, inside established societal norms, inherited tradition from the past, and in the growing up, that individual begins to sense rightly or wrongly the games that people sometimes play, the masks that people sometimes wear. Hypocrisies that are often the mechanisms of defense by means of which we make our way through this very difficult business called living. And as that individual continues to grow, should those games and those masks and those hypocrisies become intolerable to her or to him, it seems to me one of three possibilities is open to such an individual. He or she can break with that world, return to it, live in constant tension with it. Or he or she can say, I quit the fight, I don't want to fight anymore, haven't got any more strength to fight; I will join that world, marry in it, raise children in it, and watch the children grow up, and wonder which of the three steps the children will take when they make their first solo into the real world.

In the past three hundred years, on our side of the planet only, individuals have been utilizing one of the oldest forms of communication known to our species—storytelling. We, *Homo sapiens*, love a story for reasons not clear to any of us. We love a story. We're around on this planet as a distinct species for about sixty or seventy thousand years. We can track ourselves for about the last five thousand years through writing. And right at the beginning of writing there are stories, there is the attempt to structure experience, to somehow give it shape through the arabesques of the imagination, through storytelling, the poem, the tale, the epic, and so on and so forth. Some attempt on the part of members of our species to make sense out of what it is that we are and what it is that happens to us on this planet, through the imagination utilizing, as I say, the story, the tale, the embroidered arabesque of the word playing with the imagination. Individuals began to utilize this particular form of human communication for the purpose of exploring the tense line of relationship between individuals on the one hand and, on the other, the class, the group, the structured world, the system of ideas, the society into which those individuals were born, and with which, for whatever the reason, those individuals came into some kind of conflict. Some of those lines of tension are quite cool, almost indiscernible to us at this point in time. One wonders, as I said at the seminar today, what it is that is so tense about the world of Jane Austen. Some of those lines are barely visible, some of them are sweet and sentimental, as you might find in some of the works of Dickens, for example. Some of them are ironic, bitter, taut, as you might find in the early works of Hemingway. Some of them are raging and angry, as you might find in the muckraking novels here in the United States, in Frank Norris, Upton Sinclair, and so on. But this tension, this polarization of individual and society, runs like an enormous river all the way through the vast and very rich geography of serious modern fiction. It is not that it's only the river. There are many tributaries off this river, but it is certainly one of its profoundest, richest, and most characteristic features. Take *Huckleberry Finn*, though it's not a child's book. Sometimes I think the only individuals in the United States who really understood what *Huckleberry Finn* was all about, when it was first published—and it was not successfully published, it had a difficult time in the United States—were Mark Twain, and I'm not too sure of Mark Twain, and that nice, little old librarian outside of Boston who banned it from her library. It is the business of Boston librarians to understand the essentially subversive nature of books like *Huckleberry Finn*. On page five he discovers the little old lady trying hard to raise him as a bit of a hypocrite and he's very hurt. Somewhere around page thirty when his father tries to kill him, Huck heads for the river. And Carl Jung and others have pointed out how the book is structured—Huck floating on the raft between the banks of the Mississippi, while along the banks of the Mississippi are the towns of the Mississippi. A town is an aggregate of members of our species who've clustered together for the purpose of inheriting, one hopes, enhancing, and transmitting culture and commerce.

We, *Homo sapiens*, invented the town about five or six thousand years ago, on a part of the planet that's now going up in smoke, the Persian Gulf, for the purpose of pooling our energies, mutual worship of the gods, mutual security. Isn't that extraordinary, virtually each and every time old Huck steps foot in one of these centers of culture and commerce, people are shot down dead in the street, one family wipes out another family in a blood feud. There is brutality, savagery, horror, violence every time that poor kid sets foot in civilization, and alone by himself on that raft, the kid discovers who he really is as a human being, away from everything. He really finds out about Huckleberry Finn, goes on a voyage of moral self-discovery away from civilization, away from the past, away from the history that fed him, and raised him, and disillusioned him. This tension of the individual on the one hand and established societal norms on the other is, as I say, one of the fundamental characteristics of serious modern fiction. You have the individual polarized against the provinciality of small-town life by Flaubert.

The novel, the serious novel, is not a frivolous enterprise in Western civilization. It is a core, a central enterprise for Western man. It is one of the ways Western man thinks the world through the faculty of the imagination, utilizing a certain aesthetic form. Serious Western man clearly is not a frivolous being; it is not without just cause that there are whole libraries on the novel in Western civilization. From the heart of my subculture, in which all of us live today, emerged the novel. For lack of a better term, I call that a core. C-O-R-E. I don't have a better word for it. Core-to-core culture confrontation. And in the history of our species, those moments of time when for whatever the reason and whatever the occasion hearts of culture have somehow clashed, very often—not always, but very often—the tension resulting from the clash has yielded up gold that we mine to this day, and has brought us that much farther away from the dark magic of our beginnings. You see, a culture or a civilization, these words I've been using this evening, really is a very mysterious creation on the part of members of our species who, for whatever the reason, have collected together in certain areas of our planet, whether they are all stuck on an island like the English or the Japanese, or whether they're on a range of mountains, whether they're in a river valley; whatever the reason for their coming together originally, a culture constitutes the hard responses of members of our species to what I call the four-o'clock-in-the-morning question. Questions we don't like to ask ourselves during the day, so we drink beer instead. And sometimes they wake us in the early hours of the morning, and we lie there in the darkness, and we listen to them swarm all around us. What am I doing here? What is this really all about? Does anything that I do with my life mean anything in any ultimate way? What am I really teaching my kids? What am I really ready to go to the barricades for? How can I ever hope to understand another human being when I barely understand myself? What is this thin ribbon of light that I transverse between the darkness from which I came and the darkness toward which I am inevitably headed? The four-o'clock-in-the-morning questions.

Cultures are hard answers to these fundamental questions, answers unified by a style, a recognizable style. We recognize the Japanese response. We recognize the British response. We recognize the German, or the Russian, or the biblical, the Catholic response. When one set of hard responses comes up against another set of hard responses to these fundamental questions, no matter what the reason for the confrontation—whether armies are meeting in the field, or whether merchants of one culture meet merchants of a long-dead scholar, whatever the reason or the occasion for the meeting—enormous tension is generated. You'll look at those other answers and say, those are terrific answers to the four-o'clock-in-the-morning questions.

Some of those answers make a whole lot of sense. I now have to rethink my answers in light of those very significant answers. This tension sometimes will result in absolute paralysis of activity. And that's what happens to Michael in *The Promise*, the second of the novels. The boy just falls to pieces, cannot cope with this kind of confrontation. Sometimes, not always, as I said, sometimes the tension yields up a response in the shape of creativity. A book is born. A piece of music is created. New art comes to life, and we are forever changed as a result. When the medieval rabbi encounters the writings of a long-dead Aristotle, he feels himself utterly transformed by it. The tension elicits a response. The response is in the form of a great guide for the perplexed. That book has forever affected the way we think the world. Aquinas used it, when he thought his response to the same set of questions posed by Aristotle. Picasso, from the heart of Western art, knowing Western art as he knew his fingers, encountered the heart of another way of seeing the world, African art. That tension generated a new way of painting the world—cubism and modern art. Matisse, from northern life, goes to North Africa and encounters Mediterranean life. The result is a new way of coloring the world. The Samarians, Israelites, Canaanites, Jews and Greeks, Jews and Romans, Christians and Romans, Jews and Islam, and today all of us with the umbrella civilization in which we live. Culture confrontation. I'm writing about what happens when elements of hearts of cultures collide.

The story I told you isn't a story I'm going to write a novel about, but there are other encounters that I experienced and that friends of mine experienced, and they constitute the basic subjects of the novels I've thus far written. In order for me fully to understand what it was that happened in Asia, I had to go back and understand what it was that I took with me to Asia, and *The Chosen* is an effort to examine the core of my own particular subculture. At the core of that subculture are two elements at constant tension, and, by the way, this is typical of all cultures. One element looks down at the world, hungry to bring into itself the best the world has to offer. The other says, I don't want to have anything to do with the outside world. Those two elements in tension are then brought into conflict with one of the most seminal gifts to use from the umbrella civilization in which we all live—Freudian psychoanalytic theory. A notion of the world utterly inimical to the way any Western religion thinks the world. What do you do in a situation of this kind, when you encounter a body of truths utterly inimical to the way you have been brought up to think the world? Do you throw it out? Is that the price you have to pay for loyalty to your particular culture? You sense the truths in Freud; not all of it may be true, but things are happening in a way you see the world. Your eyes are changing. What do you do with truths that are inimical to your particular cultural paths? That's the problem confronting the core that I explored in *The Chosen*. *The Promise*, a conflict with another element from the umbrella civilization in which we live. A gift to us, a new way of looking at the texts of the ancient world. We call it text criticism. *Asher Lev* represented conflict with Western art. *In the Beginning* showed a conflict with anti-Semitism right at the heart of Western civilization, and new ways of regarding the most sacred texts of both Christianity and Judaism—the Bible. How do you respect the text you're being taught to dissect? This whole culture package in fiction was then explored at considerable length in *Wanderings*, which is my history of the Jews.

The whole model was put into effect at that point. Core-to-core was one kind of cultural experience that the Jewish people had, but you have more kinds of experiences, not only core-to-core. From the heart of your particular subculture, you are constantly encountering peripheral elements of Western civilization. You might not be terribly well versed in your particular subculture. You may be peripherally attached to that subculture. You go to a university; you're right at the heart of Western civilization. That sort of confrontation is a periphery-core culture confrontation, in which almost always the periphery will be swept aside by a core confrontation of that kind. There I encountered a rich, a yearning, often magnificent, and, at times, quite horrifying pagan world. I had been taught when I was a kid that Jewish suffering made some sort of sense. My father was in a unit of the Austrian army in the First World War, almost always talked in military terms, and he would say that Jewish people were leading some sort of reconnaissance troops—whatever that meant—of mankind in certain areas of human experience: morality, religion, and so on. And reconnaissance troops always take the highest casualties. I saw suffering in Asia that made me realize that absurd, meaningless suffering of individuals who were simply in the way of empires. No reconnaissance troops, no morality, nothing, stupid suffering. I remember walking into a shrine in Tokyo in a marketplace. And there I saw an old man in a brown suit, tattered gray fedora hat, brown overcoat, and standing in front of the idol with an open prayer book. Praying, back and forth, swaying, praying:

I was immediately reminded, gray beard, gray hair, of the old men in the synagogue that I grew up with.

I remember standing there and asking myself: What am I looking at? What's happening to me? Does the god that I pray to listen to this old man? If not, why not? When is there ever going to be more devotion in the being of an individual than I saw in the being of the old Japanese man, and if the god that I pray to is listening to this old man, then what are Judaism and Christianity all about? I remember walking the streets of Tokyo, and for a long time there was a feeling that I couldn't quite put my fingers on. Then it struck me one morning as I was walking that I was in a world where there was no anti-Semitism. They didn't know what it meant to be a Jew. They couldn't conceptualize hating a Jew because he was a Jew, and I cannot begin to tell you what that feeling was like the moment I was struck with that realization. What a heavy sense of freedom. There in that pagan land.

I remember being taught by my parents and by my teachers that idolatry was an abomination; indeed, that is what the Bible is all about. Just read the book of Deuteronomy. Nothing about idolatry is intrinsically beautiful. I walked through the streets of Tokyo, I saw beauty bottled by man, exquisite man-made beauty in the service of gods. It was there in that pagan land that I really began to appreciate the loveliness of God's world. I remember being told over and over again, by Christians and Jews alike, in the years I grew up what a fundamental difference to human civilization Judaism made in this world. And there in Asia I saw a world completely void of Judaism; it didn't seem to trouble it whatsoever. They get along beautifully without the Jew and Judaism. What all of this does is render the model of reality you've grown up with, that constitutes your answers to the four-o'clock-in-the-morning questions, renders that model ambiguous. That ambiguity coupled with whatever it is you're trying to think through regarding Western civilization and the atomic bomb constitutes the core question with which *The Book of Lights* is preoccupied.

This is not a neat model: Where, for example, would you place jazz in this model? Some weeks ago I was in New Orleans, walked through the streets of the old city, the French Quarter. I love jazz, and I wondered where would I put it—core, periphery, somewhere in between. You would need someone else to figure out the fine-tuning of the model, I suppose, but the model, rough as it is, has served me well thus far, and I present it to you this evening for whatever it may be worth.

I'm writing about people and events that were of particular concern to me, and to others like me, as we grew up and began to make our way into this world. My hope is that if I write about these people and events honestly enough, with as much control and intensity of focus as I can bring to bear upon them, that my very small and very particular world will open up and others will be caught up in it, just as I was once caught up in the very small and very particular world of *Brideshead Revisited* by Evelyn Waugh.

Thank you.

CONTRIBUTORS

Victoria Aarons, O. R. and Eva Mitchell Endowed Chair and Distinguished Professor of Literature at Trinity University in San Antonio, teaches courses on American Jewish and Holocaust literatures. She is the author of *A Measure of Memory: Storytelling and Identity in American Jewish Literature* (1997), *What Happened to Abraham? Reinventing the Covenant in American Fiction* (2005), and numerous other works.

Nathan P. Devir, Assistant Professor in the Department of Languages and Literature at the University of Utah, has published articles and poetry in leading journals. His interest is in the intersection of literary discourse, hermeneutics, and biblical exegesis, especially within the framework of modern Judaic cultural production.

Jane Eisner is the editor of the *Forward,* a U.S. Jewish national weekly newspaper. Previously, she worked for twenty-five years at the *Philadelphia Inquirer.* Her book *Taking Back the Vote: Getting American Youth Involved in Our Democracy* was published in 2004.

Susanne Klingenstein, Associate Professor of Writing and Humanistic Studies at MIT, is the book review editor of *Modern Jewish Studies* and author of *Jews in the American Academy, 1900–1940: The Dynamics of Intellectual Assimilation* (1991) and *Enlarging America: The Cultural Work of Jewish Literary Scholars, 1930–1990* (1998). She has written on Jewish women intellectuals and Jewish women and the Holocaust.

S. Lillian Kremer, University Distinguished Professor Emerita at Kansas State University, is the author of *Witness Through the Imagination: Jewish American Holocaust Literature* (1989) and *Women's Holocaust Writing: Memory and Imagination* (1999), as well as the editor of *Holocaust Literature: An Encyclopedia of Writers and Their Work* (2003).

Jessica Lang, Associate Professor of English at Baruch College, CUNY, specializes in early American fiction, Jewish American literature, and women's fiction. She is currently working on a manuscript entitled "Reading and the Self: Women's Narrative in the Early Republic." Her work has appeared in *Arizona Quarterly*, *Studies in American Jewish Literature*, *Texas Studies in Literature and Language*, and the *Massachusetts Review*.

Sanford E. Marovitz, Professor Emeritus of English at Kent State University, is the author of *Abraham Cahan* (1996) and coeditor of the *Bibliographical Guide to the Study of the Literature of the U.S.A.* (1959) and *Artful Thunder: Versions of the Romantic Tradition in American Literature* (1975).

Kathryn McClymond, Professor and Chair of the Department of Religious Studies at Georgia State University and Interim Director of its Jewish Studies Program, is an affiliate member of the Middle East Institute and the author most recently of *Beyond Sacred Violence: A Comparative Study of Sacrifice* (2008).

Hugh Nissenson is the well-known author of nine books, including *The Tree of Life* (1985), *The Elephant and My Jewish Problem* (1988), *Days of Awe* (2005), and *Pilgrim* (2011).

Adena Potok grew up in Brooklyn in a religiously observant Labor Zionist family. Professionally a psychiatric social worker, she married Chaim Potok and was his "first reader" until his death in 2002. She was also a consultant to Aaron Posner in the theatrical adaptation of *My Name Is Asher Lev*.

Jonathan Rosen, author of fiction and nonfiction, has written *The Talmud and the Internet: A Journey Between Worlds* (2001), *Eve's Apple* (2004), and *Joy Comes in the Morning* (2005). He is the editorial director of Nextbook.

Daniel Walden, Professor Emeritus of American Studies, English, and Comparative Literature at Penn State University, was the founder and longtime editor of *Studies in American Jewish Literature* (1975–2011). He has edited *On Being Black: Writings by Afro-Americans from Frederick Douglass to the Present* (1970), *On Being Jewish: American Jewish Writers from Cahan to Bellow* (1974), *Twentieth-Century American-Jewish Fiction Writers* (1985), and *Conversations with Chaim Potok* (2001).

INDEX